KURT,

THANKS AGAIN FOR YOUR

SUPPORT + WISH YOU

CONTINUED SUCCESS SELLING

YOUR LINKED IN TRAINING.

Praise for *Screen to Screen Selling*

"Finally a book that provides the "how to" in using the latest technology for strategic growth into new markets."

—**James Dwiggins**, CEO, NextHome Inc.

"The business of selling has changed. The problem is very few salespeople understand how the business has changed. Doug Devitre has the plan and lays it all out for you to see and more importantly how to implement it. If you're not concerned about selling faster and more efficiently then there's no need for you to read this book. If on the other hand you're looking to close more sales faster than you need this book NOW."

—**Mark Hunter**, The Sales Hunter and author of *High-Profit Selling*

"Relationship doesn't have to be a casualty at the intersection of humanity and technology. Doug masterfully connects real sales skills with practical strategies for scaling your productivity and paydays. Don't miss the opportunity to add this competitive edge to your arsenal. The future will belong to the sales rep who gets beyond connecting *to* technology and masters connecting *through* it. Grab this competitive edge. In fact, get a copy for everyone on your team."

—**Roger Courville**, CSP, and author of *The Virtual Presenter's Playbook*

"Technology can get in the way even more if you don't know how to use it confidently. Finally, a book has been published that shows you how to build trust with customers, demonstrate your skills and convert them to clients without gassing up the car to meet them. *Screen to Screen Selling* is a step-by-step guide that helps you select the right technology, conceptualize tough problems faster and develop new technical skills needed to be competitive in today's housing market. It is a must read for every real estate professional."

—**Steve Harney**, Founder and Chief Content Creator, http://www.keepingcurrentmatters.com/

"Because of advanced technologies, selling today is slowly but surely moving from face-to-face, in-person selling to virtual selling. Doug Devitre's new book on screen to screen selling is an incredible resource to help us master this new electronic form of selling. As most of our sales are over the phone and computer demonstrations, I quickly had my staff dig into Doug's book to help us become more effective and efficient at screen to screen selling. It's working!"

—**Dr. Tony Alessandra**, author of over 30 business books including *Collaborative Selling*

"Some of us have always known that selling remotely is the smartest way to sell. Now, there is no excuse for EVERYONE to do it. *Screen to Screen Selling* removes the barriers for salespeople who were reluctant to marry selling skills and strategy, the phone, and technology. Get it and master it before your competition does."

—**Art Sobczak**, author of *Smart Calling*

"Every sales professional should read this book. Doug DeVitre's new book, Screen to Screen Selling is the most comprehensive and thoughtful work I have seen on the utilization of technology to sell one's products and services. Don't make yourself obsolete by ignoring the new ways to sell when the content of this book will give you a competitive advantage!"

—**Don Hutson**, coauthor of the *New York Times* #1 bestseller, *The One Minute Entrepreneur*, and CEO of U. S. Learning and Hall of Fame Speaker

"It'll open your mind to what's really possible today. Screen to Screen Selling is filled with info, tips and resources to help you leverage technology to increase sales."

—**Jill Konrath**, author of *Agile Selling, SNAP Selling and Selling to Big Companies*

"Online collaboration and presentation tools have matured along with internet connectivity such that screen to screen should be one of the main ways you communicate and collaborate. Doug provides the when, why, and how to use your computer to remotely meet with clients, coworkers and even friends and family. Read his book, apply the strategies you learn here and you may find that screen to screen provides you with a better quality of life and a very positive ROI."

—**Glenn Sanford**, Founder and CEO, eXp Realty

"*Screen to Screen Selling* is comprehensive is covering global trends, mobile solutions, customers' expanding needs, and pragmatic sales metrics. I think it will become THE source for market leaders, start-ups, and early adapters."

—**Alan Weiss, PhD,** author, *Million Dollar Consulting* and 60 other books

"*Screen to Screen Selling* is the perfect step by step guide for selling in today's technology driven world. Doug Devitre outlines how to successfully use your existing resources to garner the most business without compromising the customer experience."

—**Eric Yuan**, CEO, Zoom Video Communications, Inc.

"Old school selling was belly rubbing sales guys. Now the best sales professionals use Screen to Screen. Doug Devitre shows us how we can use technology, time, and tenacity to drive success in sales from anywhere. "

—**Jeffrey Hayzlett**, Primetime TV & Radio Host, speaker, author and part-time cowboy

"The next generation of real estate is choosing smarter technology, raising the bar for the customer experience, and fine tuning skills to be more productive in an increasingly competitive marketplace. *Screen to Screen Selling* is the first book to pick apart the remote sales process and provide actionable and measurable checklists that will aid the astute real estate agent to increase sales and productivity."

—**Stefan Swanepoel**, *New York Times* best-selling author of *Surviving Your Serengeti* and Chairman, Swanepoel T3 Group

SCREEN TO SCREEN SELLING

How to Increase Sales, Productivity, and Customer Experience with the Latest Technology

DOUG DEVITRE

New York   Chicago   San Francisco   Athens   London
Madrid   Mexico City   Milan   New Delhi
Singapore   Sydney   Toronto

1 2 3 4 5 6 7 8 9 0   DOC/DOC   1 2 1 0 9 8 7 6 5

ISBN   978-0-07-184788-9
MHID   0-07-184788-X

e-ISBN   978-0-07-184818-3
e-MHID   0-07-184818-5

McGraw-Hill Education books are available at special quantity discounts to use as premiums and sales promotions or for use in corporate training programs. To contact a representative, please email us at bulksales@mheducation.com.

Screen to Screen Selling is a registered trademark of the United States Patent and Trademark Office by Doug Devitre International, Inc. and not to be used without written permission.

I could dedicate this book to hundreds of people. They include those who have influenced the book's creation, friends and family who have supported me in this journey, but most of all, my wife Allison.

Flexibility.

Freedom.

Financial.

What is your biggest priority?

Ultimately you get to choose all three.

CONTENTS

PREFACE

The best thing about the future is that it comes one day at a time.

—ABRAHAM LINCOLN

On Sunday morning, January 1, 2012, I reviewed my profile on TripIt, a social network that shares your travel schedule with your friends. My travel stats told me that in 2011 I had traveled to 71 cities in nine countries and had been on the road 230 days.

From 2009 to 2013, I was gone an average of 180 days a year. That's almost two-thirds of each year gone. Away from home. No connection to family, friends, or the community other than living my personal life through Facebook.

What a drag.

Before I was married, I would go on first-time dates and have to ask the date to wait another six weeks before the second date was possible. When *Up in the Air* released, I went to the theater to watch the movie by myself. I resembled almost everything in George Clooney's character—the amount of miles I was earning and achievement of the highest status on each of my travel partners, though not his good looks.

It kept occurring to me that over the preceding four years I had regularly said no to my friends' weddings, family celebrations, and any last-minute invitations of "Hey, Doug, do you want to get a beer?" because I was either out of town or preparing for a client project for my next trip. I had lost touch with my friends, lost any sense of community, and lost my identity.

It wasn't until almost a full year later, when I met Allison, the woman who is now my wife, that I knew things had to change. I needed to maintain the same level of income and be home more. I needed a new way of being able to deliver value and not have to get on a plane and go. That's hard to do when you earn a living by speaking and have to drop out of airplanes every week and live life on the road.

That's when *Screen to Screen Selling* was born.

I started to ask myself a few questions:

- How can I increase my sales and the customer experience without being physically present?
- How can I use the technology I already have that makes it easy for the customer to use?
- How can I demonstrate the value I provide in a way that differentiates me from everyone else?

After I started answering those questions for myself, I soon discovered that other professionals were asking the same questions, but in their own unique ways. In some cases, the sales professional would have to go see the customer in the customer's environment. In others, the customer would have to go see the sales professional. And this issue wasn't for just small investments or purchases. These were for highly complicated transactions that involve a significant amount of trust in order to do business.

This book is jam-packed with ideas, concepts, processes, and technologies that you can use to sell your products, services, and ideas to those who can't be physically present.

On July 5, Allison and I were married at the Cathedral Basilica of Saint Louis. Many of our friends and family were unable to make it for one reason or another. Rather than saying, "Sorry you can't make it," we decided to use Google Hangouts On Air to broadcast the event and recorded it to play back later. The sale I made when I asked Allison to marry me was available for the world to see, and it didn't cost us anything. An infinite number of ways exist to express your thoughts, talents, and time-sensitive information to customers using the latest technology. However, these opportunities can turn into setbacks. All too often, I've learned that the more things you learn, the less you actually know. And the less you actually know, the more questions you learn to ask. Some of the onerous methods for remote selling turn into obstacles that prevent performance, instead of improving the customer experience. And the sales professionals who prevail purposefully preventing their passion with the best process will improve both on-the-job and personal satisfaction.

In this book, I have compiled a plethora of *processes* to enable you, your sales team, and organization to reach peak performance using the *right technology*. However, one of our limitations is that technology changes more rapidly today than ever before, so I encourage you to focus on the decision-making process and skill set development. You can adapt these to the latest technology, both hardware and software.

Whether you sell face-to-face or from a distance, the principles of sales, communication, and influence are the same; however, the examples are different. This book is loaded with current case studies, industry research results, and tips that will help you see how you can model a proven process that works.

Before we explore the concepts, strategies, and tools in greater detail, I ask that you stay open to opportunities for improving what you are already doing. Rather than saying, "That won't work for us," ask, "How can we make this work for us?"

Will there be circumstances in which you won't need technology in sales? Absolutely.

Will there be evidence proving that technology hurts more than it helps? I'm sure of it.

Will there be better technology in a few years? Yep.

In my research, case studies, best practices, and examples, I've discovered that "visualizing conversations as Screen to Screen interactions will help you sell your ideas, products, and services more effectively using the latest technology."

What won't change is your expertise.

What won't change is your decision-making process.

What won't change are the skill sets of using technology to communicate effectively.

That's what I want you to take away from this book.

And when you have mastered the methodology, then you can begin mastering the menus. In other words, the application feature menus might seem meaningless if the message isn't methodologically communicated.

Take out your devices when you read this book. I have created a multichannel user experience with this book, so you can consume it across multiple devices and in multiple ways.

What matters most is what you implement, not just what you read. I have made it easy for you to take actionable and measurable tasks and complete them on your own schedule. Access these tasks at http://bit.ly/screen2screen.

INTRODUCTION: THE SCREEN TO SCREEN SELLING PROCESS

*The man who moves a mountain begins
by carrying away small stones.*

—CONFUCIUS

I have broken down the Screen to Screen Selling process into a customizable four-part process. First, I will prepare you with the right metrics for success and describe how inside sales is different from outside sales, how to select the right technology on a budget, which visuals to prepare for conversations, and how to set appointments for meetings that take place on time. Next, I share how to send visual summaries, incorporate digital signatures, and improve the customer experience. Then I show how sales managers and leaders can improve sales performance throughout their organization.

Anyone who needs to communicate, influence, persuade, or present ideas that solve problems without having to travel needs this book. If you have ever tried to make a conceptual sale or struggled with selling over the phone, you can benefit from adding some new skill sets and using the technology you already have. Or, if you work closely with closely with decision making teams and collaborate with peers, you can implement some of the principles we have established in this book.

Example beneficiaries of Screen to Screen Selling include:

- C-suite executives and corporate team members
- Sales management and business development
- Brand management and engagement
- Inside sales teams
- Customer support

Specific industries using Screen to Screen Selling include:

- Talent development (training, coaching, consulting)
- Technology manufacturing
- Software development and as a service
- Telehealth and medicine
- Real estate and mortgage professional services
- Energy and environmental
- Legal services
- Accounting professionals
- Banking and financial advisors
- Not-for-profit organizations and associations

Even if your primary responsibility isn't sales but you want to guide your team to make better decisions faster, you can still use in your visual conversations the same language and skill sets that I recommend for people out selling directly to customers.

Whether you are in sales or not, if you apply these ideas, you will be able to make some or all of the following improvements:

- Increase sales opportunities with customers beyond geographic constraints.
- Shorten buying sales cycle with more powerful tools and dialogue with customers.

- Increase team productivity with more effective training using technology.
- Sharpen skills with virtual coaching and peer accountability groups.
- Make it easier for meetings to start on time with all participants.
- Decrease meeting absenteeism with customers and team members.
- Cut down the amount of reworking paperwork for transactions.
- Eliminate excuses when technology won't work.
- Shorten length of meetings to focus on results.
- Improve the quality of your relationships by having more meaningful meetings.
- Avoid embarrassing mistakes using technology in front of customers.
- Cut operational costs in transportation, meeting space, and technology.
- Reduce expenses on using paper and printed materials.
- Trim down on number of reliable apps to increase productivity.
- Lower the payments on your technology setup and team administration.
- Lessen the number of mistakes made when hosting remote meetings.
- Control meeting and marketing costs in your operational budget.
- Eliminate duplication of technology that offer similar features and benefits.
- Minimize barriers and irritants to participate in remote meetings.
- Decreased likelihood of identity theft happening by adopting best practices.
- Avoid breach of confidentiality when sharing transferring files using mobile devices.
- Pay less for software, apps, and online services.
- Reduce time conceptualizing value with customers.
- Improve your quality of life by making smarter choices with how you use your time.

According to a recent report by Nielsen entitled *Screen Wars: The Battle for Eye Space in a TV-Everywhere World*, 76% of people enjoy the freedom of being connected, anywhere, anytime, and 69% think face-to-face interactions are being replaced with electronic ones. And to attract the best tech-savvy millennial talent, organizations are learning how to replicate in-person experiences in order to improve performance and contribute towards a higher quality of life. This starts at the on-the-job interview where candidates can demonstrate skills before showing up in-person, it aids them in training and reinforcing key sales training principles using hybrid learning environments, and it strengthens relationships using multiple forms of media more permanent than a handwritten thank-you note.

SCREEN TO SCREEN SELLING MULTICHANNEL USER EXPERIENCE

As a way of saying thank you for buying this book I am enabling you with multiple modalities of learning. These in turn will change beliefs about the effectiveness of your existing process and create new habits around what will make you most productive. Get the multi-channel user experience at http://devitre.co/screen2screen.

These include:

- Screen to Screen Philosophy (PDF download)
- Screen to Screen Tutorials (web video access)
- Screen to Screen Webinars (web video access)
- Screen to Screen Checklists (Wunderlist link; requires app download)
- Screen to Screen Announcements (email opt-in)
- Screen to Screen Presentation Slides (web link)
- Screen to Screen Expert Interviews (web link)
- Screen to Screen Visual Templates (web link)
- Screen to Screen Scripts (web link)

PART ONE

PREPARATION

CHAPTER 1

◆◆◆

"I CAN'T BE THERE": THE NEW WAY TO SELL YOUR PRODUCTS AND SERVICES

Is it better to sell face-to-face? Absolutely. Whether your customer is an individual, a committee, or a group of decision makers, there is no better replacement for showing up in person and meeting face-to-face. When you are physically present with your customers, you can observe body language, listen to subtle verbal clues, and watch facial expressions that allow you to quickly change course during a conversation.

When you aren't in the same room, the cards are stacked against you, especially if you haven't established credibility or a trusting relationship with the customer. The Internet connection could be slow, the audio system could fail, and both computers could go into update mode that would kill the entire meeting. Then what?

You have a responsibility to your customers, clients, and team members to eliminate as any concerns or objections when meeting remotely with technology especially when technology is in their best interests to adopt.

Have you ever prepared presentation slides and the technology didn't work? A rookie would blame the technology on the customer. A rookie would postpone the meeting. A rookie simply couldn't deliver without the technology. A pro would prepare the customer in advance with user friendly technology and be able to deliver the message in case some tech didn't work. The pro would use a combination of Screen to Screen Selling that uses visuals in a captivating way in order to solve customer problems quickly, communicate value, and decrease the amount of rework involved with transactions.

If you think travel is more reliable than technology think again. Have you ever been stranded at the airport because of weather delay or a mechanical failure? Have you cancelled a meeting from severe traffic delays caused by roadside breakdowns? Cancellations happen. And a preventive measure to decrease meeting absenteeism is to be just as good, if not better, at delivering your message screen to screen.

In this chapter we will explore the hidden benefits of selling your products or services remotely so that you think differently about interacting with customers or your team and add Screen to Screen Selling as an effective meeting alternative.

Checklist 1-1 CALCULATING THE BENEFITS OF SCREEN TO SCREEN SELLING

Take calculated risks. That is quite different from being rash.
—GEORGE S. PATTON

Glenn Sanford of eXp Realty reports a better quality of life and very positive ROI because his team was enabled to work from anywhere and still maintain a vibrant 'Culture in the Cloud.' His open door policy in his virtual office makes him accessible to his broker managers from anywhere. And, he reinvests the savings traditional brokers require to maintain the brick and mortar offices back into the technology to make his agents more productive.

Table 1.1 lists some performance areas in which you can too expect results.

Table 1.1 Performance Metrics

Sales	Productivity	Cost Savings
Number of meetings	Number of on-time meetings	Transportation
Number of new customers	Customer response time	Absenteeism
Number of call attempts	Number of files reworked	Technology
% of sales per meetings	Length of meetings	Real property
Number of sales	Customer retention	Waste disposal
Revenue per customer	% of day prospecting	Carbon footprint
Number of cancellations	Number of trainings delivered	Voluntary turnover
Customer feedback	Number of presentation errors	Hoteling
Lead response time	% of productive meetings	Administrative labor
Length of decision cycle	Employee morale	Stress management

SALES METRICS PER PERSON

C-suite executives, sales managers, and team leaders will look for the key performance indicators (KPIs) that show strengths and weaknesses in the sales process. Screen to Screen Selling will help you increase the number of appointments with new customers, decrease the customer buying cycle, and decrease the cost per customer acquisition depending on the industry and buying cycles, just to name a few.

Number of meetings per sales professional

Are you a five-star sales professional? That's when you spend more time in your car driving from appointments scattered across town than in actual customer meetings. Think of how many more appointments you could schedule with new or existing customers if transportation were reduced or removed from the equation. No delays. No nonsense. And you don't have to worry about texting drivers.

Length of decision-making cycle

Conversations typically take longer than necessary because we rely so much on verbal expression. Good visuals shorten the spoken word count because they speak for themselves and require further clarification only if the customer or team member requests it. Accuracy between what you say, what you mean, and what the customer understands increases because of the mental synchronicity around the visual. This saves time over multiple conversations, minimizes error and reworking documents because all eyeballs were present.

Customer satisfaction and reviews

Frankly, most sales technology-enabled presentations are terrible because they A) focus too much on the company, B) are loaded with benefits and features, and C) require a completely different set of skills than selling face to face. Screen to Screen Selling when done right is a differentiator. The focus is on solving customer problems, creating value, and selecting the best technology to save the customer time. When you can do all three effectively customer satisfaction will increase and the number of 5 star reviews goes up.

Customer turnover

Customers don't buy again because they don't see the value, something unfavorable happened during the process, or the competition got better. Think about how Screen to Screen Selling will help you create a productive experience for digitally adept customers who want answers and results fast. And, make it so good that it actually costs your customers more money to switch to a competitor because of how much value you can create for them.

Checklist 1-2 PRODUCTIVITY BENEFITS OF SCREEN TO SCREEN SELLING

It takes work to be considered productive. And that work is on yourself. There will always be better and faster ways of doing things. The only roadblock to maximum productivity is you and the choices you make with your time.

> *As a rule, you don't just stumble across productivity, and it doesn't strike you out of the blue like a gift from heaven.*
> —LAURA STACK, PRODUCTIVITY PRO

Start more meetings on time

Everyone has an excuse for meetings not starting on time. Your wages paid or earned (salary/commission) are affected by habits created or excuses made for not honoring commitments with technology or without.

Maybe you have heard some of these common excuses for being late or not attending:

- I didn't get the meeting notification.
- The performance agenda wasn't attached.
- I couldn't download the app in time.
- The Internet wasn't working.

Start more meetings on time by understanding where the breakdowns occur. Was the delay caused by a person, the technology, or both? Nine times out of ten the meeting facilitator is responsible for not selecting the best alternatives to decrease meeting tardiness or absenteeism. A couple prevention measures include sending a meeting invitation with clear instructions and setting reminders to prepare the participants. We will discuss this in more detail in Chapter 17.

Reduce stress with technology

Are you afraid of making a costly mistake with technology that could cost you the sale? I know I am and I still have problems. Advance preparation by deciphering best meeting alternatives, keyboard short-cuts to save time performing repetitive tasks, and recovering from both obvious and not so obvious mistakes is critical. This takes deliberate practice and with a mindset to "make as many mistakes as possible, just not the same one twice."

Improve employee morale

Sales teams and remote employees are happier with Screen to Screen Selling, because they have shorter commute times, have fewer distractions from completing important projects, and can be more flexible in their working schedule. Team members who appreciate the extra benefits will work hard to keep them and be happier about their work-life balance.

Increase customer responsiveness

You don't need to schedule a screen share meeting in advance with customers in order to help solve the problem of the day. Instant one click meetings can be initiated from mobile devices so you can have a productive conversation quickly and remove the appointment setting process if it isn't necessary. From your tablet, phone, or watch you can start a conversation in seconds, rather than postponing meetings, punishing customers with long hold times, or preventing decisions being made that require a physical presence.

Improve customer retention

Loyal customers are earned, not acquired. And, in order to retain them over time it requires consistent customized attention so they know you have their best interests at heart. Face to face follow up meetings are always best but not always realistic. Screen to Screen meetings are the next best alternative to discuss current challenges and determine visually if new opportunities exist without burdening your customer with unnecessary travel.

Checklist 1-3 COST-SAVINGS CALCULATORS

Frugality includes all the other virtues.

—CICERO

Telework, a term for giving employees flexibility to work away from the main office and connect with technology, enables employees to use Screen to Screen Selling. Research from the Global Work-Place Analytics (http://globalworkplaceanalytics.com) Federal Telework Obstacles and Opportunties Report shows cost savings from telework. In the federal government, eligible employees work remotely two days per week (Global WorkPlace Analytics). Allowing telework reduced the need for office space by 30%. The government also saw absenteeism fall by 31%, productivity improve by 12.5%, and voluntary turnover decline by 4%. Setting up these arrangements, including the equipment employees need for connecting, does cost money. The government study found that the average first-year expense for IT, equipment, virtual infrastructure, hoteling support services, and connectivity was $7,920 per person. However, the first-year savings totaled $9,630. In subsequent years, spending declined to $4,570 while the gross savings stayed the same. The Patent and Trademark Office reported a return on investment (ROI) of 21% in the first year and 54% in the following years.

Let's consider how this cost advantage can apply to Screen to Screen Selling. For each of the following costs, Screen to Screen Selling offers an alternative way to do business.

Transportation

If you total up the time and cost to travel to sales calls, you are still getting only part of the picture. The time it takes you to get ready to travel and decompress afterward is often overlooked. On the cost side, here are some common expenses associated with a one-day business trip.

- Flight
- Hotel
- Airport parking
- Rental car and gas
- Taxi or other local transportation
- Meals
- Internet charges

For these, a business traveler or customer could anticipate to spend conservatively around $1,000 to make one trip. If a flight is delayed or an accident happens along the way, it could set you back even further.

Also add up the time it takes to travel where you can't be plugged in to conduct business and make telephone calls. Instead, you just sit there, waiting for transportation, and this hurts your productivity. Multiply your projected hourly wage by the length of time you sit and wait to be transported. You will see that traveling costs you more than just expenses.

Absenteeism

No sales are made if the customer doesn't show up. Team performance is also sacrificed when a key player is missing from the equation. How many times have you experienced the lack of a decision because someone didn't show up, and how much did that cost your sales team? Calculate how many times meetings are postponed per year because attendance wasn't satisfactory to reach a quorum to make an important decision.

Reduction in technology

The worst technology is the devices, apps, and other software you bought and didn't use. Why does this happen? It is because we typically own too many tools that do the same thing. This burden in having too many tools cripples our productivity, because with each new tool, we have to learn one more thing. List all of the tools you use to serve your customers remotely with technology and eliminate those that offer unused or duplicate features you can live without, to save yourself time learning and spend more time implementing.

Real-property investment

If you could reduce the square-footage requirements for your office or meeting rooms, how much would you save in your operating budget? That might not mean much in a small town in Missouri, but on a New York City block, that might be comparable to someone else's mortgage. Calculate the operating costs needed to fund brick and mortar meetings and decide if the same or better results can be created by reducing facility costs.

Waste reduction

Have you ever told a client, "Wait till I get back to the office to send that to you"? Or have you sent a document to a customer in advance, and then when you wanted to review it with the customer, you said, "Open the document. Scroll down, scroll down, scroll up, scroll down." Or have you reviewed a website with a customer and said the same thing?

This language signals that you are probably working harder, spending more money, and spending more time because you don't have the right tools and skills for using those tools. Find performance gaps in your sales process that cause an unnecessary excess of costs and time that would be better served by meeting remotely.

Checklist 1-4 GLOBAL IMPACT

Business intelligence on a global scale needed to enter a new market, sustain demand, and explore growth opportunities is more complex than which app will you use for a meeting. Each country and/or community has their own set of decision making styles, social norms, and preferred technologies we must be well versed in inorder to serve them.

How many more customers can you serve, conversations can you infuse, and relationships can you build faster across the globe when you have the right technology and process as your friend? Now we will discuss the opportunities and considerations when applying Screen to Screen on a global scale.

Increased customer pool

International business is built on real relationships, not on apps. According to the 2014 Profile of International Buyers by the National Association of Realtors® 50% of foreign buyers were referred or recommended by someone they knew. And, if your referral partner lives out of the country and you need to ask for a referral it makes more sense to visit remotely than to wait for the next in-person visit. Screen to Screen you can strategize which websites provide the best resources, which contacts which might be best prospects, and demonstrate ways your referral partner can best refer you business.

Borderless transactions

One of the barriers to working with international customers is the need for work visas, immigration papers, and changes in immigration policies anytime you need to make a personal visit. Immigration control at the airport can delay your travel or prevent entry if officials suspect you are not carrying the proper paperwork or concealing the true intent of your visit. A series of Screen to Screen Selling meetings can reduce the number of in person visits because you are able to coordinate the details of the transaction by working remotely.

Severity of cultural intelligence

The simplest expressions, decisions, and behaviors can take on new meaning when cultural norms interpret the context differently. In Eastern Asia, decisions are made by the most senior official and so any unauthorized conversation with a subordinate would be a sign of disrespect. Also, if you point out a problem in a group setting then the Eastern Asian participant will feel embarrassed and insulted. Conversely in the U.S., some decisions need group consensus and firms address problems more directly than their Eastern Asian counterparts. Research the most applicable cultural norms for your business through David Livermore's Cultural Intelligence Research Center.

Access to experts and talent

World-renowned experts are everywhere but rarely local. If you need the world's best counsel on big data, source analytics, and information architecture then you can patch them into a video-conference all at once without having to subsidize their travel expenses. Plus, remote meetings will increase their availability because world experts won't have to factor in travel time in order to fit you in their busy schedule.

Reduction in carbon footprint

Screen to Screen Selling is more environmentally friendly than meeting face to face. In its 2013 Federal Telework Obstacles and Opportunities Study, Global WorkPlace Analytics (http://globalworkplaceanalytics. com/telecommuting-statistics) compared the greenhouse-gas emissions associated with federal-government employees going to the office every day and emissions associated with telework. The study concluded, "If the 32% of eligible federal employees teleworked at the same frequency as existing federal teleworkers, the reduction in greenhouse gases could total more than 200,000 tons a year." Furthermore, the study noted other environmental benefits, such as preservation of soil, a reduction in energy consumption, and better meeting technology. If global warming is a concern, Screen to Screen Selling will help you do your part to keep the earth green.

Checklist 1-5 MAKING THE TRANSITION TO SCREEN TO SCREEN SELLING

Your life does not getter better by chance, it gets better by change.

—JIM ROHN

There is a disruption going on right now in professional sales. According to Dave Elkington, CEO of InsideSales.com, "In the next 5 years more sales will be met by inside sales professionals than outside sales." And, according to Bob Perkins, Founder of the American Association of Inside Sales Professionals, "Inside sales jobs have increased 300% in the last year!"

This is good news for those who are proactive about change as it applies to trending market conditions. Bad news for those who will be left holding onto traditional beliefs based on what worked in the past. Here we will explore some of the changes you will soon encounter.

Inside-sales paradigm shift

Competitive organizations are re-working their sales process to increase the output of their sales representatives. And, this means re-assigning roles, removing antiquated processes, and restocking systems to serve the customer better and faster. But in order to transform a traditional sales model into a more progressive, customer-centric model, your goal or role is to help influence the beliefs as to when to use Screen to Screen Selling and when to leave sales to your team in the field. This paradigm shift is palatable in principle, but pragmatic in its application.

This starts at the top with the CEO (Chief Executive Officer), COO (Chief Operating Officer), CIO (Chief Information Officer), CSO (Chief Sales Officer) , CTO (Chief Technology Officer), and CMO (Chief Marketing Officer).

Talent identification

The hiring decision to onboard a new team or train your existing team on the new skill sets comes from your analysis on attitude more than its application. Not all field sales reps qualified to be inside sales reps just like inside sales reps may not be qualified to be in field sales. It's imperative to examine who will support a transition and who is more resistant. The technology for Screen to Screen Selling changes every day and requires new training to stay abreast of the latest advancements. A team member who says, "That won't work for me" is more expendable than someone new that asks, "How do we make that work?"

New skill-set requirements

New technology adoption for organizations means the team will need to learn new skills on how to use the features and how they help progress the sale. And sales managers are taking note through their commitments to investing in sales training. A 2014 Sales Performance Optimization study (2014 CSO Sales Management Insights) found that 75.7% of the firms surveyed expect managers to take a lead role in reinforcing/enforcing sales training concepts. Some of these new skills include visual framing, using digital whiteboards, and video-conference technology.

New systems and tools

The most common objection to investing into new technology I hear is … "We need to get the return out of our old system first before we can integrate something new." This irrational thinking presupposes that a poor initial choice has to continue to negatively affect operations.

For example, if you invested in a terrible website, would you continue to punish your customers with an unfavorable experience or eat the sunk cost as a mistake never to happen again? Before you start technology shopping, be sure you have the right decision-making process to integrate new technology with legacy systems in order to maximize your return on investment.

New selling process

Most customers are used to being served over the phone. Fewer have used online meeting tools in order to solve their problems. Once you have convinced yourself that Screen to Screen positives outweigh the negatives, next you have to persuade the customers that sharing your screen will solve their problems faster. This book will give you the right dialogue and sales process to do that effectively.

Assessment 1-1 KNOWLEDGE

We can say with certainty—or 90% probability—that the new industries that are about to be born will have nothing to do with information.

—PETER DRUCKER

The best technology and sales process are futile unless you have developed a deep reservoir of expertise which positions you as the expert in your field. Expertise is acquired over time from listening to industry experts, reading relevant books, and its practical application with real customers. Set aside technology for a moment and ensure your communication is built on a solid sales foundation using some of these ideas.

Communicate value propositions

The successful communication of value has more to do with what the customer perceives rather than what you say or believe. The creation of value propositions is an exercise that requires critical thinking, empirical evidence, and concise language in order to demonstrate how you have helped others in a simple situation as your targeted customer. A good resource to create value propositions is Tom Reilly's book *Value-Added Selling*.

Customers' preferred channels

Do you have some children or grandchildren you can get a hold of only by sending them a text message or using Facebook Messenger or sending email? Your customers have their preferences as well. The kinds of technology your customers own will affect their preferences. Do your customers have a strong enough Internet connection in order to host an online meeting?

Find out your customers' preferred channels of communication. Then place your notes about these in your contact manager for the future. That way, you don't have to second-guess yourself or others when you need to start your online meeting.

Customer history and buying cycle

Historical data can predict future buying decisions based on trends from similar customers. This can prompt you to start conversations about buying before customers have recognized the need themselves. For example, in real estate, home values are constantly using absorption rate pricing. By relying on the recent data to predict your home's valuation, a real estate professional might suggest you sell when this analysis indicates prices are rising.

Impact of data on decisions

Decision without the right data is downright dumb. And with the availability of data today there is no excuse for not being prepared, knowing a little about your customer, or how customers make decisions based on latest trends. Source analytics, predictive analytics, and big data are just a few example data sources that can help sales professionals make better decisions around acquiring and serving their customers.

Marketplace differentiation

The competitors to worry about are the ones who are always improving themselves and finding better ways to sell their services and products. Most remote conversations are over the phone or video-to-video chat. Rarely do they involve sharing screens. Why? It's because most people don't know Screen to Screen communication exists or haven't learned how to use it effectively. Therefore, if you master this skill, you will differentiate yourself from the competition.

Assessment 1-2 WHAT SKILLS DO YOU NEED?

Every artist was first an amateur.
—RALPH WALDO EMERSON

If knowledge is knowing what to do, then skills are the application of the knowledge when working with real customers. For example, you might know how to listen, ask questions, and screen share already. But, do you know exactly what to ask when a visual is being shared and the audio settings are not configured correctly? The skills we mention are learnable, implementable, and transferrable to others who will benefit.

Let's take a look at some specific kinds of skills associated with success in Screen to Screen Selling.

Active listening skills

My mom was right. She told me I needed to use my ears and mouth in equal proportions. The same concept can be applied during Screen to Screen conversations. Do you talk more than you listen during conversations? Do you ask precise questions and wait, or do you ramble until you get your point across? To remove Screen to Screen awkwardness, ask a really good question and wait patiently for the answer without interruption. Listening actively builds trust and is imperative before you can talk solutions, benefits, or features offered.

Professional competencies

A professional competency is a skill which someone possesses related to their particular trade or association. In other words, these are attributes that the professional has acquired that make them specialized in their craft, and distinguished from your DYI hobbyist. Professional competencies executed represent how much value they create for others, how much they earn, and the values which their occupation merits. These skills can be demonstrated face to face with customers or Screen to Screen depending on the situation. If you were to decide if Screen to Screen Selling was right for your role, make a list of which skills you use right now on a regular basis that could be better served remotely to save time and costs. Then continue reading to see which tools and processes fit your role best.

Knowledge transfer

It is far more effective to ask customers how the product/service benefits them rather than tell them they should buy from you. This simple step decreases the customer sales cycle, improves the customer experience and decreases the cost of acquisition because they already know how to buy from you. For example, you can use stories that share past failures/success, statistics that surface recent trends, and steps in the decision-making process that they are likely to uncover. And, if they can recite this information to their friends, colleagues, or family, then you have equipped a non-commission salesperson to do some marketing for you.

Collaborative technology

Everyone has access to the same technology, however, we use it in completely different ways. For example, a tool like the Smart Kapp digital whiteboard made by SMART Technologies can be used by one company to facilitate meetings among their team members and another company might use it to interact with customers to receive live feedback. The skill sets using the collaborative technology will be different depending upon the scenario and developed according to the expected outcome from the meeting.

Engagement tactics

Have you ever asked a question during an online meeting and nobody answered? Or, you asked participants to fill out a live poll and only a few responded? There are certainly more effective ways than posing a question and praying for a response. Participant engagement results from asking the right question and giving multiple alternatives for a response. For example, answers can be confirmed using a digital whiteboard, resource links can be shared through participant chat, and images can be collected by giving an appropriate medium to exchange files. Screen to Screen Selling encompasses every alternative in using technology to solicit feedback in addition to oral expression. We will cover these in more detail in Chapter 7.

Assessment 1-3 TECHNOLOGY CONCERNS

Computers are useless. They can only give you answers.
—PABLO PICASSO

Communication doesn't happen when the technology doesn't work. And rather than blame a device or your decision maker, take responsibility by making a list of all the potential problems and preventative measures against them happening in the future.

Unfortunately, many salespeople already know this from personal experience. In a survey conducted by IDG Research (2013), more than half of respondents (56%) using online meeting tools in sales positions report technical difficulties when trying to connect others in online meetings. Almost half (48%) reported having trouble when setting up a meeting.

Use these categories of questions to help you identify common mistakes before you have your next meeting.

Performance metrics

- How many meetings started on time with all the participants?
- What was the meeting join rate, relative to the registration rate?
- How long is the delay from clicking the link in the online-meeting invitation to actually joining the meeting?

Troubleshooting requests

- How many meetings were canceled due to technology?
- How fast of an Internet connection do I need?
- How long will it take to rejoin the meeting if I exit accidentally?

Satisfaction with usability

- How many errors were made by both salesperson and customer in completing tasks?
- How long did it take to complete a task using a technology feature?
- How satisfied was the customer when using your technology?

Learning and implementation

- How long does it take to become proficient at a new software program, application, or system?
- How responsive and adaptable are the instructions?
- Can these instructions be customized for my team?

System integration

- How will this new technology work with what I already have?
- How long will it take to integrate Screen to Screen Selling into our sales process?
- What common problems do similar companies have when integrating this process into their organization?

In Chapter 1 we discussed the impact Screen to Screen Selling is having for organizations, sales teams, and customers. In Chapter 2 we will explore the sales process in more detail in order to improve conversion and the customer experience.

◆◆◆

SELLING ISN'T TELLING: PROBLEMS WITH MOST SALES PRESENTATIONS

Selling isn't telling. You have to show them how to buy.
—BRIAN TRACY

The biggest problem most sales professionals create when they deliver a sales presentations is, "They assume the customer needs to know what the salesperson needs to know in the order that the customer needs to know it." In other words, a pre-determined order of presentation slides (assumptions) will never match 100% of the order of the questions the customer will ask and cause resistance in the conversation because the customer will think about their question while the professional is on a different slide.

These assumptions are in play when a salesperson engages in these behaviors:

- The salesperson does more talking about past experiences than listening to the customer's existing needs and problems.

- The salesperson uses a significant amount of visual aids, literature, or brochures to support his or her argument.
- The salesperson speaks in generalizations rather than supporting claims with research or past experiences.

When you are selling Screen to Screen, these problems are amplified. Here's why:

- The customer might not have developed enough trust to reveal real problems and needs.
- Sometimes you can't see the customer's facial expressions, body language, or nonverbal cues to signal awareness in conversations.
- It is easy for the customer to end the meeting with a click of the button.

This chapter identifies ways you can prepare for the sales conversation so that you can develop trust faster, increase your conversions, and have more fun in the process.

Checklist 2-1 VIRTUAL TRUST

Salespeople can't afford to take the customer's trust for granted. Consumers are wary of marketing messages. According to a study conducted by Forrester Research, 70% of consumers surveyed said they trust brand recommendations from friends. In contrast, only 10% said they trust advertising. While we don't know the share who trust sales professionals, we know their trust is earned, not given. It comes from consistently doing the right things with purpose, passion, and perseverance.

According to David Horsager, author of *Trust Edge*: "Building trust is the #1 answer to solving the world crisis."

To establish trust with new customers, ask yourself the following questions.

Social search for customers

- How many different ways does your customer gather intelligence about you and your company?
- How quickly can customers find pertinent information they need?
- Can customers find a combination of both personal and business profile information about you?

Social-engineering contacts

- How long does it take to build rapport with a new customer?
- What is your customer conversion rate from inquiry to appointment?
- How fine-tuned are your sales scripts for specific customer segments?

Social introductions from peers

- How often do you request introductions from past clients and customers?
- How often do you receive introductions from past clients and customers?
- How many different ways can you be introduced to future prospects?

Social sharing of value

- How accessible is your intellectual property?
- How quickly can you share your digital content library after receiving an initial request?
- How usable is your digital content library on mobile devices?

Social affirmation in reviews

- How many different ways can you collect testimonials or endorsements?

- What percent of your customers write recommendations or reviews about your performance?
- How detailed are your reviews in explaining specific benefits or methods used during the transaction?

Build a professional website

Have you ever said to someone, "Don't look at my website. It's really bad?" If you think your website is poorly designed, imagine what your customers think. And if you think it's fine, ask them how you can improve it in order to improve the customer experience.

Creating a well-designed website requires expertise. There are plenty of freelance website designers, but only a few of them understand how behaviors affect conversion, how user testing improves the customer experience, and how design affects usability from multiple devices. Find website designers that understand usability so your website delivers results, and doesn't just look nice.

Optimize your LinkedIn profile

Your LinkedIn profile is selling you more than any of the other social networks. If I can't find you on LinkedIn, I won't trust you, just as a homebuyer won't visit at a property until there are photos with detailed descriptions on the agent's website. Find ways to optimize your LinkedIn profile with highlights that reinforce past successes, digital resources, and trusted recommendations.

Improve your Klout Score

A popular tool to measure someone's effectiveness on social media is their Klout Score. This algorithm takes in the participation from your social-media activity and assigns you a score based on how much interaction you have with others. A high Klout score can quickly reveal who has the most influence in social media. Conversely, a low Klout score means someone is silent on social media. And, like in real life, if someone is too silent socially, we tend not to trust them if we don't have an existing relationship.

Increase social shares

The more others share your videos, tweets, and posts in social media the more quickly you build trust with those whom you haven't met. Robert Cialdini, author of *Influence*, talks about "social proof" as a psychological phenomenon: if enough people are talking about a common conversation it can influence others on how they perceive the topic.

Maintain online reputation

Whether you realize it or not, anyone can post something about you, your business, or how you do business. Right or wrong, what they post is out in the world, and how you recover from online reputation attacks will determine how others who don't know you will perceive you. Set up alerts (ex. Google Alerts) that automatically notify you when someone has posted online a statement, article, or video that has your name or company on it.

Checklist 2-2 CONSULTATIVE SELLING

Remove the term *sales presentation* from your vocabulary.

In Screen to Screen Selling, you don't present to a customer. You *talk* with a customer.

You don't show services to a customer. You *uncover* needs from a customer.

You don't do something to a customer. You do something *with* a customer.

Consultative selling seeks to understand before spewing out features and benefits for how your product or service can help. And, when you have visuals to aid the discovery process, the conversation length shortens.

When I think of the word *presentation*, I think of trying to wow someone rather than win his or her respect. And the best way I've found to earn respect is to listen. Here are some ways you can reverse the customer's perception of a presentation by turning it into a conversation that truly helps them make informed decisions.

Do's/Don'ts of relationship building

A relationship in its infancy stage can improve or decline based on the decisions you make in-person or Screen to Screen. Limit your mistakes by avoiding these screen share faux pas.

- Don't enable the participant camera upon start. You never know if the other person is dressed. Let them enable their own camera themselves.
- Don't share your screen until you have the customer's permission. Assuming a screen share too soon can make someone think they are being controlled.
- Don't abuse visual control. The speed of the screen share is controlled input from the customer, not how fast you can manipulate the screen.

Accidental or observational, these blunders are mitigated over time and deliberate practice.

Diagnosis before prescription

Doctors don't give out medicine until they have asked a series of questions, run some tests, and attempted to diagnose problems. You should approach Screen to Screen Selling conversations the same way: first diagnose the customer's problem, and only then offer your prescribed solution. Are your sales conversations prescriptive or diagnostic? Take a look at Table 2.1 to see how these approaches compare.

Table 2.1 Prescriptive vs. Diagnostic Sales Presentations

Prescriptive	Diagnostic
More talking by salesperson.	More listening by salesperson.
"Here is what you need to know."	"What concerns you most?"
Assume customer has technology for presentation.	Ask technical requirements before talk.
Share screen without permission.	Share screen with permission.
Slides appear in predetermined order.	Questions guide order of slides and conversation.
Slides flip back and forth with delays.	Best visual appears quickly for customer.
Questions asked according to script.	Questions asked based on customer choice.
Present without tests of comprehension.	Test comprehension after every slide.
Limited or no customer feedback.	Consistent requests for feedback.
Poll participants verbally.	Poll participants visually.
End with "Do you have any questions?"	All questions answered before end.
Follow up without requesting permission.	Request permission to send visual summary.

PowerPoint and Keynote presentation slides are prescriptive ways of delivering material, because they are ordered based on perceived past problems from others, not specific issues with specific customers. Have you ever been on a 60-minute webinar where only 5 minutes were actually useful? Don't put customers through that pain when you can cut to the chase by using Screen to Screen tactics to diagnose the customer's problem.

Prioritization of needs over wants

Often customers talk about what they want, though your goal is to help them pinpoint what they actually need. I've heard executives say they want to recruit new talent when their culture is in the dumps. I've had meeting planners say they want a full day of training when the implementation from knowledge transfer would only take two hours.

Visuals accelerate the separation of needs from wants because they are created together and understood in real time. See Checklist 8-2 on visual framing for the how-to.

Interpretation of value

The value of your product or service solely depends on how well you can conceptualize it with someone else. In Alan Weiss's book *Value Based Fees* he shares a methodological approach for calculating value based on the tangible, intangible, and peripheral benefits a customer might receive. And, this exercise involves asking better questions to surface the value that remains uncovered until probed. This way the customer shares with you your contribution to value rather than you telling them.

Cross-screen conversational control

The best conversations are rhythmic. In other words, there is an even flow of questions and answers, talking and listening, and who has control. What if you are the host of an online meeting but the customer wants to explain with their screen, navigate a website with their mouse, or fill in the blank with their mouse? You should know which tools to use inside your meeting to make that happen. Not only should your meeting be technically smooth, but you and the customer should be able to work together to conceptualize or recreate the problem.

Assessment 2-2 COACHING CUSTOMERS SCREEN TO SCREEN

Some customers already have all the answers. They just need to be reminded, reinforced, and recognized when they are on the right track. This is why coaching your customers can create a deeper connection than telling them what they already know. Learn to use the following coaching skill sets during Screen to Screen Selling.

Ask precise questions

Vague, more generalized questions like, "What type of satisfaction do you get from your work" are great for building rapport at the start of a relationship. And, as the relationship progresses then you can more effectively coach your customer by asking more precise questions that narrow the focus as to the outcome the customer can expect. For example, a precise coaching question might involve asking, "Because you love your work and you want the best for your people, how might they be better served if they had access to X?" This eliminates assumptions that might be otherwise withheld if the "coach" hadn't probed deeper by asking more precise questions.

Listen carefully

According to Marshall Goldsmith, "So many people have spent a life-time preparing themselves for technological skills, yet have spent no time training themselves on how to influence people so that their technological skills make a difference." It might seem that people influence others the most by talking, but in fact, listening is at the core of influencing. If you listen well, you can learn what people want and what they care about. Pay attention to more than the words; also listen for what is not being said. Ask yourself, "Did I understand what they said and didn't say?"

Offer solicited advice

As I noted earlier in this chapter, coaching your customers can create a deeper connection than you build by lecturing. A coach is a guide on the side, not a sage on the stage. When you are coaching your customers, the language you choose will ultimately decide whether conversations are constructive or combative, helpful or hurtful, and pragmatic or pithy. Try starting your recommendations with openers that signal you are coaching, not lecturing:

- "Would you like some clarity around that?"
- "Are you open to a better alternative?"

Reduce cognitive dissonance

Buyer's remorse begins with misunderstandings from a lack of communication. Either the salesperson promised to do something but didn't do it, or the customer took away a whole new meaning from the salesperson's interpretation. These customer misunderstandings can form before the conversation, during the conversation, and following the sale. Remote meetings with an assortment of visuals ensure that all participants are looking at the same link on a web page at the same time, same line item on the same contract at the same time, and same financial calculations at the same time to avoid any misunderstandings from the details.

Checklist 2-3 BARRIERS

As much as you would like to host a Screen to Screen sales conversation with a customer, you will encounter some roadblocks you might not be able to avoid. These include security prevention tactics, confidentiality concerns, device compatibility, Internet access, and customer unfamiliarity with technology.

Customer's network security

Fortune 500 companies, which store massive amounts of intellectual property and descriptive financial records, and which supply their team with protected laptops and other devices, are very strict about forbidding employees from downloading untested third-party apps and other software. This barrier is almost impossible to remove, because the customer's IT department—not the customer—controls the technology. If you are working with customers at a company with strict security, you may need to sell using their online meeting solution, work with the customer's IT department on finding a more effective app or tool, or make the trip in person yourself.

Confidentiality concerns

If you use the Internet for online delivery, storage, and file creation, there is always a risk someone can hack into your computer or that of your customer. And, this risk of breaching confidentiality is the big reason why industries such as finance, banking, and insurance have been reluctant to embrace Screen to Screen Selling as a tactic to increase sales. We will suggest some best practices in Chapter 12 to limit your risk and protect your customer more effectively.

Device functionality

Computers or devices five years or older will suffer online meeting performance issues as a rule of thumb. If your computer requires an upgrade to a new operating system to perform then it will prevent or delay the meeting from happening until you seek another alternative. Also, if the customer experiences the same issue and they don't have a backup device then you are back to relying on the telephone or face-to-face for your meeting. Two things. Verify your technology has the latest software updates and double check with new customers to see if their devices are compatible to participate in online meetings with both clear audio and video.

Internet and data plans

The Internet is the life support for Screen to Screen meetings, as oxygen is for the heart. A fast Internet might not be available for all customers because of where they live, your current location, or either party's Internet/data plan subscription level. Take the time to learn about Internet access from multiple locations and compare wireless data plans. Video uses more data than audio. And, if the meeting with screen share is slow, transition the meeting option from video to audio only. Or pick up the phone if all else fails.

Unfamiliarity with technology

Age is not an excuse to prevent adoption of new technology. Unfamiliarity is. My father, who is 74 years old, bought his first iPad and recently had Internet service installed at his house. My mother is 67 years old and has been using Skype with me for the last five years. Right now, I can have a Screen to Screen conversation with my Mom on Skype and my Dad on FaceTime through the iPad.

But there was resistance to the technology because they didn't know what to click, when to click and how often to click. This took patience on my part to help them become more comfortable in the beginning and now that's how they want to communicate because they are more comfortable.

As Jackie Joyner-Kersee says, "Age is no barrier. It's a limitation you put on your mind."

Checklist 2-4 IRRITANTS

My favorite Whoopi Goldberg quote is, "I don't have pet peeves; I have whole kennels of irritation." I've had more problems with technology than most people I know because I subject myself to potential mistakes and failures that come along with it. But most people don't have that much patience. When the customer and sales professional experience these irritants during a meeting, it can erode the customer experience. Therefore, you must address possible irritants before launching any Screen to Screen meetings.

Not starting on time

According to a study conducted by Ovum, employees reported that when meetings start late, the average length of the delay is 10 minutes. Multiplied by the number of employees, this is a lot of wasted time and unnecessary payroll expense. To prevent delays in Screen to Screen meetings, look for the causes of late starts: Was the meeting invitation sent? Was the phone number incorrect? Did we send the wrong link to the wrong people? Meetings can start closer to the scheduled time if you remove the excuses others give for being late. Take responsibility for the factors you can control, and schedule meetings with the appropriate meeting notification setting discussed in Chapter 5.

Resistance to download

Customers won't want to download your meeting app. Here's why…

- It takes extra time to download a new app.
- There are security concerns around downloading a 3rd party program.
- Apps take up extra storage on devices.
- Unused apps clutter up navigation menus.
- Customers might not know how to remove the app.

Unless you can convince them that downloading a meeting app is in their best interests then it can cause resistance from those who are not as familiar with the technology. Some meeting apps do require an extra download and others don't. We will discuss these options in more detail in Chapter 3.

Assumptive attention

Conference calls reliant on only audio are filled with assumptions. These include:

- Assuming participants on the invitation list are all on the call, all at the same time. You can't see who is there until someone speaks.
- Everyone is equally prepared with the same supporting documentation, files, or resources. Bet on them not bringing anything with them to the meeting.

- Everyone is mentally focused on the same line item on the agenda at the same time. Chances are participants are disengaged and multi-tasking.

As a result, conversations easily drift off topic which hurts productivity in meetings. New video conference call features allow you to see who is participating, allow for real time collaboration supported by screen share, and decrease the amount of assumptions made over traditional conference calls.

Delays in Internet speed

I   have   something   to   tell   you.
Can   you   hear   me?
I   can't   see   you,   but   I   can   hear   you.

A slow Internet connection can cripple a conversation, even if you have the best online meeting tools. In Chapter 3 we will discuss multiple alternatives to accessing the Internet so you can adjust your technology quickly to keep the meeting going without having to cancel.

Font and visual size

Picture your last vision test at the Department of Motor Vehicles or eye doctor. The letters at the bottom are always harder to read than those at the top. And, in remote meeting technology, the smaller the device the greater the need for a larger-sized font.

Design your visuals so they can be readable from a laptop, tablet or mobile device (minimum 32 point type face). Also when using digital whiteboard tools, make sure your handwriting and annotations are large enough so a participant doesn't have to squint or ask for clarification.

Checklist 2-5 VISUALIZING THE CONVERSATION

Olympic athletes visualize their entire performance many times over before the race begins. Professional salespeople do the same by reciting common objections, visualizing the meeting space, and identifying the decision makers before they join the meeting. The same principles apply in the Screen to Screen Selling environment. Here's how.

Visualize before, during, and after

Your visualization should include what is involved in every stage of the Screen to Screen Selling process. (For an overview of that process, see Figure 2.1). The three major parts of the Screen to Screen sales call are preparation, delivery, and follow-up.

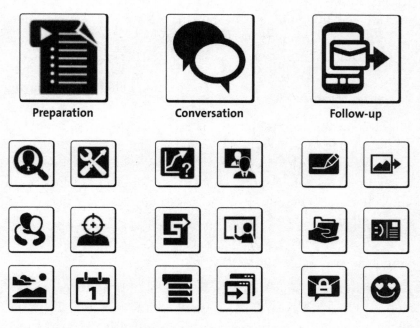

Figure 2.1 Screen to Screen Selling Process

Preparation begins with knowing your scripts, which technology you will use, how fast your Internet connection is for participants, and what problems you might experience during the conversation.

Next is delivery. Visualize how the conversation starts, how often you ask questions, and how well you listen. Visualize which visuals you will use for unique situations and how you will communicate them.

Finally, visualize how you plan to follow up with your customers. Will you send a visual summary? Do you need to send a screenshot of an important point?

Prepare visual FAQs

Prepare for your customers' frequently asked questions (FAQs). Most likely, you can answer every FAQ verbally. However, people can process images 40 times faster than words, so think about how to create visuals that answer customers' frequently asked questions. For example, I could spend five minutes explaining the financial benefits of owning versus renting, or I could show you a visual that helps you understand in five seconds.

Review documents and web pages

The customer's interpretation of financial spreadsheets, contracts, and web pages begins with having the appropriate visual aid ready and accessible to use when you need it. Prepare and review these files before the conversation starts. Think of how you will explain certain line items faster when the customer asks a question. We will discuss the preparation of these visuals in Chapter 5.

Rehearse software shortcuts

I don't handle a hammer with two hands, because it's harder to hit a nail that way. That's like trying to use Screen to Screen Selling without knowing the shortcuts to find and deliver what you need when the customer needs it. The types of shortcuts to master include keyboard quick keys, browser navigation, and application shortcuts. The goal is to develop an unconscious competence around these shortcuts, so you don't have to think about what to do when you need to do it. These are discussed more in Chapter 7.

Demonstrate with technology

The transition from asking one question to probing deeper with another needs your audio to work seamlessly. Your transition from video camera to screen share, and back to video needs to seem natural. And, deciding which visual to use at specific times all are a part of staying in the moment with your customer. You demonstrate your professionalism by acting in congruence with how you normally react in person with a customer, by looking them in the eye and using traditional presentation aids. The difference with Screen to Screen Selling is how easily you transition your expertise into outcomes without the technology getting in the way.

CHAPTER 3

◆◆◆

TECH TUNE-UP: THE TOOLS YOU WILL NEED FOR SCREEN TO SCREEN SELLING

Technology doesn't hold people accountable.
People hold people accountable.

—SAM SILVERSTEIN, AUTHOR OF *NO MORE EXCUSES*

Before you get all excited about the app of the month, I would like you to remember this one statement: Technology is a solution to a problem, not a problem looking for a solution. I'm always reluctant to recommend any specific technology, for five reasons:

1. I don't know yet who your customers are or their communication preferences.
2. I don't know yet know the skill sets of their team.
3. I don't yet understand your team's fundamental beliefs about adopting new technology.
4. I don't know what existing tools and systems you are using that you can integrate into a new sales process.
5. I don't know if you have existing policies around using technology or whether new ones need to be created first.

So instead of telling you what to buy, this chapter focuses on alternative working arrangements, features you must have, and how to more effectively allocate your resources for multiple meeting environments.

Table 3.1 compares the multiple communication options, selection criteria, and tips to ensure a successful implementation.

Table 3.1 Technology Decision Menu

Communication Options	Selection Criteria	Ideas for Implementation
Phone teleconference	Platform support	Assess team belief system
Voice over Internet phone	Pricing and licensing	Hire talent with skills
Web Real Time Communications	Cross-platform functionality	Select systems
Instant video meetings	Cross-platform usability	Create policies and rules
Screen-share applications	Multitasking functionality	Adapt existing resources
Whiteboard interaction	Current updates and bug fixes	Train using best tools
Participant chat	Security access and protection	Train team on new skills
Mobile meetings	Wired or wireless	Observe team in the field
Text message response	Compliance with legal and IT policies	Coach team on skills
Wearable technologies	Installation requirements	Coach team on tools
Mobile notifications	Integration with infrastructure	Measure impact
Social media	Return on investment	Celebrate

Checklist 3-1 SCREEN TO SCREEN ENVIRONMENT

If you are not physically in the same room with a customer, how can you create an environment of trust, demonstrate your expertise, and make it easy for the customer to buy? There is no silver bullet answer to any of these questions. And, you will make mistakes as you experiment with each step in the process. Take a pragmatic approach in recreating the same environment you would be meeting in face to face and decide which technology is best suited to meet your customer's needs.

Here are some considerations.

Alternative working arrangements

Where will the customer be when you start your meeting? Will they be working from home? Will they be in their office? Are they out of town but still have access to the Internet and have the right devices? Answer these questions for the customer, and then ask the same for yourself. Don't always assume that your customer will be in the same location as yesterday. Your office needs to be clean, organized, and clutter free. The Webaround (www.thewebaround.com) is a portable backdrop to remove distractions or can be used last minute if you don't have time to clean your office.

Customer-friendly options

As you start to dissect technology, applications, and features, you will find out that not all of them are as user-friendly as you would hope. Can the customer find the mute button, hide video, or locate how to share their screen quickly? These considerations will help you prioritize which tools to use in certain situations.

Verbal and nonverbal elements

Screen to Screen Selling is 10 times better than over the phone. When a customer gives you permission to enable their video camera in a remote meeting you get to see them smile, make observations about your customer in their natural environment, and see if they are really paying attention or multi-tasking on something else.

Camera position and eyeball attention

Pay close attention as to how others see you from the camera preview feature of your meeting software. You don't want your web cam pointing neck down at your waist or worse, looking in the other direction.

Also, if your webcam is too close to your body, your head will consume the entire screen for the participants. The camera preview feature of tools like Skype, FaceTime for iPhone, or Zoom.us allows you to see yourself as others will see you in order to position the camera correctly. Finally, write a little note that says, "Smile!" Post it at the top of the screen, next to the webcam. No one ever buys from a grumpy face.

Screen-share application menu

The most powerful and underutilized feature of online meetings is the screen-share feature, and many meeting tools have this feature built in. Whatever is showing on your screen can also be seen on others' computers, laptops, big screen televisions, and wearable technology.

I recommend developing new skills around how to use it more effectively from your laptop or mobile device. The command to start the screen-share feature is usually a button to click to share screen or an option available in the application menu. Remember, software offers several different ways to use each application feature. Find the most efficient way, repeat it over and over again, and ingrain those tasks into your subconscious.

Checklist 3-2 WORKING ARRANGEMENTS

Telepresence is the new trend that allows team members to work while they are in different locations. And, depending on how simple or sophisticated of an environment you want to create, you can have everyone join by webcam or appear in virtual 3D. Let's take a look at some alternative working arrangements you can consider.

Home office

Do you already have a home office? Great. Ramp up the Internet connection with your Internet service provider, because Screen to Screen meetings soak up bandwidth like a sponge. You are relying upon a strong signal and a strong wireless router to connect multiple devices. Your computer, tablet, and smartphone all need to be on the same network if they are being used simultaneously. And, if the connection is too slow to handle your equipment's demands, the meeting experience will suffer.

Office adaptations

You don't have to overhaul your company's office equipment to add the Screen to Screen benefits and flexibility to your sales meetings. If you have a conference room, you can add a high-definition flat-screen television or projection screen at the front of the room. The conference room's computer must download all the popular meeting applications that are OK'd by your company's IT department. We'll cover this more in Chapter 12. Then, as long as the sound is plugged in from the laptop to the room speakers and you have a conference phone system available, dialogue will flow smoothly.

Hotel and meeting rooms

How much does it cost to use the Internet at your favorite hotel chain? I'm always in awe of how much Internet access costs at hotels. Here are some options to consider:

- BYOR. Bring your own router. Some hotels will give you a hard-wired Ethernet cable to plug into your computer for Internet access. Rather than plugging the Ethernet cable into the computer, plug the cable into your own router which (depending upon firewall settings) will allow you to connect multiple devices to the same network for a seamless connection experience.
- Hotels sometimes give each of your devices its own Wi-Fi password to get connected to the Internet. But just being on the same wireless network doesn't mean your devices are connected to one another for quick data transfer.

- The strength of your wireless signal will depend upon the facility, distance from the router, and operating system speed of the device you are using. Plug a USB wireless-signal booster into your laptop to get a faster connection.

Internet cafes

If you are in field sales, I'm willing to bet you have tried to take calls with customers from a Starbucks or Panera café (St. Louis Bread Company in St. Louis). However, you can't have effective Screen to Screen meetings in locations like these, for a couple of reasons.

1. Risk of being interrupted is far too great.
2. The Internet signal isn't something you can control.
3. The audio quality will decrease from background noise.

If anything, the Internet cafes are great places to do digital administration tasks.

Extreme locations

I've Skype videoed while snowboarding at Durango Mountain Resort, called from an American Airlines plane using Skype (not accessible anymore) and made Skype phone calls from cruise ships that had Internet access.

And, the strength of the Internet connection is always critical to have a successful conversation. If the Internet connection is weak, then switch the meeting to enable audio only in order to demand less broadband from the network.

Checklist 3-3 TECHNOLOGY REVIEW

Meeting online is becoming an ordinary part of business life. In its 2013 Sales Engagement Study, CSO Insights found that 72.4%

of the nearly 500 sales organizations it surveyed said they were using "web-based collaborative meeting technology." This is an impressive number, but I wonder how many companies are really using it well. The technology you own is only as good as your ability to set it up, use it, and get help when it breaks down. It is easy to blame technology for breakdowns, but it's also important to take responsibility for how smoothly your meetings go by understanding the following priorities when choosing which online meeting technology to use.

Platform support availability

Customers don't care if your technology doesn't work, so what do you do when you have a technology issue? The biggest consideration when deciding whether to choose a freemium tool (initial cost is free with an upgrade upsell) or an enterprise solution (customized software sold to businesses) is the availability of customer support. Each of the meeting platforms offers support options by phone, email, and online chat at different price points. Before you go all in on a meeting solution, enroll in the free trial and test the customer support experience.

Pricing and licensing options

Right now, you can host meetings with up to 25 people using Zoom. us video-to-video, screen share, and participant chat for free. The premium version of Join.me allows you to start a meeting from your Apple Watch and mobile phone. The all-in-one sales engagement platform ClearSlide has deeper analytics to show real time customer engagement. Many of these online meeting platforms have allowed their application programming interface (API) to integrate the customer database, website, and other company support tools. Enterprise solutions that integrate with API require specialized computer programming knowledge to be used under the platform's license agreement.

Meeting setup and participation

66% of buyers are looking to acquire new web collaboration tools.

OVUM, COLLABORATION 2.0 DEATH OF THE WEB CONFERENCE

Here are questions to ask about the technology setup.

- How quickly am I able to start a meeting from invite to engagement?
- How quickly is the participant able to join the meeting?
- How familiar are you and the participant with the online meeting tools?
- What are the common mistakes or questions participants have about the platform?
- Does the participant need to create an online account to join the meeting?

Functionality and usability

Here are some platform features to add to your wish list:

- Meeting duration. Start to finish some meeting tools allow more time than others for participants to interact.
- Video-to-video chat. I see you. You see me.
- Audio teleconferencing (international phone numbers). Phone numbers are great backups when VOIP is not available.
- Screen share (with audio from laptop speakers). You see my screen too.
- Participant chat. I message you inside the meeting without sending an email.
- Whiteboard. I draw on your screen similar to transparencies and chalkboards.
- Mouse control. I give you control of my mouse to use on my screen.
- Meeting room vanity URL and branding. We easily remember the link to the meeting room.

- Mobile co-browsing. Screen share on mobile devices.
- Browser plugins and add-ons. Additional features made by 3rd parties.
- Meeting recording options (video). We watch meetings for quality control and training purposes.

Software installation and security

Organizations that supply their team with laptops may have high privacy restrictions, and employees may need approval from the IT department before installing new software. Similarly, customers may need approval too from their IT department. You don't have to be the expert on network security on every meeting platform. Search the web for the security and installation FAQs ahead of time to find the most appropriate link(s) to send to IT in order to save them time and build confidence that you know where to find the answers.

Network security will be covered more in Chapter 12.

Checklist 3-4 MOBILE-APPS REVIEW

There are more apps in the app store than you have time to figure out how they work. Similarly, you already have invested in other apps that may perform similar functions or need to be integrated into the apps you have already invested in.

Here are some tips for becoming more selective in choosing apps for working from your tablet or smartphone, as well as updating your apps.

Cross-platform integration

The most popular apps are those that create the same experience regardless of whether you are operating from a laptop, tablet, or mobile device. And, you can preview the experience using the screenshots from the provider's website, app store preview, and in YouTube demonstration videos.

Before I download any app, I ask myself these questions:

- Is this app available for iOS (Apple), Android (Google), and Windows (Microsoft)? If it is available for all three, then any customer with a mobile device can use it, regardless of their device.
- Will the app synchronize data between my laptop, tablet, and smartphone? If so, it will be more useful.
- What additional in-store app upgrades do I need to invest in? Some features will remain dormant until an additional purchase is made.

Responsive features

The best meeting and presentation apps are those that offer the same features as the desktop version packaged tightly into a mobile app display. For example, Zoom.us has a menu at the bottom of the phone where you can quickly set the audio, enable/disable video camera, invite participants with quick share copy/paste meeting URL, control the audio of participants, and share screen. Zoom doesn't sacrifice the functionality or user experience in transition from desktop to mobile.

Quick link share

When you're engaged in a Screen to Screen meeting, you want to be able to share links to online content as quickly as possible. Sharing a link is often the way you'll start meetings. Also, during the meeting itself, you can send a link to share important files, documents, and images. That means you want apps in which links are easy to share and fast to use.

Here are some questions to ask to determine how sharable your meetings are:

- How quickly can you start a meeting?
- Was it easy to create the meeting URL (the link's address) for participants to access and click?
- How fast can you copy and paste links and share them with chat?

Content portability

Presentation visuals created for different meetings need to be available at a moment's notice stored as files. Images, process maps, and slides can be saved into the photos app of the device whereas documents might be stored in Google Drive or Dropbox. Meeting apps now integrate with the photos and other storage apps in order for hosts to decrease the response time in accessing important visuals for conversations.

In choosing your apps, it's best to identify those that require the fewest keystrokes and clicks when cross-navigating multiple platforms.

Updates and bug fixes

After you have selected and downloaded apps, consistently update them when software developers release new versions. Benefits include repairing bug fixes, installing security patches, adding feature enhancements, and improving usability.

Updates should be performed at night, not right before customer conversations. Most customers won't have the patience to wait five minutes for your software update to finish for a conversation to start. Plus, if the update dramatically changes the interface right before a meeting and you can't find platform then it could hurt the conversation flow and overall first impression.

Checklist 3-5 MANAGING BUDGETS

New tools are expensive. It costs the initial investment to buy them. It costs the team productivity in unlearning old tools and developing skills around new ones. And, the sunk costs in previous tools are now realized. Take a pragmatic approach to calculate the true investment in adding a new tool each time one is in consideration and avoid making costly mistakes before it is too late.

Initial-setup budget

What does an initial investment cost to get started? That of course depends upon the experience you want to create using the tools you already have. Consider these items as a wish list for multiple Screen to Screen Selling environments.

- Computer and operating system, price varies
- Tablet computer, $300 and up
- Smartphone, $400 and up
- Webcam (if not built in), $100
- Kubi robot $700
- Double presence robot on wheels (http://store.apple.com/us/product/HE494LL/A/double-telepresence-robot), $2,500
- High-definition flat-screen television, $2,000
- Projector and screen, $1,000
- Logitech Conference Cam Connect, $500

Renewals and recurring charges

Online-meeting software and web-based software (known as SaaS, which stands for "software as a service") will have a monthly or yearly fee. I recommend starting the free trial before signing a yearly contract and setting an appointment on your calendar in one month to measure the return on investment before the annual billing cycle renews.

Warranties and upgrades

When you buy hardware, also buy the warranty with a duration as long as its useful life. I've been issued new computers or refurbished models and received discounts because I enrolled in the warranty upon purchase. More importantly, a warranty gives you quicker access to support to resolve issues faster than a prospective customer inquiring about the product.

If you are a heavy user of technology then it makes sense to load up your devices with the most amount of upgrades, like processing speed, storage, and camera features. Repetitive tasks performed with the best technology should (not always) increase your productivity because the performance of the device is faster. If you move at a slower pace, try a model comparison in the middle. Rarely would I recommend getting the least expensive version because too many useful features are unavailable.

Obsolescence

Each technology you acquire will lose value over time just like fruit spoils if you don't eat it. It's realistic to assume that your phone today won't have the same value ten years from now because newer models will have features that don't exist today.

One way to address technology obsolescence from software is to choose SaaS (software as a service), because the software company hosts the software online and any updates are included in the annual billing price. This allows customers to add the latest features, updates, and bug fixes without requiring the customer to buy the product every time a new release is made.

Checklist 3-6 WIRELESS DEVICES

The best meeting environments are those reverse engineered from the customer experience and availability of the best choices in technology. And, this experience can be enhanced with the meeting host using multiple devices synchronously in order to create a visually stimulating experience. Examine a few of these common scenarios.

Wi-Fi and the Internet

There is a difference between Wi-Fi and the Internet. The Internet is access online to information networks for computers and devices throughout the world wide web. Wi-Fi is a networking technology for sending and receiving wireless signals that connects multiple devices in the same location. For example, when you visit Starbucks and want to access their Internet, you connect through Starbucks' Wi-Fi wireless network so that you don't need to find an Ethernet to plug into your computer for Internet access.

Examples of when you want to use Wi-Fi (in addition to using the Internet):

- Mirror the display on your tablet to your desktop computer in order to use other desktop applications at the same time. Ex. App demo.
- Mirror the display on your tablet to a projection screen wirelessly.
- Make slide annotations using the Doceri Desktop iPad presentation app on slides in PowerPoint.

Projection screen options

Traditional group presentations have the presenter connecting their laptop to a projector to a projection screen. But according to a case study in Ovum's Collaboration 2.0 Death of the Web Conference, screen sharing is often taking the place of this face-to-face approach. Customer conference rooms equipped with a computer, projector, and screen (or flatscreen TV) can display your presence with the right Screen to Screen meeting app without you being there. And so, it is incredibly important to prepare the group with the proper A/V setup so that the projection screen image (or TV), room layout, camera positions, and sound quality are optimal for a two way conversation.

Routers and wireless signals

Meeting setup for a hybrid of face-to-face/remote participants can live poll, interact with social media, or collaborate with technology as long as everyone has Internet access. The facility that hosts the face-to-face participants needs a powerful router and a simplified process to enable participants to join the Wi-Fi network quickly without delay. Here are some tips for preparing your facility or that of your customer:

- Find out whether your customer's facility has Wi-Fi with Internet access, how many devices it can handle, and if it can support the bandwidth demand.
- Ask for the name of the wireless network, password, and the URL for the meeting invitation to be stored in a quickly retrievable location. Paper post-it notes and pre-printed access instructions work great.
- Distribute meeting instruction notes to the participants ahead of the meeting with any preparation materials to review.

A year ago I had 20 participants join video-to-video from the same Wi-Fi access point in the same room and crashed the network because the facility wasn't properly equipped and I didn't know any better at the time. I hope you don't make that same mistake.

Bluetooth cameras and audio

My Bose headphones, Apple Watch, and Swivl recording device connect the audio to my phone using Bluetooth technology without using wires. These devices communicate with one another wirelessly which has removed the need for cords and freed up my ability to do more things without being physically tied to a location. Bluetooth cameras started in home security protection and have now evolved into creating collaborative environments with remote teams. The Kubi and Telepresence Robot mentioned earlier are specific examples of Bluetooth cameras with audio available.

Checklist 3-7 AUDIO OPTIONS: PHONE, VOIP, OR WEBRTC

Customers have their own preferred ways of communicating with technology using the phone. Some will prefer calling in through a land line connection, some will prefer VOIP (calling through the software), and others don't care just as long as the instructions are easy. Take a look at some options and considerations in using each one.

Landline vs. mobile phone

If there is a choice between better quality audio or video (screen share), choose audio. And, the audio connection can be dramatically improved by calling from a landline phone or using a reliable high speed Internet connection for VOIP. Landline phone calls are more stable than dialing in from a smartphone. With a mobile device, the battery could die, another app could cause the device to restart, or app notifications can continuously interrupt the conversation. When possible, use a landline connection to dial in.

VoIP app installation

Web conference calls that don't require video or screen share can be accessed using VoIP (Voice over Internet Protocol). With this technology, you don't have to dial a phone number to join the conversation. Instead, click the "Join audio" button and "join meeting" link. VoIP requires both parties to download the meeting app in order to participate using the audio feature.

WebRTC

Have you ever delayed an online meeting because someone needed to install an app first? This irritant has been removed by WebRTC (Web real-time communications), which lets consumers co-browse with one another, with or without the sales professional. The audio and video conversation is hosted inside the Internet browser, not as an application. Think of it as online chat on steroids.

WebRTC offers several benefits to consumers and sellers:

- No software download
- Only a few lines of JavaScript installed on website

- Analytics to track customer behavior during discovery and buying process
- Lead capture using quick forms

International roaming

The cost for long distance phone calls has dramatically reduced with
the availability of the Internet in more locations and the addition
of VoIP. However, use for some technology or websites is restricted
because of government influence to prevent foreign competition
with local businesses. For example, if you want to use Skype while in
China, you have to download a special version and buy credits from
a Chinese bank account if you want to Skype with a Chinese resi-
dent. Whether you are for or against net neutrality in your customer's
country, you must be compliant with each country's Internet service
provider regulations, and have back up options just in case.

◆◆◆

CHAPTER 4

BEFORE THE APPOINTMENT: HOW TO PREPARE SCREEN TO SCREEN CONVERSATIONS FOR CONVERSIONS

Sales are easy. Salespeople make sales hard.

—MIKE WEINBERG, AUTHOR OF *NEW SALES SIMPLIFIED*

To increase sales, you need to increase the number of meetings with the right people at the right time. In previous chapters, I identified the irritants and barriers to hosting remote meetings, and then I outlined the technology that can help you facilitate these conversations. Now I will show you how to use those tools to better prepare for as many appointments as possible without leaving your desk.

Checklist 4-1 SALES PERFORMANCE

In her book *Nonstop Sales Boom*, Colleen Francis mentions the sales leader clarification model as a way to define the types of accounts to pursue in order to attract new business and sustain long-term growth in sales. According to Francis, the salesperson should focus on growth and key accounts while allocating fewer resources to service and maintenance accounts. I agree and would add to conserve some travel expenses and time by meeting existing maintenance accounts Screen to Screen, and conserve resources for face-to-face meetings with greater opportunities. Read on to find steps on how to establish your Screen to Screen Selling model for optimal performance.

Establish a Screen to Screen strategy

Low cost, low margin or low valued products or services don't need Screen to Screen Selling because the customer acquisition cost and risk is relatively low. The Screen to Screen approach is most beneficial for any type of customer relationship that is focused on complex processes that involve high risk/return decision-making, performing of critical tasks, and demonstration of specialized expertise by educating customers through a series of steps. And, it may take several meetings with a prospective customer face to face or Screen to Screen in order to influence their decision. Establish a focus on which customers, products, or services would benefit most based on their buying behavior and adapt your model to include Screen to Screen as you best see fit.

Sales enablement innovation

Sales enablement refers to the recent trend of making the buying process easier for buyers and those who are selling goods and services. Customers are presented with their best options at the right time during the sales cycle from sales professionals. New tools empowered with real time data allow sales professionals to serve their customers faster and sometimes before the buyer knows they need to buy themselves. For example, tools like Salesloft, Toutapp, Yesware, LiveHive, and ClearSlide can tell you how many times a customer opened up an email, if they forwarded it on, if they opened up the attachment and other important customer behavior salespeople can use to modify their approach.

Sales process customization

Selling which widgets isn't as important as how you sell widgets differently from everyone else more effectively. And, what works for someone else might not work for you. I've learned that in order to break rules, first you have to know them. Follow these basic steps and see how you might customize your sales process accordingly.

- Identify and respond to customer.
  - Reply by text message with video.
  - Send video email.
  - Instant screen share meetings.
- Build rapport and trust.
  - Send a handwritten thank-you note.
  - Research social media profiles to find similar interests.
  - Supply referrals and ideas while using screen share.
- Select the most effective technology.
  - Select most customer friendly tools.
  - Identify distinctive demonstrative techniques to communicate ideas.
  - Eliminate barriers and perpetual irritants from experience.
- Visualize the conversation with framing skills.
  - Create diagnostic visuals.
  - Improve use of digital whiteboard.
  - Anticipate quick access of frequent websites.
- Arrive at a conceptual agreement.
  - Fill in the blank annotations from visuals.
  - Calculate customer ROI using table or chart.
- Customer signs agreement.
  - Sign accurately, completely, and in real time screen share.

Customer anticipated questions

Do you have a list of questions your customer typically asks when meeting for the first time? Common question themes include, "Will this make my life easier? How much money will I save? How much time can I save? How much better will I feel as a result?"

Similarly, a customer might have questions they don't know they need to ask until you can frame their situation in a way that demonstrates an opportunity they might be missing.

Build a list of questions your customer is likely to ask. Then prepare a visual that answers each question quickly without the need to explain every detail. For example, if someone is facing foreclosure, then a lender could use an image that lists the advantages on one side and the disadvantages on another side. Because this is a question a lender faces often, it's critical to have a visual prepared to answer clients' concerns.

Checklist 4-2 PHONE CONVERSATIONS

Despite the advantages of Screen to Screen Selling, the phone is still an effective sales tool. "'Cold' calling might be dead, but not SMART prospecting," says Art Sobczak, author of *Smart Calling*. Surprisingly, even salespeople with leads don't always bother to call.

In the context of Screen to Screen Selling, the question is not whether to contact your leads (of course you should!), but whether to use the phone and additional technology to influence decisions. This section compares phone conversations with Screen to Screen Selling conversations so you can decide when to use each one.

The advantage of using the phone over email, text, or social media is that you can express great enthusiasm, change meaning according to tone, and sometimes solve a problem faster. However, the phone has its limitations that when overlooked might decrease the impact you might have during a sales conversation:

- **Reliance on clarity and tone:** In the movie *Wolf of Wall Street*, Leonardo DiCaprio's character does vulgar physical acts when on the phone with a customer, while keeping his voice calm, collected, and in concert with the customer's aspirations. The reverse could be happening for the sales professional, who can't see the customer's body language, facial expressions, and posture. When you rely only on the phone, you are missing out on 85% of your customer's communication.
- **Metaphors are verbal:** What I say doesn't necessarily equate to what I mean, what you understand, and what you see. Meaning can sometimes get lost in translation, especially when you rely on the spoken word. Visuals can enhance that meaning and make the message more memorable and can be archived for future viewing.
- **Visual learners are handicapped:** If some of your customers rely on visuals to reinforce their understanding, then a phone call to them is not adapting to their preferred learning style. Therefore, you might lose them while explaining advanced concepts or processes. In contrast, Screen to Screen Selling conversations involve auditory, visual, and kinesthetic learners, because they are actively involved with their devices.

Checklist 4-3 SCHEDULING MEETINGS

How many customer meetings did you set and attend today? Since Screen to Screen appointments depend upon technology and not physical transportation you can attend more of them in less time. Prepare yourself by choosing the most effective meeting scheduler, supporting tools, and notifications settings. As a result you can prevent remote participant absenteeism and increase the overall sales productivity of your team.

Follow these appointment preparation tips when scheduling Screen to Screen meetings.

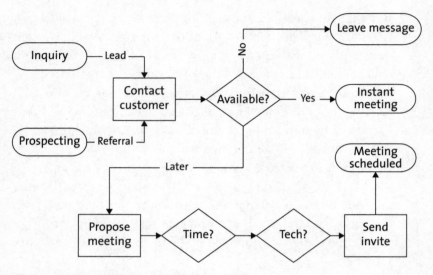

Figure 4.1 Process for Apointment Setting

Meeting scheduler characteristics

Your online-meeting tool should have some scheduling options that can save you time scheduling and allow the customer to save the meeting in their calendar. Using such a tool can decrease absenteeism as a result. In your software's scheduling tool, look for and learn to use the following options:

- Email invitation with instructions for joining the meeting
- Link to join a meeting in progress
- Calendar attachment that saves meeting information in the customer's appointment book
- Meeting notifications sent by email, text, or social media

Power dialer for making calls

How many telephone prospecting calls can you make in 60 minutes to the customers who already know you, like you, and trust you? The more calls the more appointments and referrals you can request.

Integrate a power dialer with your customer relationship management (CRM) system in order to automatically dial customers directly from your computer or mobile device. The investment in a speed dialer saves you time finding phone numbers, dialing phone numbers, and preventing long times on hold waiting for an answering machine.

Setting a results-driven agenda

Each meeting invitation sent should include a results-oriented agenda for the topics covered or questions to be answered. A quick summary might say:

1. Calculate the lost opportunity by conducting business as usual.
2. Identify cost savings from mutually agreed solutions.
3. Decide the investment necessary in order to meet specific needs.

The summary is quick, to the point, and shares what will happen as a result of the meeting.

Before you send your next meeting request, include a results driven agenda inside of the meeting invitation message template provided by your meeting technology solution.

Calendar integration

A common problem with scheduling meetings is that the salesperson and customer don't know one another's schedule. The two of them send email back and forth, proposing one time after another until they find a time that works for both of them.

This approach is time-consuming and delays the meeting.

Remove this delay with a shared public calendar using Meet.me or TimeTrade.com that gives customers access to dedicated time slots reserved for sales conversations and synchronizes with each other's calendars. This calendar appears to customers as a widget on a company website and to the salesperson as an RSS feed inside the salesperson's calendar application in order to prevent having to update multiple calendars one by one.

Meeting notifications

Delayed meetings cost money. Postponed meetings as a repetitive practice cost even more. Best practices to confirm a next-day appointment include sending an email, texting the meeting notification, and making a phone call to ensure the time has been protected by the customer. All three executed may be a bit overboard so choose your reminder options carefully based on customer expectations. Then research the Screen to Screen Selling meeting apps to see how to automate and integrate meeting reminders into your sales process.

Checklist 4-4 MANAGE MULTIPLE BUYERS

Preparation to persuade multiple decision makers at the same time during remote meetings without causing conflict or losing control of the conversation is a very complicated task. This requires more attention to multiple decision-making styles, more accurate questions to provoke dialogue, and better choice of visuals to frame conversations in their best interests. Here are some special circumstances to be prepared for when engaging multiple buyers.

Participation preferences

One client might love the details, but their colleague might want to see just the big picture. What do you do? I recommend catering to both. Start with big-picture visuals, ask how decisions are made, and then break them down sequentially from less detail to more. Also, ask your customers if they prefer to use online chat or other features inside the online-meeting software. You could save a customer time finding a pricing guide by copying and pasting the link to the PDF inside the online chat during a conversation. You could send a quick tweet with a hashtag if Twitter is preferred. What matters is what the customers want and how they want to receive it.

Participant interface usability

The more customers involved during the web conference meeting, the more the likelihood one will use a different operating system or device increases. This can cause issues in helping the customers access hidden online-meeting features, because the menus on your screen will be different from theirs. For example, if a customer uses an Android operating system and you have a MacBook, you might have to help the customer navigate the menus on their device. This would involve walking them through step by step to troubleshoot any technical issues that might occur.

Web-conferencing features

The most important web-conferencing features are audio, video, and screen share. To use audio features well, you need to know how to mute yourself, mute the whole group at once, and silence an individual who starts to cause trouble. With video, you will need to know when to show video, when to share screen, and when to pass over control of your screen. Online polling, participant chat, and whiteboard features will be explored in later chapters.

Handle conflict among group members

Sometimes conflicts arise in a group of customers. Here are a few signs that conflict may be arising during a Screen to Screen meeting:

- Participants don't allow you to finish asking questions and complete your statements.
- One customer keeps posting remarks to the online chat that distracts attention away from the objectives of the meeting.
- One customer repeatedly speaks out of order or without regard to others during the conversation.

The best way to handle conflict during these situations is to appreciate the feedback, seek to understand the customer's intent, and determine if the meeting should continue. Obnoxious behavior is inexcusable; depending on its severity, the host may need to eject the offending person from the web meeting room.

MEASURE ENGAGEMENT LEVEL

Patrick Lencioni, author of *The Five Dysfunctions of a Team*, says, "Absence of trust, fear of conflict, lack of commitment, avoidance of accountability and inattention to results are the reasons why teams do not succeed." It's important to continuously measure the commitment of your customers by how much they participate during the meetings from the signals you receive.

These signals represent the level of customer commitment:

- The dialogue is not dichotomous. Everyone in the process engages as a team, not hidden agendas that work in department silos.
- Participant chat reinforces the rigor. Customers pat each other on the back by supporting one another with positive remarks in the online chat.
- Latitude for laughter. Count how many laughs lasted after the conversation. The more fun you have, the more likely they are to buy.

CHAPTER 5

◆◆◆

PROVISIONING AND POSITIONING: WHAT YOU NEED TO GET READY FOR THE CONVERSATION

You very likely have seen visual presentations in which the speaker displays a series of slides—one boring bulleted list after another. When I talk about using visuals in Screen to Screen Selling, I have in mind something quite different:

- Visuals are diagnostics. They help solve problems, just as doctors perform tests to diagnose the cause of the patient's symptoms.
- Visuals appear extemporaneously. They appear in the order prompted by customer requests, not a predetermined order.
- Visuals can be sequential. Like branches from a tree, the order of the visuals springs from the root of the problem. An answer from one visual might suggest another set of visuals, depending upon the hierarchy of the questions.

In this chapter, we will equip you with the types of visuals to use with different types of customers based on trends from data, knowledge management, decision styles and how to access them quickly.

Checklist 5-1 DATA SOURCES

According to a Cisco Visual Networking Index: Global Mobile Data Traffic Forecast Update 2014–2019 White Paper, monthly global mobile data traffic will surpass 24.3 exabytes (1000^6 bytes) by 2019. And, it's no wonder why organizations have a Chief Data Officer to mine through what data is relevant, how to process it, and how to protect it. In order to save you time sifting through stockpiles of data here are a few useful data types to consider making visuals that will support buyer decisions when sharing your screen.

Demographic trends

According the U.S Census bureau, in 2015 Generation Y will surpass the Baby Boomers in comparative population. And, companies seeking new alternatives to capture the Gen Y market are forgetting the Baby Boomers who have all the money. A visually stimulating image illustrating the significant statistical discrepancy in assets would demonstrate this much better than me just writing or saying it. The visuals speak for themselves.

Historical patterns

According to the National Association of REALTORS® International Profile of Home Buying Activity, in the last year foreign clients paid on average nearly $500 thousand for a house, compared to the overall U.S. average house price of about $256 thousand. An infographic-like image would show the dramatic price difference to support a listing agent's international marketing campaign directed at foreign buyers.

Table 5.1 Ways to Visualize Historical Patterns

Charts	Graphs	Diagrams
Trend focused	Data focused	Relationship focused
Data required	Data required	Data not required
Characteristic driven	Correlation driven	Process driven
Linear	2-dimensional	3-dimensional

Psychological needs

Emotions come from customer sentiment as to how they feel about a specific product, service, or event. And, data sources that support feelings can help you craft visuals to reinforce them in conversations with customers. For example, an investor from Sao Paolo, Brazil might choose New York City because it's safer to walk the streets, whereas a Chinese investor might buy because the investment in the U.S. is safer than keeping the assets in the local economy.

Geographic considerations

Maps are fantastic tools to demonstrate geographical constraints, buyer activity, and help teams allocate resources more appropriately. Type in your customer's home location or destination in Google Maps, and you can analyze distances, draw map routes, or target regions using an electronic highlighter from your computer. Your narration as you navigate will save your customers time trying to visualize every step all at once.

Search your industry, software provider, or company toolkit for visual templates you can use in your screen share conversations. A great example for the real estate industry is Keeping Current Matters (http://kcmblog.com) who supply both PowerPoint and images.

Checklist 5-2 FILE MANAGEMENT

My mom, used to say, "Everything has a home, so you can find it later." And, that's good advice for managing digital files found on devices and in the cloud to answer customers' questions. Organize your files into logical places, so you can find them fast. Consider all of the electronic files that you use to support the sales process, including forms, applications, and recordings of the conversations to be shared with your customer. Arrange it logically. Then, when the customer asks, "Can you help me with X?" you can quickly share the answer based on their preferred method of communication.

Document storage

Printed promotions, agreements, and invoices can be stored in the cloud, not sent to the printer. A customer might request an example sales agreement and you can either show it to them in real time through screen share and/or send it electronically. And, the most reliable access to store these documents is in the cloud accessible on all devices, mobile included. This way sales professionals can respond quickly with the right documents if they are hosting a meeting from their laptop or tablet device

Bookmarks in the cloud

As of today there are 308 million search results for "screen share" each of which contains recommendations on which tools are the most effective, videos on how to screen share more effectively, and images that support the process. The problem is finding the right link to the right answer because A) quantity of content is high, B) quality of overall content is low, and C) we don't have the time to sift through all the answers. That's why in professional sales for higher value transactions it can never be automated.

Instead of files, think of links that can be saved as bookmarks for frequently used documents, requested videos, and supporting research as favorites that synchronize across you Internet browser. That way when the question comes up you can find the link quickly from your Internet browser to copy/paste share by email, text message, instant messenger, and more.

Risk management and security

A security breach isn't a matter of "if it is going to happen", "it's really a matter of when." The larger the organization, transaction, and risk associated the deeper the need for an enterprise level document storage solution. Enterprise solutions offer the best security but in most cases are not affordable for the startup entrepreneur. Review the security protection measures offered by each solution and compare pros and cons using online forums with trusted user feedback. We will explore risk management and security best practices more in Chapter 12.

Compatible file types

Create files for distribution in a universal format that anyone can download if they are using a Mac, PC, Android, or Windows. Save word processing files as PDF to avoid broken formatting mistakes when transitioning from Microsoft Word files, Apple's pages, or incompatible versions. Save audio as MP3 files, movies as MP4 and presentation slides as PDFs in order to increase the likelihood they can access your files without contacting customer support.

Checklist 5-3 CREATION OF VISUALS

Begin by learning to draw and paint like the old masters. After that, you can do as you like; everyone will respect you.
—SALVADOR DALI

The process of creating visuals starts with results first and then brainstorming more visually appealing ways of explaining an idea in order to get conceptual agreement or persuade someone to take action. We will discuss process maps, fill in the blank templates, and how to narrow down choices through visual selection or de-selection of alternatives.

Process maps and flowcharts

Process maps are a great overview to an extensive buying process. And creating one ready to explain the steps involved can save time and minimize errors by you and the customer. For example, a customer could save hours searching for a house by not looking at ones not pre-approved to buy. A mortgage professional could demonstrate the home buying process in a way the customer understands with a process map so it makes sense to get pre-approved first.

Easy to use software to help you create process maps:

- Draw.io is a free web-based tool that integrates with Google Docs.
- The Grafio iPad app creates great decision-making templates.
- MindMeister creates mind maps which are spider web-like outlines that brainstorm alternatives in clusters around the center of a main idea.

Forms and registrations

Any existing blank forms or registration templates will work during screen share conversations to authorize transactions. This step requires you to have forms accessible, ready to preview, and to allow customers to sign electronically. Seek legal counsel when adopting new forms and be especially leery of those found easily on the Internet.

There are two types of forms to consider: first, forms you collaborate on to obtain conceptual agreement; and second, forms you sign, print, and store for record keeping. One visual form could be a quick rating scale that customers use to show their urgency. The next example form is their official commitment by electronic signature or sent overnight for printed signatures (if required by your legal jurisdiction).

Spreadsheets and calculators

The financial breakdown is more complex for every row and column of data you add. Multiple accountants could give you a different perspective even though they have the same data. Visuals can demonstrate a reliable process for calculating common answers and increase the trust between both parties because the numbers are transparent throughout the screen share.

Application screenshots

Every software program or app you have downloaded is in and of itself its own visual. Apps are becoming more universal in cross-channel design, so familiarity across operating systems is less of an issue. For example, if you are demoing your company app to a customer, you will need to explain locations of features and guide customers through their own questioning process. You don't have to be a creative design expert to design images for conversations when, chances are, you already have these images created as website images, website forms, or inside of your own company literature. Take a computer screenshot of the visual, table, or form data to create a list of options from which the customer can choose. Not only will this increase engagement with your customer, but you also can include it in your visual summary.

Checklist 5-4 VISUAL TEMPLATES

The best way to engage a customer screen to screen is to ask a really good question, ask permission to share your screen, and then insert a blank visual template in which the customer supplies the answers in the blanks and for you to address. This template could represent a blank Venn diagram, blank table, or blank process map saved as an image. Used at the right time, specific customer needs are solved with visual templates rather than making assumptions about what they really want.

Here are some examples.

Fill-in-the-blank

The easiest way to create fill-in-the-blank visuals is with Microsoft Word, Excel, or PowerPoint by creating tables. Just add the appropriate number of columns, rows and label the headings for the table. Then, take a screenshot or export the table as an image to be used in your screen share meetings so customers can fill in the blanks. For example, a table to pursue one option has advantages and disadvantages. After you display the table on screen share, the customer tells you what answers to fill in the blanks using your best annotation tool.

Selection and de-selection

Visuals can provide customers choices they didn't know were options and make selection faster than over the phone. Some customers prefer to see all of the options and then narrow them down one by one to get the best result. Others want you to help them select the best option without having to explore every detail.

These options are represented by images of benefits, features, products, and add-ons and by asking which are the most important for the customer. They help you prioritize the conversation. For example, an insurance agent could use a visual template that displays auto insurance, home insurance, personal property insurance, life insurance, and commercial insurance plans. A customer who owns a business in addition to a home might not know the insurance agent sells commercial insurance if it weren't listed as an option to select. Visual templates aid in the cross promotion of multiple products or services and recapture lost sales, even if you forget to mention, "Oh, by the way."

Ranking priorities

Every day we commit money, time, and energy to specific needs and wants. And, prioritizing needs over wants is a challenge we don't have an expert to help. Use a blank checklist as a visual template so you can help a customer list what's most important in their order, make recommendations to improve their condition, and prioritize the steps in the right order to help the customer reach their goal.

Project management

In order to successfully manage the timeline of a customer transaction, its typical to have a timeline with important milestones before, during, and after the customer walks away happy. Successful collaboration in sales happens when the salesperson and the customer work as partners.

And, presenting the transaction outline as a fill in the blank visual template for the customer to supply input increases the accuracy of details and improves the recall for when important events are supposed to happen. Take a screenshot of your existing customer funnel or have a designer create a more customer friendly model.

Brainstorming

Sometimes the best template is a blank one. In Chapter 8, I will go into more detail about brainstorming using a whiteboard, mind mapping, and extemporaneous thinking with visuals. Going into the conversation, you don't have to have all the answers—just the questions inside your process confirmed visually.

Checklist 5-5 CO-BROWSING ELEMENTS

Before you start sharing your screen with others, you can adjust your settings to improve the conversation experience. Settings to consider adjusting include the cursor, placement of links on web pages, and display size. Also be ready to help customers navigate your company's website.

Cursor size, shape, and color

Your operating system should allow you to change the way the cursor displays. For example, if you or your customers have vision trouble, you simply increase the size of the cursor. It takes a few weeks to get used to the new cursor placement, but your customers will be better off for it. You even may be able to set up the cursor to act as your logo.

Call-to-action clicks

On most websites, there are multiple images, words, and buttons that incorporate links the user can click on (or tap on a touch screen) to move to another web page. However, when there are too many options, the customer can become confused and not be able to follow along. Prepare yourself by locating where to find call-to-action links for frequently used website behavior.

Zooming in and out

Always assume your customer is using a smaller screen than you are. That way, your visuals on your screen will always be viewable on their screen. Your customers may be using screens as small as smartphones and as large as flat-screen televisions during conversations. Since you are responsible for initiating the screen share, you control the size of the information displayed by zooming in and out quickly. Also, you might need to advise your customer to enter the "full-screen mode" on their meeting software, so what is on your screen takes up the entire area of the customer's screen.

Search, filters, and navigation

Your customers will never know more about your website design and layout than you do. (If they do, then that's a whole other issue.) If customers ask questions that can be answered easily on your website, you can save them time in the future and make it easier for them to buy if you show them how. Be ready to show customers how you found the answer by using the website search function, the sort menu, or a shortcut in the website menu navigation.

Also prepare to help customers by asking yourself, "What could go wrong during the buyer purchase or application process online?" Develop a list of errors and solutions. You can use the solutions as talking points inside of the Screen to Screen conversation. For example, if customers frequently experience excessive time spent in a shopping cart, have difficulty adding options, or miss an important feature, you can take responsibility by walking them through. Also, consider asking your web designers and programmers to improve the website by addressing these issues.

Checklist 5-6 QUICK-ACCESS MEMORY

When I throw a tennis ball in my backyard for my French bulldog, Burton, to retrieve, he runs like heck to bring it back. During a Screen to Screen conversation, customers might ask you to find a file or access a website. How fast can you retrieve it? Thus, a final part of preparation is to practice navigating to information on your computer until pulling up answers is fast, easy, and smooth.

Let's say a customer asks you to review their contract with you Screen to Screen. Does finding and opening that file take you five seconds or five minutes? Or suppose a customer asks you to recalculate their investment according to new criteria. How quickly can you access the program to recalculate? The longer someone has to wait on the phone or watch you fumble around with your computer, the more credibility you might lose because of your disorganization.

To improve the performance of your quick-access memory, find the content sources listed in Table 5.2. Choose a few to practice opening. See how quickly you can access each of them by using the best tool and preferred delivery.

Table 5.2 Quick-Access Memory Practice

Requested content	Tool options for creating and hosting content	Delivery options for sharing links
Blog post FAQ	Wordpress, Blogger	Face-to-face
Video FAQ or playlist	YouTube, Vimeo	Screen share
		Email
Slide presentation	SlideShare, HaikuDeck	Text message
PDF report or e-book	Dropbox, Google Drive	Live chat
Image	Instagram, Pinterest	Phone call
		Facebook IM
Infographic	Visual.ly, Piktochart	Skype IM
Audio recording	Dropbox, Evernote	Twitter (mention/hashtag)
Task list	Wunderlist	Participant chat
		Desktop notification
Mind map	MindMeister	Mobile notification
Meeting invitation URL	Meeting software	Wearable technology
		AirDrop Handoff
Meeting notes	Evernote	Push notification
Latest news	Storify	Bluetooth beacons

If you're slower than you expected, don't despair. The following suggestions will help you master the art of fast retrieval and delivery of information.

Link references and repositories

Create a list of important links to files you may want to share. For each of these, you have only three questions to answer:

1. What is the content?
2. What is the tool?
3. Where does it go?

Sort your content types into the following categories:

- Blog post that includes multimedia
- Video with description, prescription, and transcription
- Presentation slides with images and narration
- Image designed as a process visual, infographic, or road map
- Online-meeting invitation
- Project management checklists

The right tool for hosting content depends on the type of content. Here are my recommendations for what to use:

- Wordpress for blog posts (your articles)
- YouTube channel for video
- SlideShare for presentation slides
- Instagram or Pinterest for pictures
- Zoom.us or Join.me for meeting invitations
- Wunderlist for checklists

The final question—Where does it go?—refers to the way you will provide your customer with links to these resources. Each tool I recommended will create a URL for the customer resource you created and posted with the tool. You can then copy and paste the link into whichever of the following modes of communication your customer prefers:

- Text message
- Email
- Facebook instant messenger
- Twitter

Information asset quick links

Even better than giving customers the full URL, create short versions using bit.ly. For example, when customers ask to receive my email updates, I don't give them this link: http://dougdevitre.us4.list-manage.com/subs cribe?u=abe091936f3c5e1038af34638&id=3283dc9414. Instead, I give them http://devitre.com/screen2screen. Both links will go to the same page, but I set up the shorter link because it's easy to remember.

Not only does bit.ly shorten the long link, it also allows me to customize it. Furthermore, I can track to see how many people navigated to my page by typing the URL and how many clicked on a link to go there.

What long links do you share with customers that are hard to memorize and take up too many characters? What links do you want to track? Convert these links using the free http://bit.ly tool.

Information-scented labels

Every visual needs a label (or filename) in order to be found quickly when it appears in the menu of your file folders. And, the label needs to be specific, short, and relevant to the visual based on outcome or process in the conversation. For example, if someone asks me about growing his or her business I will refer to the image labeled "Business Model Generator" in the "Strategy" folder. A quick tip is to label the folders by customer type, transaction type, or process type and synchronized across all of your devices for faster retrieval.

Social-intelligence directory

The dumbest thing a salesperson can ask a customer is, "Hey, what have you been up to?" Unless your customers are Amish, the likelihood of the Internet not having any information on them is pretty slim. Your customer relationship management system can tie into social networks, customer history, and conversational history to prepare you quickly for a productive conversation. Learn about their most recent updates, accomplishments, and online commentary before calling, so you can have more meaningful conversations.

Search-and-find techniques

Finally, speed up your searches for information if you take full advantage of search software. Whether you are using the search menu in your device's operating system to find files on your device, or a search engine on your web browser to hunt down information online, today's search engines try to help you out. One incredibly powerful feature for retrieving data quickly is suggestive search: as you starting typing, suggestive search offers words and phrases that might complete the term you are entering. If you select a suggestion, the search engine immediately fills in the rest of your search term. The best resource on how to do this is Sam Richter's book *Take the Cold Out of Cold Calling.*

The more ways you can search and find, the better equipped you will be to handle a variety of scenarios when you are navigating multiple screens.

PART TWO

CONVERSATION

You are now equipped with the best technology, have the right visuals prepared, and are ready to start having Screen to Screen conversations. However, as Jerry Weisman, author of *Presenting to Win*, says, "What presenters say and how they say it are of far greater importance than what they show."

The next few chapters will share with you what to say during a Screen to Screen conversation, as well as how to navigate through the applications and end the meeting appropriately to ensure your customer takes action.

CHAPTER 6

IT'S SHOW TIME!
WHAT TO SAY WHEN
THE CUSTOMER CONNECTS

Conversation should touch everything,
but should concentrate itself on nothing.

—OSCAR WILDE

According to the CSO Insights 2013 Sales Engagement Study, 72.4% of the nearly 500 sales organizations surveyed are using web-based collaborative-meeting technology. However, how sales organizations are using the technology, what they are saying when using technology, and what customers perceive might not be level with expectations moving forward. This chapter will prepare you with the right questions to ask, so you and the customer can make quick decisions when using technology together.

Checklist 6-1 PREPARED QUESTIONS

The best part of giving a speech is that the customers don't know your lines. However, if you don't know your own lines, then making a sale becomes a more frustrating process—not only for you, but also for your customer who is waiting for the answer.

The problem is that while you are hearing, you're not
listening, no matter how good your intentions and
how hard you try.

—MARK GOULSTON, AUTHOR OF *JUST LISTEN*

Rapport building

Prepare your conversations by doing a little advance homework by knowing who you are talking to first, before jumping in and asking problem-solving and opportunity-seeking questions. Rapport is earned by finding similarities between yourself and the customer, not by asking a magic-bullet question. For example, if you discover from your customer's bio that you both went to the same college at different times you could start by striking up a conversation around past memories, campus activities, or collegiate sports. This step is critical. If you haven't established rapport with a customer, you haven't earned the right to share your screen with them. You can't skip this step. Period.

Objective-seeking questions

There is a fine line between what the customer wants to accomplish (objectives) and what steps to take to get there (alternatives). In the case of home sellers, some objectives (results) they are looking for include negotiating the highest purchase price, moving within a specific time frame, and minimizing the number of repairs they must make before they sell. These types of objective-seeking question then help you prioritize follow up questions and visuals to use during the screen share conversation to help narrow down the alternatives. In the home selling case, alternatives might include aggressive pricing to sell quickly, professionally staging the home to help with showings, or advertising the property as farms/acreage . You don't need to talk about the alternatives until you have confirmed the customer's objectives.

Technology preferences

In order to initiate a screen to screen meeting you must be able to quickly identify the technology your customer is using in order to improve the meeting experience. This involves asking questions about which technology they are most familiar with, speed of their Internet bandwidth, and how to troubleshoot common mistakes. If the technology doesn't work and you don't know what questions to ask to get the meeting started, it can hurt your credibility even though it might not be your fault.

Learn the lingo, so you can limit the number of mistakes made when you do any of the following:

- Selling the benefits of sharing your screen during conversations
- Starting and ending online meetings on time
- Making sure customers can see your screen
- Enabling multiple participants to use multiple web browsers and devices
- Enabling and disabling meeting features such as audio, video, screen share, and online chat

Sequential-process thinking

Our minds are fascinating electronic machines. It's as if God implanted an infinite number of if/then questions that resolve an absolute answer based on our experiences, existing process, and subjective interpretations. Prepare follow up questions to ask after frequently asked questions in order get deeper into the mind of the customer and improve the accuracy of your recommendations. For example, if a customer asks you what the best life insurance is then you might ask them about their age, health, habits in a predetermined sequence supported with or without visuals.

Follow-up preferences

The purpose of the Screen to Screen meeting is for the customer to make an informed decision, not just for you to share information.

And if the customer doesn't reach that decision, then they might have other preferred ways of you following up with them, rather than having another Screen to Screen meeting.

How do you follow up? The easiest way to figure that out is to ask, "What is the best way to follow up with you?" Also, it's much easier to ask this question when the conversation begins than to wait until the end or guess later.

Checklist 6-2 QUICK DECISIONS

Productive conversations happen when you can sort through all of the complex details by asking some critical questions before, during, and after the call. Your goal is to decrease the time spent on meetings, choose the most effective technology for special situations, and focus on the customer experience.

Verbal agreement on agenda

In the meeting notification you sent to the customer ahead of time, you should have included a quick summary of the objectives. But although you included these remarks in an email, that doesn't mean the customer has read them. After you have introduced yourself and made pleasantries, you can verbally review what you both hope to accomplish as a result of the call.

Will video chat hinder or help?

Screen to Screen video can help as much as it can hurt a conversation, depending on the Internet connection, customer's familiarity with technology, and your relationship with the customer. Disable the customer's video upon meeting start as a best practice. Customers may not be aware their camera is on, and that could cause an uncomfortable meeting start if they are not appropriately groomed (or dressed for that matter). If there are frequent pauses or delays in a video to video conversation, this is usually caused by a slow Internet connection. If it happens, you might need to ask the customer to disable the video and just use the audio. If the customer doesn't know how to turn on the video or has a hard time adjusting the audio settings, you might need to revert to the trusted telephone.

Will sharing screens save us time?

If you need a yes/no answer then a text message is fine. If you need more detail then an email will work. And to save time exchanging emails sometimes its better to pick up the phone. You don't need screen share for every meeting. It's only for when you need to frame a complex idea using visuals, demonstrate a website or online tool, or review a document together to avoid reworking the same details over and over again. Be prepared to make the quick decision to share screens as long as it is an added benefit to support the conversation.

Participant's technology requirements

Would you tell a customer, "Sorry, if you can't get your technology to work, then I can't help you"? That would be the last conversation you had with them, their coworkers, and their friends. Instead of telling yourself, "This won't work," ask yourself, "How can we make this work?" Educate yourself on the customer-friendly technology alternatives. Some customers still prefer the phone, and others will demand you visit in person. Don't let the technology get in the way of serving your customers, no matter your bandwidth.

Participant's file-receiving preferences

During a conversation, a customer might ask you to send a file, an image, or a link to a website to provide support information. You can send these files inside the Screen to Screen meeting platform or by email, text message, or social media, depending on what the customer prefers most.

Invitations sent by email, SMS, or SMM

There will be special circumstances when your customer has more than one decision maker and you want to invite more participants into the conversation during your dialogue. For example, a real estate professional might be talking with the husband about contract negotiations and quickly need the wife to be involved visually to see the terms. Your Screen to Screen meeting software has the ability to add more participants during the conversation quickly without having to start over. Every Screen to Screen meeting creates its own unique URL specific to the meeting. Inside the software, you can quickly copy the link to the clipboard, determine the desired participant's communication preference, and paste it and send it to their device. In other words, if the extra party is on the fly, you can paste the link into a text message, and they can join the meeting in seconds, rather than you trying to reschedule for another time, which only delays the decision making time.

Checklist 6-3 QUESTIONING STRUCTURE

Asking more questions reduces the need to have all the answers.
—DONALD PETERSON, FORMER CEO OF FORD MOTOR COMPANY

Do you know what to ask when you are supposed to ask it? Try these tips to improve your line of questioning.

Ask a precise question

Half of solving any problem is asking the right question. A customer might tell you what they want, but only through your diagnosis through questions will you ever find out what they truly need. Rather than asking a why, what, or how question, combine them in order to get a better answer to help you help them. Here are some example questions:

Why are you searching for new talent? Is your company in a growth cycle, or do you want to replace nonperforming team members? You say that revenue is important to sustain your organization, but you are leaving money on the table by not making it easy to buy online. Is that because of strategic oversight or because your team's performance isn't evaluated on outcomes?

The better the question, the better the answer, and the better you can understand your customer's needs.

Ask probing questions with visuals

When the customer supplies you with an answer, do you take their word for it, or do you dig deeper to conceptualize their true need? You need to ask probing questions, and visuals can help.

Visuals are just as great for asking questions as they are for demonstrating answers. Sometimes the only way for a customer to understand a problem is to experience it or recreate it. A Screen to Screen meeting with a customer can include revealing a problem on their website, calculating lost opportunities on a financial calculator, or developing better language for a document. The impact of those decisions will depend on the quality of the questions you ask and the extent to which you allow your customers to discover for themselves.

Affirm answers verbally

There can be a difference between what a customer says, vs. what they mean, vs. what you understand. For example, a prospective home buyer might say they want to live "close" to a hospital. In a city "close" could mean blocks and in rural communities it might be a 30 minute drive. You have a responsibility to clarify meaning behind the words they use by saying, "Close, what is your definition of close?" Ask for the customer to elaborate on what they said if a statement has the likelihood of being misinterpreted.

Confirm answers visually

If you were face-to-face with a customer, you might pull out a pen and napkin to interpret the context of a conversation, summarize key points, or draw a quick diagram. When you are meeting Screen to Screen, replace the pen and napkin with the screen share application of your meeting software, and use whiteboard annotations to confirm the customer's concerns.

For example, a customer might say they need help with finding the best prices, don't want to worry about their product breaking soon after they buy it, and need personal attention setting up their product to work correctly. You, the salesperson, would use the whiteboard feature and screen share application to write on their computer screen, "1. Cost savings, 2. Warranties, and 3. Installation." When you summarize the key points in a few words the customer can identify with, then they feel confident you understand them, and there is order to the rest of the conversation that follows.

Narrow down alternatives

Your 20-page product or service brochure might be loaded full of features, benefits, or alternatives, but chances are that not all of them are going to be relevant to your customer. This is why asking precise, probing questions is much more valuable than putting your customer on overload. Chapter 8 will show you how to do this by conceptualizing value with visuals.

Checklist 6-4 AGREEMENTS WHEN CO-BROWSING

In Jacqueline's Whitmore's book *Business Class*, she uncovers the etiquette required in order to act professionally in the business environment. Essentially this is a list of unspoken rules professionals engage in to demonstrate their sophisticated manners. This is the opposite of how the title character behaved in the controversial movie *Borat*.

Unfortunately, he was cast out from every place he visited because he unintentionally offended every person he met.

When you share your screen with a customer, realize that there are some unspoken rules you can abide by so that you can have professional conversations that demonstrate your expertise and don't unintentionally offend a customer. Let's take a look at a few of these.

Seek permission first

We've established that phone conversations are different from Screen to Screen conversations because sharing screens involves more work on the customer's behalf. The customer must have a device connected to the Internet, know how to use their device during a conversation, and be willing to engage with you through their device. Don't assume that because you have the screen share option to co-browse websites, documents, and files, the customer wants to use it. Instead, after you have established rapport with the customer and determined there is a need to co-browse, then you can ask them to enable this option. You will have to use special language that sells them on the idea of why this will shorten the conversation time, discover missing opportunities not available on the phone, and help them make a more informed decision.

Don't move the cursor or type when listening

Have you ever noticed during a conversation when someone is not paying attention to what you are saying? Maybe the other person is thinking about something else, thinking more about what they are going to say next, or checking their phone and saying they are multitasking (not cognitively possible). You create the same dynamic when the customer is sharing their thoughts during a Screen to Screen conversation if you are moving your mouse, browsing for files, or searching the web, even though you have the best intent in helping your customer. When your customer talks, do nothing but listen. When they stop talking, then you can perform whatever computer task or shortcut progresses the conversation further.

Tell the person what you are doing

If you quickly move from one browser to the next, application to application, or file to file without telling the customer what you are doing, they might assume you are lost in your own computer. This frustration is amplified if you are silent or tell them to wait a minute, and then another minute until the task is finally performed. Instead of remaining silent when working across applications, tell the customer what you are doing and why you are doing it. Here are some examples:

> "Right now I need to open up my financial calculator, so I can show you how much money you will save."
>
> "Right now I'm going to open up your website to show you that the language on your website is actually different from your desired customer's behavior."
>
> "Right now I'm going to insert a process-map image on your screen [using screen share], so you can see what important step you might have overlooked. Is that OK?"

Send and receive URLs from devices

Do you have an important link to share during your Screen to Screen conversation? For example, that blog post you wrote a couple years ago might answer a similar question another customer has now. However, don't assume your customer sees a need for the link. Before you copy and paste the URL into the meeting chat room, seek their permission to send the link. Otherwise the customer will see it as marketing, not providing a solution, or will miss the link altogether because of their unfamiliarity with chat. Before you hit send, always ask the customer for permission to share the link and verify that they know how to receive it.

CHAPTER 7

◆◆◆

APPLICATION AGILITY: THE SKILL SETS OF SCREEN TO SCREEN SELLING

Being an agile seller in today's business environment virtually guarantees a prosperous career. In short, it becomes your competitive edge.

—JILL KONRATH, AUTHOR OF *AGILE SELLING*

Software will change over time; however, skill sets won't. Skill sets can be broken down into industry-specific skills and Screen to Screen–specific skills. For example, industry-specific skills for a real estate professional might include calculating absorption rate pricing for home valuation, calculating a rent-versus-own analysis for a first-time home buyer, or calculating a seller's net sheet, which will dictate how much equity the home has or how much the seller has to bring to closing to sell. Screen to Screen Selling skills transfer those industry-specific skills to use of the recommended Screen to Screen software. They include mastering the keyboard shortcuts, setting up instant meetings, and collaborating with multiple customers on multiple platforms all at the same time. Gaining speed at maneuvering between

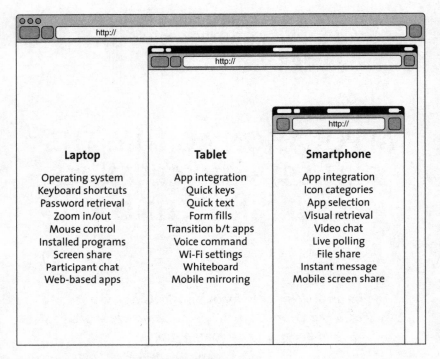

Laptop	Tablet	Smartphone
Operating system	App integration	App integration
Keyboard shortcuts	Quick keys	Icon categories
Password retrieval	Quick text	App selection
Zoom in/out	Form fills	Visual retrieval
Mouse control	Transition b/t apps	Video chat
Installed programs	Voice command	Live polling
Screen share	Wi-Fi settings	File share
Participant chat	Whiteboard	Instant message
Web-based apps	Mobile mirroring	Mobile screen share

Figure 7.1 Screen to Screen Skill Sets

different applications demonstrates your expertise and increases the productivity of meetings without compromising the customer experience. Figure 7.1 lists some skill sets needed for Screen to Screen Selling.

Checklist 7-1 PARTICIPANT APPLICATIONS

Each application requires the development of skills as prescribed by the availability of useful software features. And the choice as to which software application to prioritize skill building around depends upon the tool the customer is most familiar with. For example, corporate customers will prefer you use their meeting software, like CITRIX or WebEx, whereas ordinary customers might prefer Skype or FaceTime.

In this section we will help you narrow down the alternatives so you can increase your productivity by performing fewer tasks better.

Choosing preferred applications and tools

Selecting the most customer friendly app is a skill set in itself. There are more than a hundred different software options, which can be overwhelming in selecting the best one. Remember, your objective is to spend time with customers, not learn every feature of every software application and every operating system. You can spend all day down-loading apps and creating accounts and never host a meeting. Here on some tips to find the most appropriate option:

- Browse your device's app store for the category or search terms "Business, Productivity, and Education."
- Search your device's app store for the keyword "meeting."
- Read one-star reviews first. Unhappy customers are good at revealing problems you will most likely experience but they also need to be filtered according to the tone of the review. For example, I will take a one-star review more seriously if the customer constructively empathizes with the developer than demonstrating a harsh tone.
- Prioritize app options with the most amount of positive reviews.
- Ask industry forums, colleagues, or trusted advisors for a recommendation.

Customers who use popular apps on their mobile devices will assume you know how to use them, too, especially if the apps are industry specific. For example, if a customer is using the Zillow real estate app on their phone and you don't know how to navigate through the popular features, then they may ask themselves, "Why do we even need this agent anymore?" Therefore, make a list of the popular industry-specific apps in addition to the online-meeting apps, and install each of these apps on your devices. Then learn the nuances of each, so you are prepared to discuss them during your Screen to Screen conversations.

Cross-operating-system performance

In some situations, your customer might have a different operating system than you do. And, in order to prepare, it's best to have a basic understanding of each type in order to quickly locate menus, features, and where the customer should click next on their device for each operating system. The software or application interface might also change based on the operating system. For example, if you have a PC and your customer is using Apple, the Skype application uses a modified software design which can cause confusion if you only understand how to navigate the PC version. Operating system skill sets are imperative for those who work with less tech-savvy customers because of their unfamiliarity with technology or Screen to Screen software.

Cross-application performance

ClearSlide, an all-in-one solution, has many built-in features that enable Screen to Screen meetings without combining several different tools to produce the same result. This saves time learning new skills on multiple platforms and troubleshooting problems from multiple vendors who might not otherwise be accessible for support. However, the price point might deter a solo entrepreneur or startup from its adoption and require a combination of different skills using multiple tools without diminishing the experience. For example, you might have seen a presentation where someone exits a PowerPoint presentation, opens, up a YouTube video in an Internet browser, plays the video, closes the Internet browser, and then re-opens PowerPoint. Each transitional delay quells the experience and can be mitigated by using an all-in-one solution or shortcuts between applications in order to improve the experience.

Voice commands

If you can speak ten times faster than you can write, then seek to improve your typing performance by issuing verbal commands into your devices. Operating systems in newer computers, Internet browser extensions, and smartphones already have this functionality built in— for example, Google and Apple's Siri. These voice command features have amazingly accurate transcription into text and only require a couple of clicks to summarize your thought into a sentence.

File format conversion

In some cases, a customer might ask that you convert your Microsoft PowerPoint presentation to a PDF or your website into a print-friendly file. You don't want your customer to wait while you ask IT for help with these small tasks or to listen while you admit your lack of skill in making these conversions. Instead, learn to use some quick-conversion tools for file formats you are likely to need:

- Make any web page print-friendly with Print Friendly (http://www.printfriendly.com).
- Capture an image of a website with Screenshot machine (http://screenshotmachine.com).
- Convert a PDF to a Word file with Nitro's PDF-to-Word converter (https://www.pdftoword.com).
- Convert a PDF to another file type with Baltsoft's PDF converter (http://www.freepdfconvert.com).
- Convert any file format to any file format at Online-Convert.com (http://www.online-convert.com).

Before you send your customer a file, ask them what their preferred file format is. Then use your file conversion skills to send them the information in the format they want to use.

However, before you use a free online tool, read the terms of use page to see how that service will handle file security. Take into consideration how confidential these documents are to your customer.

Checklist 7-2 TIME-SAVING FEATURES

Quicker conversations benefit both you and the customer. Avoid keeping your customer waiting while you maneuver your technology at your fingertips by learning time saving features that improve the overall

Screen to Screen experience. Read on to implement these shortcuts to boost your meeting productivity.

Table 7.1 Keyboard Shortcuts

System and software	Web browser	Meeting apps
Copy and paste	Open new window	Start and hide video
Create new file	Open new tab in window	Mute or unmute audio
Open new file	Zoom in or out	Enter full-screen mode
Open existing file	Reload or refresh page	Minimize or maximize screen
Search and find local files	Page back or forward	Conference call prompts
Menu sort, filters, and tags	Access downloaded files	Annotation tools
Open new programs	Save bookmark	Exit meeting
Presentation view	Add to reading list	Whiteboard
Switch programs quickly	Browser extensions	Participant chat
Blank screen	Form fill	End meeting
Program-specific features	Password generator	One-click meetings
Check system properties	Create new hyperlink	Audio/video preferences

AutoCorrect

Software programs offer a variety of ways to simplify the job of keying in words you enter often. Microsoft Word, for example, has a powerful function called AutoCorrect that replaces a set of characters you type with what you intend to display. If you turn on AutoCorrect and type a *c* between parentheses, it inserts a copyright symbol, ©. You can use this tool as a time-saving feature by customizing it, adding your own combinations for frequently used terms. Open up the AutoCorrect Options menu, and enter an abbreviated version with each longer word or phrase. The iPhone has a similar feature for text messages called Quick Text, which is equally a tremendous time saver.

Form fill

Data entry into online forms has never been easier. Complete an online application, pay with a credit card, or automatically populate agreements with the same data you use most frequently by saving them once into your web browser extension. If it normally takes five minutes to complete a form by manually entering data, now it only takes 5 seconds. Enable the form fill feature in popular browsers like Safari, Google Chrome, and Firefox.

Suggestive search

At times a customer will ask you questions you don't know the answer to and it will be necessary to perform Internet searches while you are both Screen to Screen in order to find the right answer. As you begin typing words or phrases in sites like Google, Amazon, and realtor.com, similar results others have used will populate under the search bar as options to consider in addition to your original request. This saves you time typing popular results and provides ideas on related searches you might not have thought about before.

Password retrieval

How often do you forget passwords for your software or to access your technology? If you do forget, how long does it take you to reset one? And, if you are meeting Screen to Screen and need to reset your password during a conversation because you forgot it, what type of message does that send to your customer? The more apps and tools you use, the more passwords you have to remember. It's unrealistic to try to remember every single one unless you are the Rain Man or have them written down somewhere.

In Chapter 12 we will dig into the security risks and best practices of password management.

Operating system shortcuts

The Apple, Microsoft, and Android operating systems have short-cuts to complete tasks quickly regardless of which applications are being used. And the quicker these tasks are performed, the better the Screen to Screen customer experience. Conduct exercises including the switching back and forth between applications, controlling the speaker volume, and zooming in and out. Find a list of these short-cuts and other quick keys that work with your operating system by performing a quick Internet search with the name of your operating system followed by "+ shortcuts." When you have the list, make an effort to try using these quick-key shortcuts.

For example, you may need to take a screenshot of a website for a customer to show a value/price comparison listed on a competitor's website and share it with them as an image sent as an attachment or link for them to view. You could take a picture with your phone; however, the quality isn't great and also requires extra work in using another device. Press Command-Shift-F4 on a Macbook Pro com-puter to turn the cursor into a plus symbol, drag across the desired area to capture the outline of the image, and when released the highlighted area will be saved as an image in your folder to share later.

Application quick keys

Each application or software supplies a list of their own shortcuts (also known as quick keys) to save more time. Research these through the software menu (ex. File, Edit, View) or as listed under the Help Menu available online. Next, master the most frequently used tasks performed by typing a few keystrokes to avoid keeping the customer waiting and watching you during screen share. Every time you can shave 5 seconds or more off a task, the more you can focus on the customer, and the more productive your conversations will be.

Have you ever watched a professional graphic designer use Photoshop? Most actions are conducted from the keyboard by com-bining the command, option, shift, or control buttons with a letter, number, or symbol. The mouse or dropdown menus are rarely used. This form of mastery is a result of habitual practice to press the right keys to perform the right task at the right time without looking at the keyboard. Strive to develop an unconscious competence when performing application quick keys and you will have much more productive meetings as a result.

One-click meetings

Put yourself in your customer's shoes for a minute. How many clicks would you guess to be the easiest for customers to start a conversation Screen to Screen? Three? Two? Ten? Limit the number of clicks by 1) choosing the Screen to Screen technology they are most familiar with and 2) narrowing the "join meeting" process down to as few clicks as possible.

The more instructions you give to someone in order to join is a sign you've selected a platform with a poor user interface, and the likelihood of them having trouble joining increases considerably. Assess your current "join meeting" process and eliminate as many clicks as possible. One click to one link after receiving the invitation is ideal.

Checklist 7-3 IMPROMPTU MEETINGS

Suppose you have been waiting for months for an important customer to return your call. Finally and unexpectedly, the customer calls with questions. Are you going to ask that customer to call back in 30 minutes so you can prepare? My guess … probably not.

Of course, there will sometimes be occasions when you have no choice but to postpone. But if that call comes when you are between sales calls, delegating administrative tasks or preparing proposals for customers, will you be ready for an impromptu meeting? Here are some quick tips on making those meetings impactful.

Quick Internet setup

Avoid putting the participant on hold while you set up your Internet connection. Ask them something personal about a recent event, or about a shared memory to keep them talking. Assuming you have applied the advice in Chapter 3 to plan for alternative working arrangements, you have already prepared for your Internet connection to work from wherever you might be in any instance.

Quick tool selection

Spur-of-the-moment meetings need user-friendly solutions that don't require the customer to install any software. Join.me is a terrific tool for Screen to Screen meetings because the service doesn't require the participant to download any software to participate. Once a customer clicks on a link and/or enters in the meeting ID code in an Internet browser, now you have control of their screen inside of their browser window. Once you have made a list of the most user-friendly technology, customer-preferred technology, and downloaded each tool, then organize them into your desktop file folder or category of apps to access the right one for the job quickly.

If this, then that

High revenue transactions with multiple decision-makers simply involve more meetings than smaller investments. And, some meetings will only require the telephone with one person while some meetings will entail a multi-camera video display with many participants. Our job is not only to be adaptable to multiple environments preferred by the customer, but to also suggest the best meeting option in order to progress the sale one more step forward.

Develop an "if this, then that" mentality for your customers. For example, *if* you are working with a customer for the first time *then* perhaps you will use the phone. If you have built some trust and the customer requires more specific details or is having a hard time comprehending your then, then perform a screen share. If the customer trusts your ability and isn't afraid to meet with you in person, then request a video to video with screen meeting. Role play a few scenarios with your team in order to develop a process to use the right technology that works best for your customers and your team.

Quick summaries

Think ahead before you send your follow-up email in order to capture teachable moments during your conversation. During a screen share there will be opportunities to take screenshots of websites with annotations that reinforce the dialogue afterwards and demonstrate the customization that no sales brochure could ever do by itself. And, once the conversation is over, be prepared to send over the modified visuals. This will differentiate you from the pack and add value to the customer immediately.

Chapter 11 will dive into more detail on how to create and send visual summaries.

Checklist 7-4 STEPS TO CO-BROWSING

Co-browsing, also known as screen share, is an effective way to increase customer satisfaction. Add productivity skills to co-browsing features and now you can create more happier customers faster.

Let's take a closer look at the steps to mastering your co-browsing productivity with your team, customers, suppliers, and more.

Sign-on instructions

Screen to Screen meetings are usually delayed because an app must be downloaded to start or the host isn't able to troubleshoot the customer through the sign-on to start the meeting. Test your preferred co-browsing tool on multiple devices in order to discover common issues potentially to surface so you know the language ahead of time in order to help customers in need of assistance. The co-browsing tool you use will depend upon what the customer is most familiar with or the one you've found to be most usable.

Listen for opportunities to share screen

During your online meetings, your customer will give you verbal cues that will prompt you to enable screen sharing. Listen for these customer questions or statements:

- Can you clarify the options for me?
- I'm having a hard time telling the differences between the options.

- What is this going to cost?
- I want to know exactly where my money is being invested.
- What criteria should we be looking at together?
- What page of the document are you on, and which paragraph are you looking at?
- This is a lot of data.
- What row or column should we be looking at together?

Prepare your computer before sharing screens

When you share your screen with a customer, you are ultimately exposing anything and everything that appears on your browser or desktop. Protect your privacy and minimize intrusions. You should close programs that aren't relevant to the Screen to Screen meeting. Here are a few quick tasks to perform before you share:

1. Close down all applications not needed for your conversation.
2. Close down all online-chat applications.
3. Disable instant notifications from other software and applications.
4. Open up any appropriate documents, files, or websites to be used in your demonstration.
5. Locate how to stop or pause screen sharing if you take a quick break or put the customer on hold.

Share invitation code link

Each Screen to Screen meeting tool has a participant meeting code and/or link to be shared with your customer. Find the location of the participant invitation code/link inside your tool either from the application navigation menu, icon, or quick key shortcut. If you aren't sure what icon performs which task, hover your cursor, mouse, or touchpad over the icon, and a pop-up will describe what will happen when you click.

Control the customer's screen with permission

In some cases, your customer will need to recreate the same problem they experienced earlier and will need your help navigating through websites, files, or other documents. Check your Screen to Screen meeting platform for two options: handing over mouse control and customer screen share inside meeting. Ask permission before you use either of these options.

Before you start co-browsing a website together with a customer, make sure you know how to reassume control. In other words, if a customer has control over your mouse and starts opening up files from your programs without permission, you will need to stop the mouse share option immediately. Also, some Screen to Screen meeting software has the option to set limits on what you share: either an entire desktop, specific applications, or specific screens if you are using multiple screens. It's your responsibility to know how these options work. Make it a priority to learn before it becomes your liability.

Checklist 7-5 BALANCING CONVERSATION

Begin your demo by showing the best, most compelling screen or handful of screens. You have to complete this in less than 2 minutes.

—PETER COHAN, AUTHOR OF *GREAT DEMO*

The desired temperature in the human body is 98.6 degrees Fahrenheit or 37 degrees Celsius in order to retain equilibrium in the body. If that temperature rises too far above or below, then fever or hypothermia will set in. In a similar way, during your Screen to Screen conversation with your customer, you need to gauge your customer by observing behaviors. If customer responsiveness decreases and the meeting goes cold you have to find a way to escalate the engagement.

If the meeting gets heated with high emotions or verbal attacks, you also need tactics to bring the meeting back to a safer environment. Try some of these tactics for creating a safe environment for them to participate in, taking their temperature during the conversation, and moving them closer to saying yes to your offer.

Prioritization of visuals on screen

The order of your visuals at the start will either engage the customer or signal another slide deck full of assumptions that miss the mark every time. The skills involved are knowing which image works best for specific situations and how to use that image in a way that engages the customer.

The first visual displayed after rapport is established with the customer ultimately sets the tone for the conversation. If you start by co-browsing the contract before you discuss their most pressing issues, then the conversation can get cold really quickly, or it gets too hot if you mention the benefits and features before you have uncovered the customer's needs.

The diagnostic visuals we discussed in Chapter 5 are a great tool to assess customer needs first. Then, the next visual (image, web page or whiteboard annotation) depends on the answer from the customer, not the next slide in your deck.

Customer signals across screens

If your customer can see your screen but you can't see them, you will need to continuously check their interest level by asking a few key questions to get them involved in the conversation. It's far too easy to assume a customer is engaged because you can't see them in screen share only mode. Also, carefully listen for signals to tell you if you need to change the conversation to focus on another issue.

Here are some questions you can ask to measure their engagement level:

- Are we looking at the same website that shows the value matrix?
- How would you answer this question that appears on your screen?

- What do you *not* see here on this website that you wish you would see?

These customer signals will tell you that you need to adjust your conversation:

- **Talking more than the customer:** If you are saying more than the customer is, take a deep breath and ask yourself what the objective of the conversation is. Long-winded explanations show that you aren't listening and require that you ask better questions.
- **The customer saying, "Keep going":** You don't go with the customer; the customer goes with you. If the customer says, "Keep going," that's a sign to ask, "What specifically interests you about what we are talking about?" Put it back on them to tell you what they want to hear more about.
- **The customer doing all the talking:** Don't fall into the trap of letting the customer ramble on about every insignificant detail when it's your job to shepherd them through by asking them impactful questions. To regain control of the conversation or interrupt their thought pattern, insert on their screen a visual that frames the problem for them in a different way, and then continue on.

Cross-application agility

To get a license to fly, an airplane pilot must understand meteorology, aircraft systems, navigation, air-traffic control, regulations, and physiology. If a pilot makes a poor decision, the impact could go unnoticed or become catastrophic, depending on many factors that are sometimes out of their control. The complex controls in the cockpit require years of practice and precision to master. So does selling and influencing decisions Screen to Screen. How quickly can you navigate from one application to the next in order to serve the customer's best interests and increase overall satisfaction in the sales process?

Here are some examples of the salesperson's need for agility:

- Transitioning from a presentation visual that identifies historical costs of making a common mistake in the transaction into a financial calculator that demonstrates real costs
- Transitioning from a presentation visual that shows the steps in the buying cycle to a third-party website that supports the customer's decision-making process
- Transitioning from a website that shows an inventory of products to a checklist of steps the customer needs to follow in sequence
- Transitioning from an online financial calculator or spreadsheet that outlines costs to a sales agreement to be completed together online

The two goals of cross-application agility are precision and speed. Precision measures how accurately you are able to conceptualize the conversation into next steps. Speed describes how quickly you can perform these tasks so you can maintain a high level of productivity and performance.

Chapter 8 will explore how to conceptualize conversations with visuals in order to simplify how you can help them achieve their goals Screen to Screen.

◆◆◆

CONCEPTUALIZING THE SALE: HOW TO PAINT THE PICTURE USING VISUAL CONVERSATIONS

Customers make buying decisions based on cognition, divergent, and convergent thinking.

—ROBERT MILLER, AUTHOR OF *THE NEW CONCEPTUAL THINKING*

I've had customers ask me if there was a way they could download all the information from my brain using a USB memory stick from Office Depot, stick it in their ear, and then have the same knowledge in order to make an informed decision. Maybe that technology will be available someday, but for now we as sales professionals need to become not only masters of communication but also masters of being able to paint the picture using the latest technology Screen to Screen. In this chapter, we will explore new ways of visual thinking, visual expression, and conceptualization, so you can connect with customers at a higher level than you would achieve if you were relying solely on the telephone.

Checklist 8-1 EXTEMPORANEOUS VISUALS

Back in 2005, I was encouraged to attend Toastmasters in order to develop my communication and leadership skills. This group uses an exercise called table topics, which requires you to take one random idea and create a powerful story around it verbally—with no preparation, no visuals, and no technology. Little did I realize at the time that table topics were a kind of exercise to improve my extemporaneous thinking and delivery, which I would later use in the sales process. Here we will explore some ways to think quickly on your feet, which also will allow you to create a collaborative environment with your customer Screen to Screen.

Idea streaming

In his book *The Einstein Factor*, brain expert and psychologist Win Wenger says not to differentiate between the left brain and right brain. There is only whole brain. Even though the left side is primarily used for sequential intelligence and the right side is used for spatial intelligence, Wenger says we can connect both sides of the brain in order to perform at a higher level by using an exercise called idea streaming. Here's how it works. When a customer tells you their story—problems they are experiencing or results they anticipate—you don't write down the notes in the form of words, but instead structure their thoughts in a more visually appealing way as if you were painting a picture by using annotations on their computer screen.

The customer benefits from visual conceptualization because images are faster to read than text, easier to understand, and require less time for you to show them you understand. You benefit because it increases your understanding of customer needs, avoids making incorrect assumptions, and saves you time in summarizing the conversation to be used in your follow up.

On your next phone call take out a sheet of paper or digital whiteboard and attempt to draw out a visual that summarizes the customer's needs, recommendations made, and next steps simplified. Master this practice as a habit and it will differentiate how you communicate with customers and add value to the sales process.

Brainstorming

Customer brainstorming sessions can be some of the most effective ways of building rapport, discovering roadblocks, and creating more effective solutions. They demonstrate you are listening and enable you to solve specific problems quickly, rather than loading a conversation full of assumptions.

During a Screen to Screen meeting, open your favorite collaboration tool to generate the most ideas in real time. The tool you use will depend on your customer's familiarity with the brainstorming tool, permission to view/edit settings, or if you take full responsibility for summarizing ideas with the tool while your customer gives input through audio. Some of my favorite web-based tools and apps for brainstorming with customers include the following:

- Google Docs and Sheets – Type answers to current problems, prospective solutions, and anticipated roadblocks on a shared web-based document.
- Red Pen (redpen.io) – Get real time feedback on projects with multiple participants, explain your thinking, and organize projects.
- Mural.ly – Process out ideas with sticky notes, organize thoughts, and vote on best ideas.

List building

When you ask a customer to list all of the issues they are facing, problems they want solved, or expectations they have, you can summarize the responses on the customer's screen with lists. You can do this by quickly launching a screen share and opening your favorite list-building tool. The following tools are examples of options you can use to build lists from customer responses:

- Bulleted or numbered lists in Microsoft Word are the easiest to build and most recognized.
- Microsoft PowerPoint (outline view) – This saves time converting lists into presentation slides used online for customers or internal purposes.

- Wunderlist. Save time rewriting lists for customer implementation by entering action items in Wunderlist mobile project management system.

Mind mapping

Normal linear note taking and writing will put you into a semi-hypnotic trance, while mind mapping will greatly enhance your left and right brain cognitive skills.

—TONY BUZAN, AUTHOR OF *MIND MAPPING*

Customers who are involved with strategic decisions need to see the big picture, how one objective breaks down into a series of alternatives, and how moving parts are interrelated with one another. And, to simplify the 30,000 foot view, mind mapping will save you and the customer time during a screen share.

Mind mapping isn't something you do with every customer. It's one tool to use when you want to start with an original concept and explore the details with your customer Screen to Screen.

When you mind-map Screen to Screen with a customer, you put them in the driver's seat by asking them what they want to accomplish. For example, here is one process I use in my consulting work:

- Determine objective
  - Write down the fewest high-impact alternatives to reach the objective.
    - Show metrics that demonstrate the impact from each alternative.
    - Calculate the anticipated value from pursuing each alternative.
    - Determine the cost feasibility of each alternative.
    - Determine the completion time for each alternative.
    - Determine the risk associated with selecting each alternative.

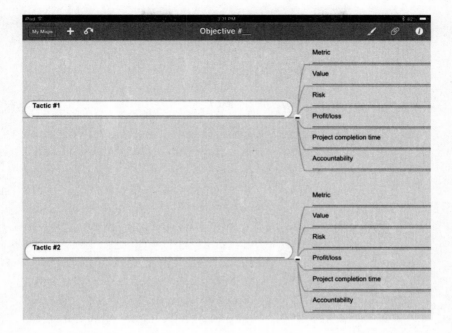

This mind map is something you can't do on your own without the input from your customer.

You can use my process for creating a mind map or your own using some of these tools I recommend for using Screen to Screen:

- MindMeister
- Coggle
- Mindjet
- MindNode

Note: You only need one mind-mapping tool. Choose one that meets your requirements for accessibility, transferability, and exportability.

Checklist 8-2 VISUAL FRAMING

We've covered what questions to ask, what visuals you can use, and how to think on your feet during Screen to Screen conversations, but what does the process actually look like? In this section we will provide some examples as well as specific actions to take so you can improve the customer experience with visual frames.

Diagnose problems with visuals

Sales brochures commonly address the process from identifying problems, suggesting solutions, determining important benefits, and analyzing features of a particular product or service. And examining the buying process together Screen to Screen will undercover opportunities that require the most attention first. Homeowners selling their house by themselves having never done it before get quickly overwhelmed with the many responsibilities once the sign goes in the yard. Also, little do they realize how much liability is involved or how costly a mistake can be without input from a trusted real estate advisor. To help them diagnose these problems in a Screen to Screen meeting, real estate professionals can insert one visual (an Infographic) that lists the steps and costs of hiring a professional versus selling the house. Then they can ask the would-be "for sale by owner" sellers which of these activities, costs, or mistakes are most relevant. Ultimately, the customers will see the disconnect for themselves.

Building value with visuals

In his book *High-Profit Selling*, Mark Hunter says the number one reason why sales professionals fail to earn the sale or keep their commission is that they fail to articulate their value to their customer. Visuals aid you in articulating the value verbally and amplifying the value visually (in communicating lower costs, higher earnings, ease of use, etc.) by making it clear in the customer's mind that the value received is substantially greater than paying the commission on the sale when closing the sale.

To apply this concept, make a list of all the value propositions your customer can expect as a result of doing business. For each value proposition, create a visual that demonstrates its tangible and intangible benefits. And organize these visuals into your Screen to Screen meeting tools so that you can quickly retrieve the right one according to which benefit is most appealing to the customer and annotate as necessary.

Demonstrate process with visuals

Process maps are great visuals to outline the steps in the buying process and solve specific problems. If, during a Screen to Screen meeting with a customer, a question comes up about the process or a step inside the process, pinpoint which step the customer worries about most by inserting a visual to save time that asks where the breakdown did or might occur. For example, if an investor is interested in transferring their equity from a 10-unit rental property to a commercial shopping center using a 1031 exchange, they can visualize the process using a graphic to show how soon they need to close on their existing property, identify the new property, and close on the new property using a qualified intermediary. A mistake made or a delay beyond the 180 days required can cost thousands, if not billions, of dollars. For an investor who is unfamiliar with the process, showing a visual not only saves time explaining the details but also clarifies which steps need to be performed in what order.

Assessing risk with visuals

Customers can reduce their risk visualizing the alternatives and identify which decision(s) will produce the greatest benefits with the least risk. A visual that rates the customer's risk level will demonstrate unexpected long-term and short-term consequences with your assistance. For instance a financial advisor who educates customers on choices for asset allocation will use tables and charts to demonstrate investment characteristics, financial projections, and historical performance. Tables, charts, and rating scales can significantly reduce the amount of time customers need for evaluating risks and making an informed decision and can be used as visuals in Screen to Screen conversations where appropriate.

Checklist 8-3 WHITEBOARD BASICS

Visual thinking means taking advantage of our innate ability to see—both with our eyes and with our mind's eye—in order to discover ideas that are otherwise invisible, develop those ideas quickly and intuitively, and then share those ideas with other people in a way that they simply "get."
—DAN ROAM, AUTHOR OF *BACK OF THE NAPKIN*

Do you remember when teachers used to teach with flip charts and transparencies? The principles are the same in sales and now we are using technology to create a similar effect Screen to Screen. Add flexibility and power to the way you articulate ideas from a blank canvas which, during screen share, draws on other people's computer screens by using the whiteboard feature inside the Screen to Screen meeting tool or using our own digital whiteboard app. This section will share which whiteboard tools to use and skills to develop in order to customize the conversation even more and enhance the buying experience.

Interactive-whiteboard apps

A wildly popular iPad interactive-whiteboard app in professional education, universities, and public schools is Doceri. I've found Doceri to be one of the most impactful apps I've ever used, and use it every day. The Doceri iPad app acts as an overlay or telestrator on top of your desktop or laptop computer so that you can make annotations on top of visuals, images, and web pages.

Here is a list of some practical applications of using Doceri:

- Drawing on presentation slides to assist in decision-making.
- Inserting presentation slides as images at any time regardless of the Screen to Screen meeting tool.
- Telestrate over documents to clarify ambiguous language.

- Drawing circles, rectangles, and arrows to highlight key points on visuals.
- Recording videos of Screen to Screen conversations to be used for quality control or future digital marketing content.

Many Screen to Screen meeting platforms already have a whiteboard feature that allows you to draw on whatever visual you display to your customer; however, I've found many of them to be less user-friendly than Doceri. The reason is that it's quicker for me to tap an icon on the iPad than to search for and find the right button to click on a mouse.

Does Android have an app like Doceri? Probably. It's nearly impossible to cover every operating system, device arrangement, and connectivity option, so in order to give you the most value, I'll use Doceri as the standard and let you explore the app store to find other alternatives that might have the same features and benefits.

Select and download a whiteboard app

Your first step is to select and download a whiteboard app. If you use an iPad, I recommend that you visit http://doceri.com and download Doceri to your iPad for free. The Penultimate app (for Android and Apple) is a close comparable but offers nothing close to the amount of features and usability of Doceri.

Note: The Doceri iPad app also is incredibly useful for outside sales presentations because you can create a napkin effect on your iPad and insert visuals as needed during face-to-face conversations.

Practice drawing on your interactive whiteboard

Do you remember when you were two years old and your parents gave you crayons and paper? If not, do you have kids or grandkids who are experiencing this new phenomenon for themselves? Engage in that level of exploration yourself. Start with a blank canvas and try writing words, drawing shapes, and alternating colors as you go. Forget about accuracy and staying in between the lines. Let your mind just write down or draw whatever comes to mind. The more you learn the nuances of the app, where features are located, and mistakes that you make, the better you get. My advice is to click on everything. That's how children learn and how I suggest you learn, too.

Then start to apply your practice to your Screen to Screen visuals. Reexamine your existing marketing materials and visual aids. Look for types of visuals that are common in your industry—equations, charts, diagrams, and tables that appear industry-wide to support common decision-making processes—and practice drawing them. Sketching these common visuals on a whiteboard app in the moment can seem more meaningful to a customer than a visual already created, because most sales professionals depend upon their slides. If you can draw the kinds of visuals that are common in your industry, you will differentiate yourself quickly from the amateur who cannot perform this exercise.

Mark up templates and slides

You can use Doceri to mark up the templates and slides stored on your computer. To do this, you'll need to connect the Doceri iPad with your computer: download the Doceri Desktop application to your computer, and connect both iPad and computer to the same wireless network. Then whatever appears on your computer will mirror on your iPad, so you can enable the feature to draw on your computer screen.

Highlight desktop and web application features

Use the whiteboard app to highlight key features on the screen that can sometimes seem hidden to customers. Don't assume that because you can find something in a couple of clicks, your customers can figure out how to do it themselves. The ability to mark up screens gives you a powerful teaching tool: a way to help customers learn through practice. When Apple customers participate in One to One personal-training appointments in an Apple Store, they are forced to perform the tasks themselves, rather than give up their device and say, "Fix it for me." I've tried. It doesn't work. Apple's "teach the customer how to fish" policy prevents customers from repeatedly encountering the same problems because it forces them to learn how to use their tools with their own fingers. Similarly, when you pass over mouse control for a customer to recreate a problem, you can use the whiteboard tool to highlight the next button or link the customer should select, draw an arrow to reinforce it, or draw a big circle over it.

Checklist 8-4 WHITEBOARD BENEFITS

One of the most frustrating things about slide-based training is that the information is transferred to sales reps in such a way that it can't actually be used to facilitate customer conversations.

—COREY SOMMERS, *WHITEBOARD SELLING*

A Screen to Screen conversation that starts with a blank canvas will have more authority than any presentation built around slides. How do I know for sure? My customers give me feedback like this:

- "I'm so glad I didn't have to sit through another slide deck."
- "Wow, you made the experience real for me and didn't bury me with details I couldn't care less about."
- "You really listened to my needs and were quick to respond."

Let's consider some of the advantages the whiteboard has over traditional screen sharing, webinars, and presentation slides. Then you can make the decision to learn the necessary skill set.

Demonstration of differentiated expertise

How many sales professionals use a digital whiteboard in their sales conversations? My guess is not that many because the traditional salesperson is accustomed to selling verbally, with presentation books, or with presentation slides.

In order to use a digital whiteboard effectively it takes time to adjust one's beliefs, attitudes, and behaviors to use the technology. And our hope is this book encourages you to think differently about how you have conversations with technology.

Enhanced focus

When selling over the phone there is less chance for cognitive overload than Screen to Screen because there are no visuals. The customer is intently listening to what you are saying. That's it. There are no distractions except what's sitting in front of them you cannot see. In face-to-face meetings, the conversation includes body language, posture, and hand gestures that impact how messages are understood. This involves being aware of not just what you say, but how you say it.

In contrast, Screen to Screen meetings include many more moving parts that may distract customers away from the message if you aren't able to involve them effectively using the technology. The digital whiteboard is a blank slate. It's an opportunity to discover and listen. There aren't hyperlinks or buttons, or distractions that take attention away from the purpose of the meeting. The focus is on asking the question and confirming in writing what will help summarize and clarify the customer's thinking on the digital whiteboard. These annotations become part of the final visual summary to share with customers after the conversation: similar to sharing a drawing on the back of a napkin with your customer.

The power of selection

Let's pretend a customer is given three options to choose from and each one is listed on your digital whiteboard. How will they decide which option is best? Take the annotation highlighter and draw a line over their preferred choice once in agreement or highlight your recommended option if the customer is undecided. Then you can break down a more detailed analysis of that option on the digital whiteboard if more explanation is requested. The highlighter visually confirms answers and is used in the visual summary in case a dispute arises following the call. There is no more, "But I thought you said _____" because the whiteboard annotations are your backup.

The power of de-selection

Another tactic to gain agreement visually is to use the power of de-selection.

Given three options, a customer can narrow down their choices more quickly by crossing off what they know they don't want and examining fewer options more closely. Let's say a certified public accountant uses a digital whiteboard to write on a prospective client's screen a list of commonly requested services, such as bookkeeping, payroll, asset allocation, and advice for mergers and acquisitions. If the customer tells you they do not need mergers and acquisitions or asset allocation assistance then the CPA will cross them off the list on the whiteboard and continue talking about bookkeeping and payroll.

The benefit of this tactic is that customers might not know or think about all the options until you express them. Therefore, de-selection helps clients identify more options of what to buy. Also, they select for themselves what they want, rather than you asking them five questions that reinforce those options. Time is saved, revenue opportunities increase, and the *focus is on the customer.*

Time savings when used with prepared visuals

In some cases, you won't have time to hand write all of your options on the whiteboard, especially if your handwriting is poor or you can't draw a straight line. Frequently used fill in the blank visuals prepared ahead of time will save time framing conversations to address customer concerns rather than spending valuable talk time drawing them out individually on the whiteboard. Store these fill in the blank templates in your laptop or mobile device for fast retrieval and use only them when the conversation calls for it.

Digital archive of markups

Using a digital whiteboard offers a way around some of the practical disadvantages of using visuals that are handwritten on napkins or flip chart paper:

- You will eventually lose the paper.
- Something will eventually spill on the piece of paper.
- Paper notes easily become disorganized.
- Your dog might eat a few pages.

In a pinch, you might create a digital record by using a camera to take a picture of a handwritten visual. But honestly, you can't expect that you or a customer will remember to do that for every handwritten note or drawing. It's much easier to use a digital whiteboard. You can save the digital-whiteboard markups and in the future easily retrieve them and quickly share them as visual summaries (discussed in Chapter 11).

CHAPTER 9

BEFORE THE FINISH LINE: DO THESE THINGS BEFORE YOU END THE CONVERSATION

Why do we take notes of meetings that last for hours and call them minutes?

—DAVID WILLIAMS, AUTHOR OF *ENTERPRISE PROGRAMME MANAGEMENT*

Meetings that last 5 or 50 minutes are more meaningful after resolving a set of objectives and next steps are conclusive. Otherwise, conversations that meander from one point to the next without a specific agenda extend the time commitment necessary to make the sale, and in some cases, lose it.

Before you end the conversation with the customer, it's important to review the meeting objectives, assess for comprehension and be prepared to schedule another appointment on the call if necessary.

This chapter represents the tasks that occur in the last minutes of every conversation so that you move your customer one step closer to making the sale. Screen to Screen.

Checklist 9-1 ASSESSING COMPREHENSION

When all questions have been answered to the customer's delight, it's time to review the discussion for comprehension, so that each party knows their next steps before the meeting ends.

Affirm objectives with customer

Is there consensus that the decision-making team knows where they are going? The more people involved, the more complex this can be, because there still could be lingering questions that will surface only when you ask participants to affirm the objectives. Therefore, simple and essential ways to affirm objectives with your customer include:

- **Summarize meeting objectives.** For example, "We agreed that we would determine how much renting vs. owning would cost and explore financing alternatives. Do you feel comfortable in what we discussed today?"
- **Set clear expectations for follow up.** In the case of an attorney responsible for drafting a living trust, living will, or estate plan you will need to set clear expectations, deadlines, and responsibilities for each party. Otherwise, if someone overlooks a step, it could end up wasting multiple exchanges of emails, transfers of multiple versions of documents, and unnecessary time reworking the transaction.
- **Ask, "What haven't we discussed that you feel is missing from this conversation?"** Sometimes hidden objectives will surface at the end and not asking this question can prevent the sale because the objection remains buried in the customer's mind.

Rework is waste disguised as busywork in the customer buying cycle and can be eliminated when meeting objectives are clear, understood, and mutual agreement of responsibilities exists after each meeting is over.

Confirm by writing answers

Writing customers' answers on your screen using an annotations tool while in screen share mode confirms to the customer that they were understood. If you inaccurately drew a number, wrote a word, or penned a dollar amount they will correct you on the spot. And, that's a good thing, especially when the audio connection is having difficulty. These annotations can be edited in case handwriting isn't legible prior to sending in a visual summary and they support the decision-making process following the meeting.

For example, if a mortgage professional is hosting a Screen to Screen meeting about financing a property, the mortgage professional confirms amounts with annotations on the whiteboard, while sharing screens so the customer can see:

1. Application $100.00
2. Pre-approval $200,000.00
3. Underwriting $175,000.00
4. House $170,000.00

The mortgage professional can highlight steps, change amounts, and elaborate in more detail to help the customer make a better decision.

Review list of links

If you and the customer visited websites that the customer will later need to explore more on his or her own, it will be helpful for you to create a list of links to each site and then review your list with the customer. The list will be easy to create if you navigate the Internet in a way that keeps all the websites open in your browser: for each new site you visit, open up a new tab rather than retyping the URL in the same tab, and don't close the tabs during your meeting. On each of the tabs opened in your browser, you can find the link near the top of the page, in the address bar of your browser. Before you close your browser, make sure you copy each of the links and paste them in a location that will appear in your meeting summary. This will save you and the customer time trying to remember each link.

Checklist 9-2 THE NEXT VISUAL AGENDA

The secret of your success is determined by your daily agenda.

—JOHN MAXWELL, AUTHOR OF *THE 360° LEADER*

If the original purpose of the first meeting was to build rapport and conduct a needs analysis, more meetings might be necessary to build your customer's confidence to say yes by demonstrating your expertise. The next meeting will have a new set of objectives, new participants involved in the decision-making process, and maybe a change in the Screen to Screen environment. Save time coordinating the next meeting's logistics while you are still Screen to Screen by using these next set of tactics.

Write the next objectives

To create the next meeting agenda, start by stating new or revised objectives. Objectives will evolve from previous meetings or change completely, depending upon your needs analysis and recommendations. At the start of your first meeting, one customer might have said they wanted X, but you might find out they really want Y. This Y now ignites a sequential series of questions, processes, and visuals to support those processes in your next meeting.

To prepare for this step, during the screen share portion of each Screen to Screen meeting, make notes of any changes in the customer's objectives, as they might have changed as new information presents itself. Before you end the meeting, review the changes and clarify your understanding of outcomes the customer wishes to receive. Then, summarize the outcomes as objectives for the next meeting you'll make an effort on between the end of the meeting and the beginning of the next meeting.

List the participants

Your agenda also should include a list of those who will participate in the next meeting. Therefore, an important question to ask before the first call ends is, "Who else needs to be involved with the decision-making process to support this initiative?" For example, you might need to involve a significant other, a team member, or a subject-matter expert to reach a conclusion. At that time, list the participants Screen to Screen, to ensure everyone comprehends which necessary parties are involved. Creating this list can be as simple as writing the names and relationships (to one another) on the whiteboard, typing them in a co-browsed collaboration tool, or using a fill-in-the-blank visual in order to gain consensus.

Set time and date together

Don't forget to establish the date and time of the next meeting. Here, too, Screen to Screen tools help you communicate these decisions. With a generic calendar tool or a screenshot of a calendar, you can quickly narrow down an infinite number of meeting times, saving multiple email exchanges to select the best time. Rather than sharing your entire business or personal calendar that contains confidential information with all your appointments, find a tool that displays a generic calendar to find out which time works best. Or if you use a screenshot of a calendar, you can use the process of elimination by crossing off weeks, days, and times that don't work.

Sometimes you and the customer cannot set the time and date for a follow-up meeting during your initial meeting, because additional participants will be required. In that case, you can use a tool like Timetrader, Appointy, or MeetMe.SO to publicly give your available meeting times, which would eliminate even more dialogue in nailing down the best time.

Next meeting environment

If you work in outside sales, you might meet a customer at a Panera Bread or St. Louis Bread Company restaurant to get to know them, and then the next appointment might be in your office to sign the paperwork. Why would you switch locations? It all depends upon what is in the best interests of the customer. The same principle applies to Screen to Screen Selling. You might respond to an online inquiry using the phone and then meet with Join.me, transitioning to Zoom or WebEx to add the video element for more effective conversations. As in these examples, your final agenda decision involves what physical and technological environment will best serve your customer's interests.

Checklist 9-3 CREATING VISUAL CHECKLISTS

Atul Gawande's book *The Checklist Manifesto* supplies examples of how surgeons, pilots, and teams use checklists to increase performance, reduce cost, and mitigate risk from the unexpected. In Screen to Screen Selling, you will use visual checklists that you have either created ahead of the meeting or brainstormed in the moment using different tools recommended for Screen to Screen meetings. This section provides some actionable ideas that will help you execute with your customer following the conversation.

Brainstorm tasks

During your meeting, you and your customer may need to brainstorm the tasks required to meet the customer's objectives. For some sales processes, such as in real estate and mortgage lending, the tasks are always the same. In contrast, consulting on a business strategy might involve the same consulting process with each customer but lead to very specific and different tasks from customer to customer.

As you identify these tasks Screen to Screen, it increases the likelihood the customer will collaborate with you because they will have a deeper understanding of what deadlines need to be met, who is responsible, and when tasks need to be completed. Then you can share your project management timelines and hold each other accountable the next time you meet Screen to Screen.

Break tasks into subtasks

Completing a task sometimes involves carrying out several additional smaller tasks. For instance, in order to get pre-approved for a loan (task) you need to submit your driver's license (subtask), submit copies of W-2 returns (subtask), and submit copies of your bank statements (subtask). If one subtask isn't performed correctly the original task cannot be completed and will delay the entire transaction.

Create a list of tasks, subtasks, and a visual timeline to demonstrate the entire buying cycle from interest until the sale occurs. Show customer responsibilities, salesperson responsibilities, and mutual responsibilities so that each of you can hold one another accountable Screen to Screen in case something slips through the cracks.

Arrange tasks by priority and sequence

After brainstorming a list of next steps, you might find that the last item is actually most important and is a prerequisite to all of the other tasks. For example, a real estate professional might wait to set up a next meeting with a homeowner to list their house until they clear up an issue with the title or verify that the homeowner has enough equity in the house to be able to sell it. If the real estate professional started with marketing tasks before the house was salable, the professional just wasted their time and the homeowner's time by not following a prioritized sequential order.

Thus, for any list of tasks, you need to put them in order based on which must be completed before you can move to the next task. If you prioritize the tasks Screen to Screen, you and the customer will be able to reach agreement faster on which steps are most important.

Set task notifications

Finally, remind the customer what to do by sending notifications by email, text message, or mobile app (whatever the customer prefers most). This involves creating your own messaging campaign using your existing technology or buying a license to use an industry accepted solution. Before our first son was born the BabyCenter app sent us weekly notifications to prepare for each stage in the process and included checklists, videos, and resources. And, when we had questions about specific parts of the process we were prepared to ask better questions before our next visit.

Checklist 9-4 ADDING HUMOR

Have you ever noticed when customers laugh out loud because of something you said or when something unexpectedly happened and reduced tension during the conversation? In December of 2009, I was on a conference call with my first big consulting opportunity with a large trade association that needed my help architecting their online-communications plan when social media was becoming increasingly popular. The client was in their conference room. I was outside Cleveland harbor. The client began by sharing their challenges, problems, and setbacks and then asked me, "Doug, what do you think?" Out of nowhere a huge cargo ship from the harbor let out one of the loudest blow horns I've ever heard. Rather than trying to cover it up or ignore it, I said, "You have to excuse what I had for lunch," and the decision-making team started howling with laughter together. The details of how we would work together soon fell into place.

The blow horn was completely unexpected, as soon will be problems you experience with the latest technology. Add humor to help you downplay unexpected technology problems, build rapport faster with your customers, and augment the human side of meeting Screen to Screen as much as possible.

Here are some ways you can add humor in those unexpected situations.

Point out the obvious

As the Screen to Screen meeting host, you are in control of what the customer sees through your laptop's video camera, what's behind you, and what's on your screen during screen share. If you initiated an instant meeting without any preparation, you must be cognizant of how you look at the time.

Ask yourself the following questions:

- **Is your physical appearance groomed, or is your hair a mess?** Just because you are having a Skype call doesn't mean that you have to enable the video-camera feature. You could start a conversation by welcoming the customer and saying, "I'm having a bad-hair day, so I have turned off the video." Or try this: "I wanted to focus more on the details of the discussion rather than enable the video camera, so I've turned it off."
- **Is your office clean, or is it a disaster?** When your office is a mess, enabling the video camera will make it pretty obvious to someone else and could start sending signals that you are disorganized. You could turn off the video camera or leave it on and say, "This is all of the research I've been preparing for our conversation today, and I'm excited to learn more about what you need."
- **Do you have 20 applications open in your laptop or just 2?** Some Screen to Screen meeting tools allow you to share one application window or the entire desktop, depending on your specific needs. If you share the entire desktop and haven't closed all your windows, the customer will be soaking in every detail on your screen, even though you didn't mean to cover some of what is there. Put the screen share on pause and say, "Can you hold one minute while I pay my Internet bill before we get disconnected?"

Prepare "save lines"

Judy Carter, author of *The Comedy Bible*, says, "A person in the funny business can even make it without getting on stage." She turned me on to "save lines" that have helped me in daily communication with others, when delivering workshops, and during Screen to Screen conversations. Save lines are what you say when something goes wrong. The difference between a professional and an amateur is that an amateur will blame the technology when it doesn't work, focus on the negative when the Internet connection is slow, or try to fix the problem without regard for others' time. The professional will use save lines under the same circumstances in order to minimize the disruption or impact of the unforeseen dilemma.

Following are some common problems that arise in Screen to Screen meetings and some save lines for you to use when you experience these problems:

- **Slow Internet connection:** "I'm waiting for the government to pass the tax bill in order to fund high-speed Internet in my area."
- **Customer unable to join the meeting:** "There is this new technology called the phone. We can try that, but I don't have a manual to use it."
- **Text on screen too small to read:** "Oh, by the way, did I send you the magnifying glass in the mail, so you can read what I'm sharing?"
- **Delay in loading programs and documents:** "Do you remember the *Jeopardy* theme song? Sing it with me."

Apply the rule of three

Use the rule of three when you want to break up tension when making a list for a customer. The first two items on the list are serious business and the last one (total three) represents a humorous derivative of the first two. Let's say the three things you will need to get approval for a home loan are credit, cash, and cutbacks. The first two are simple, obvious, and memorable. The third is also true but completely unexpected and will get a laugh when used appropriately.

Show personal metaphors

When you learn how to use the power of personal metaphors, others will be able to relate to you as someone who is like themselves in order to increase the level of trust ... And, a quick way to share personal experiences is by slipping in visuals during a screen share to reveal mutual interests.

Since we have four dogs (a bloodhound named Bella, two Plott hound mixes named Fred and Fergie, and a French bulldog named Burton), I will sometimes use their pictures to show how leaders make decisions based on their personalities. The bloodhound is the authoritative one, who is the loudest and always snooping around to find out what is going on. Fred is a big, quiet, and gentle dog who only speaks up when he has something important to say. Fergie will follow you around wherever you go and is always trying to people-please. And then there's Burton, who acts a lot tougher than he really is. When I insert the image of the dogs in the Screen to Screen meeting, others start to see themselves and their decision-making styles through the personal story I have created.

Draw a smiley face

As conversations get deeper into the details during the screen share feature, you will want to find other ways to humanize the conversation. After all, during a screen share, you can't see the customer, and the customer can't see you, only your screen. The quickest way to show that you are listening is to draw a smiley face when you hear something positive. Use the smiley face when there has been agreement on ideas, the customer is completely satisfied with the experience, or the customer is ready to buy.

Everything we've discussed so far represents what to say and how to say it during Screen to Screen meetings. Our next section explores how to best follow up with customers in order to finalize the agreement as a way to improve the customer experience.

CHAPTER 10

◆◆◆

SCREEN TO SCREEN FROM MOBILE: HOW TO INITIATE SCREEN TO SCREEN MEETINGS FROM ANYWHERE

The world is being re-shaped by the convergence of social, mobile, cloud, big data, community and other powerful forces. The combination of these technologies unlocks an incredible opportunity to connect everything together in a new way and is dramatically transforming the way we live and work.

—MARC BENIOFF, CEO OF SALESFORCE.COM

A common objection to overcome when scheduling a meeting is the response "I will be out of the office." What does that really mean? Does that mean the customer is unavailable at the specific time and date suggested? Does that mean they don't have Internet access wherever they are going? Does that mean their technology doesn't work outside their zip code?

Other times, customers suggest postponing the meeting opportunity because of commuting delays or weather conditions. You could do that. But why wait if an urgent decision needs to be made ASAP? You could just use the phone to have a conversation. But why take longer than you would have to if you relied on your voice alone to explain processes, lists, etc.? You have another option that would let you launch the conversation Screen to Screen right away: a mobile Screen to Screen meeting. Mobile Screen to Screen meetings differ from regular Screen to Screen meetings in that you and the customer are each operating from a mobile device.

If the customer didn't know they could meet with you Screen to Screen from their mobile device, it is your responsibility to guide them with the best options in order to start the dialogue. Otherwise, meetings can keep getting delayed, rescheduled, or negatively affect a customer's equity position if the decision requires an urgent response.

This chapter contains advice on which tools and processes create meaningful conversations Screen to Screen without the need for a computer. As an overview of this topic, Figure 10.1 shows options for using mobile devices when you connect with customers online.

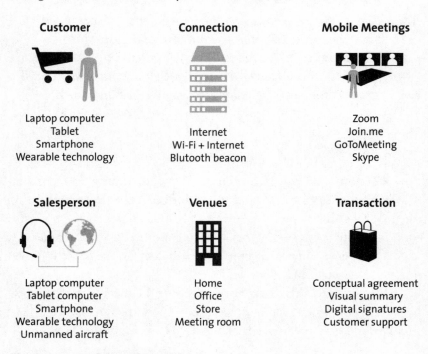

Customer	Connection	Mobile Meetings
Laptop computer Tablet Smartphone Wearable technology	Internet Wi-Fi + Internet Blutooth beacon	Zoom Join.me GoToMeeting Skype

Salesperson	Venues	Transaction
Laptop computer Tablet computer Smartphone Wearable technology Unmanned aircraft	Home Office Store Meeting room	Conceptual agreement Visual summary Digital signatures Customer support

Figure 10.1 Mobility Alternatives

Checklist 10-1 CONVERT WEBSITE TO MOBILE

To be happy in this world, first you need a cell phone and then you need an airplane.

—TED TURNER

First things first. Your reputation is being judged every minute as customers experience the design, layout, and features of your website. Proactive customers will have already done their research on your website and may ask you to retrieve web pages from your mobile device before, during, and after the meeting. If you know most meetings will start from mobile, start by making some critical changes to your website to include the following characteristics.

Choose responsive design

Your website design must be responsive for mobile meetings. This means the layout of elements changes based upon which device is being used. Common device options include mobile phone, tablet, laptop, big-screen television and wearable technologies. Does the customer receive the same experience with one device when accomplishing tasks as with all the others? If not, consider the assistance of a user experience (also known as U/X) professional to work with your website developer in order create a seamless mobile browsing experience.

Rethink features for mobile

Customers who work from a mobile device might have different uses for your website than they would from their laptop. For example, I might do research from my laptop, but when I need to check the status of an order, I might pick up my phone to access the information. This requires companies to rethink features on their website to cater to behaviors more likely to originate from a mobile device and so mobile visitors can perform certain tasks more quickly. Also, when you change the name (label) of a feature it can also change browsing behavior because customers can identify with the new labels. A simple change (as in renaming the label from "more here" to "buy now") will increase conversions from mobile.

Browser testing

Have you tested how your website looks across multiple operating systems, web browsers, device types and manufacturers? It takes time that many of us don't have, never mind the patience to test each on ourselves. What once would be a full time job testing browsers now is available on CrossBrowserTesting.com as a premium service. You will be surprised to learn how your website can take on new forms that customers can see now. On your website analytics you can see how many visitors use specific devices and browsers to prioritize with your web developer what design changes are most urgent.

Improve calls to action

Delays in Screen to Screen conversations happen when the customer can't find which button or link on your website to click next during a screen share. The customer will either blame themselves for not being able to find it or blame your company for having an unusable website. Both situations can be avoided by placing highly visible call to action images or buttons for the most important next steps. This could mean either designing an image to be a clickable button, changing the name of the clickable link, or placing the image in a more obvious place on your website to find.

Improve shareability

During a conversation, there is much to share in addition to the dialogue. White papers, case studies, document files, infographics, and meeting invitation links are all examples of what you can share during a Screen to Screen meeting. However, sharing information with a laptop is much different from sharing with a mobile device.

Learn the different ways to use a laptop and a mobile device for performing these tasks:

- Copy text or other content to your clipboard and paste it into a window.
- Open up a website, new tab, or new browser.
- Send a meeting invitation link by text message and email.
- Share a file stored from the Dropbox mobile app, rather than sending an attachment (benefits include link tracking, saved upload time, files accessible from anywhere).
- Share the screen of a website or document.

Checklist 10-2 DEVICE CONNECTIVITY

In the majority of this book we discuss situations where you will be meeting with a customer Screen to Screen from a remote location. There will be times when you will use similar technology in meetings face-to-face around a board room, one on one with a customer, and displayed on flat screen TVs or projection screens.

One question I get asked regularly is, "How do I get all of these devices to talk to one another, so I can use them all at the same time?" And my best lawyer answer is that it depends. It depends upon your answers to the following questions:

- Will the client's condition be better off using Screen to Screen technology? If not, don't use it. The reward for using technology must be greater than any anticipated risk.
- Do we have a reliable Internet connection in order to connect the devices wirelessly with one another? If not, you are risking the quality of the meeting and limiting the ways participants can collaborate with one another.
- What camera angles and positions are necessary to capture participant feedback and involvement? If you don't test ahead of time you could ending up embarrassing yourself.

This section will organize the right questions for you to ask yourself on which technology will best help you communicate, persuade, and influence decisions from one screen to the next.

Wired meeting options

An ideal situation exists when the technology works without wires. But because of antiquated systems, device incompatibility, or under-performing Internet connections, wires will continue to exist, at least in my lifetime. What scenarios require wire?

- Absence of knowledge of using wireless devices
- Wireless out of order, requiring use of Ethernet cable for Internet
- Cameras that need USB cables to perform
- Projectors that need VGA or HDMI cables
- Flat-screen televisions that need VGA or HDMI cables

Don't assume that your customer has the same setup as you do. When you ask a customer if they have used Screen to Screen meeting tech-nology in the past or determine their comfort level on using mobile, you can quickly troubleshoot some wireless options because you have analyzed multiple wired scenarios in advance.

Wireless settings

A participant might use their mobile phone for live polling, share pic-tures from their tablet, and view slides from their computer all at the same time. And when devices are on the same Wi-Fi network it saves time transferring data, synchronizes applications, and eliminates one more code you have to remember.

This applies to Screen to Screen meetings and face-to-face envi-ronments when participants are using multiple devices in the same location. Example data transfer mechanisms include:

- Sending pictures taken from iPhone to iPad in order to edit them on a bigger screen.

- Synchronizing the Doceri iPad app to the Doceri Desktop application.
- Mirroring the iPad screen on top of the computer screen during screen share.
- Mirroring the iPad display directly to an Apple TV.

Media streaming player

Have you ever walked into a conference room and discovered you couldn't connect your laptop or tablet to the projection screen because you didn't have the right cord or adapter? If this happens to you, you might not need to make that extra trip to Radio Shack or rely upon IT to help you. If you have an Apple TV, AirPlay can connect the devices wirelessly. Businesses have been equipping their conference rooms with Apple TVs, Rokus, and Google's ChromeCast media players because they easily integrate with a flat screen television to act as a multimedia billboard or screen for an interactive demonstration without the use of more cords.

Bluetooth

Back in 1994, Ericsson invented the Bluetooth technology that allows devices to communicate with one another wirelessly. Examples of devices that work with Bluetooth include the following:

- Mobile phones and tablets
- Desktop and laptop computers
- Wireless headphones and earpieces
- Portable media players and DVRs
- Heart rate monitors, scales, and thermometers
- Remote controls
- Wireless cameras, speakers, and microphones

Bluetooth is an alternative to using Wi-Fi to connect devices located in the same room only. As it pertains to Screen to Screen meetings, wireless speakers and microphones are connected to the host computer using Bluetooth across longer conference rooms. This requires an initial setup and testing to avoid troubleshooting audio/video issues during real meetings with real customers.

Security and risk management on mobile devices

How embarrassing would it be if a customer took over control of your screen because you weren't familiar with the collaboration settings inside of the Screen to Screen meeting? All credibility can go out the window when a participant shares a purple pony on your screen for everyone to see. Or better, the participant starts drawing on your slides without your awareness or approval.

Fortunately, you can prevent these mishaps. AirPlay, Bluetooth, and Wi-Fi connections all have a password option to protect you from anyone else gaining control of your devices. Failure to set a unique and memorable password will put you at greater risk of this happening. Humuhumunukunukuapuaa is a pretty fish but not a good password because of how long it would take to type it out every time you needed it.

Checklist 10-3 MOBILE MEETINGS

Because in a mobile Screen to Screen meeting you and the customer are using mobile devices, you need a different set of tools, a different set of skills, and a different format for communicating information from one device to the next. Let's consider the details of what you'll need to conduct mobile meetings.

Mobile-meeting feature list

Mobile technology is changing every single day. Between the time this book was written and when you are reading, some of the Screen to Screen meeting platforms will have added more mobile-meeting features that used to be available only for use with a desktop or laptop computer. Keep that in mind as you use the following list to identify features you demand for your Screen to Screen conversations:

- Hosting instant and scheduled meetings from mobile
- Teleconference phone numbers and VoIP
- Video-to-video chat to turn camera off and on
- Mute (for your own device) and mute participants
- Whiteboard
- Screen sharing of files from mobile
- Sharing websites from mobile
- Multi-participant access

App demos

Apps navigate much differently from websites because they involve touch and swipe rather than click and scroll. And to increase the number of downloads or get customers to use hidden features you will need to show them how to use it, not just tell them these features exist.

There are two primary ways of demoing an app for a customer. First, you can create a web page that maps out the options for the customer to explore on their own or create a video that highlights important features. Examples include Appdemostore.com and Preapps.com. The second, more powerful way is to demonstrate the app in real time with customers using screen share and mobile mirroring software. The app (from phone or tablet) mirrors the same display onto the computer, and with screen share, mirrors the app on the customer's computer screen in order to review the features together in real time. You would ask the customer questions about what is most important to them, and enter in data, click on menus, and solve problems with your customer as if they were using the app themselves. This real time approach is far more effective than sharing a link with a customer to download the app and asking them a few days later, "What did you think?"

Menus, filters, and sorting

We have discusses already that responsive websites will change their design according to the type of device being used. And, designs will continue to change as new standards are adopted by Google and suggested by the Internet of Things Consortium. Specifically regarding mobile, we need to pay close attention to how apps are using menus, filters, and sorting features to help us access the right data as quickly as possible to produce desired behaviors both as a communicator and as a customer. Wearable technologies and mobile device screens have far less real estate than a laptop allows. This pushes engineers and software developers to re-examine design to focus on how customers experience their platform across multiple devices. Apps such as Kayak, Uber, and Hotwire have crammed the most important search and scheduling options simplifying a very comprehensive set of data on mobile. Try using the menus, filters, and sorting options. They have made the process so simple you shouldn't need a tutorial to learn how to operate them.

App agility and shortcuts

Switching back and forth between the most suitable app for specific parts of the conversation will make the difference between someone who is seen as credible or not. It's the same as someone who retrieves the exact contract from their briefcase and shuffling through many files and saying, "that's not it."

In Chapter 7 we discussed some time-saving shortcuts using different operating systems and web browsers, and to execute the same tasks on mobile device there's a little twist.

Perform a quick Google search by using the name of the device and the word "shortcuts," and master them to increase your productivity in meetings.

Here are my favorites for mobile:

- Search and find apps instead of using app list. Devices overloaded with too many apps cause delays in finding the one you need when you need it most.

- Select Wi-Fi settings. Sometimes you will be forced to switch Wi-Fi networks quickly because bandwidth speed can change without notice.
- Categorize apps based on similar type. For example, all meeting apps go in the folder named "meetings."
- Transition to recently used apps with swipe, not buttons. A four finger swipe left or right on an iPad display can switch to most recent or previous app being used without touching buttons.
- Adjust background brightness settings. Meeting rooms might require more light to brighten the device display or darken the screen to conserve battery.
- Pan and zoom. Zoom in and out takes place by pinching fingers instead of keyboard shortcuts on a laptop.
- Mobile screenshot. Take a picture of your screen from your mobile to be used in visual summaries.

App developers have also created shortcuts that are specific to their own native app. When you download an app, they usually appear as quick tips in the introduction before you begin use. Instead of tapping Skip, take a few minutes to learn these shortcuts, because they will save you hours in the end if you frequent the app regularly.

Checklist 10-4 MOBILE-MEETING ETIQUETTE

To win today's competitive world of business, you have to know how to play the game. Of course, to excel in any game, you must know the rules.

—JACQUELINE WHITMORE, AUTHOR OF *BUSINESS CLASS*

Would you consider a meeting to be productive if everyone were on his or her mobile phone while it was taking place? Maybe it would not be for those who demand that the attention of participants focus on them. But those who are more focused on collaboration to get results might see it differently. If an investment group were told they needed to "bifurcate their investments" but didn't know what *bifurcate* meant, what would the group do? One individual might ask for clarification, another would perform a Google search on their phone, and the rest would hope that the financial adviser would cover it again but in simpler terms. The meeting host and participants MUST agree as to what is considered to be Robert's Rules of Order to determine what behaviors move the agenda forward and what is seen as a disruption with technology.

Doug Devitre's 12 Musings for Mobile Meetings

1. Each participant agrees to act as if they were participating in a meeting with one another face-to-face.
2. Each participant is prepared to start at meeting time, not join to then troubleshoot technology. Join meeting early to avoid delays that happen from last minute software downloads, audio/video malfunctions, problems from having an unanticipated weak Internet connection.
3. Each participant is entitled to participate using their own device (BYOD = bring your own device), regardless of operating system used by other participants. Teams in the same company should agree upon best device and adopt companywide to decrease costs and service time in troubleshooting multiple devices.
4. Each participant is responsible for obtaining the fastest and most secure Internet connection (either bring your own Internet [BYOI] or provided by host) before the meeting begins.
5. Each participant must know how to mute their own audio by themselves before the meeting starts. You would be surprised how many people cause distractions from crunching potato chips and shuffling papers while waiting to contribute.
6. Each participant is permitted to disable his or her webcam when not needed. Webcams for video, like microphones

for audio, should be turned off when a distraction is about to occur and turned back on when ready to engage in the conversation.

7. Each participant must share the exact URL of online resources in the participant chat for all to access it, not just mention URLs. This saves everyone time typing in the URL, writing it down in their notes, or asking, "How do you spell that again?"

8. No participant may record a video of the conversation or take screen capture photos unless all parties have granted permission in writing. Just because you can doesn't meet you should. Screen to Screen meetings fall under the same privacy guidelines as telephone calls and are reviewed regularly to protect the confidentiality of meetings.

9. Each participant agrees during face-to-face meetings to place their phone face down on the table in silent mode unless app access adds value to the conversation.

10. Participants agree to perform actions quickly on mobile devices when requested by the facilitator. This doesn't mean everyone has an extra minute to check email, Facebook, or other social media.

11. Participants agree to eliminate distractions by turning off notifications, instant messages, and ringtones by putting the mobile device on silent.

12. Participants using wearable technologies with audio and video recording must remove them before the meeting starts unless agreed to by all parties in writing.

Device acceptance

Mobile meetings can be a challenge to initiate when your devices have different operating systems. For example, you might be working from an iPad, and the customer is using an Android tablet, or vice versa. Do you cancel the Screen to Screen meeting, rely solely on the telephone, or make it work by selecting apps that work across operating systems? It would be silly to limit your ability to serve your customers based on what device they use. Instead, choose popular applications that are available for download on devices with different operating systems. If you are unfamiliar with other operating systems, spend an hour at the electronics store and ask the attendant questions, play with the devices, and try to access certain websites and tools the way your customer would.

Video chat vs. verbal

Most newer Screen to Screen meeting tools have added the webcam feature so you can see your customer and your customer can see you. The upside includes the ability to observe body language, facial expressions, and observe your customer in their natural environment. Downsides include advanced preparation of background surroundings, attention to grooming (ex. bad hair days), and increased bandwidth requirements from your Internet connection.

A video chat isn't always necessary and shouldn't be the focus of the meeting. The focus should be on meeting the customer's objectives in the least amount of time. If trouble occurs when signing on a meeting with video, don't waste the entire conversation trying to fix it. Simply revert the dialogue to audio, screen share, or as a last resort, pick up the phone!

Permission to share screen

Customers want to talk with you, not at your screen. The minute you activate the screen share feature on your mobile device the dynamic shifts to presentation mode and will turn off customers if the screen share isn't presented as if it is in their best interests. There's a point in the conversation when a customer says the following:

- What does that look like?
- Can you share or show me an example?
- How does that compare with what I'm doing now?

Then you ask the question, "In order to save us time in communicating the details can I share my screen with you so you can see what I'm talking about in addition to my words?" or "I can try to explain it over the phone or I can share my screen with you so you can see exactly how I can help you. Which do you prefer?" Screen share is more cumbersome from mobile to mobile: it requires even more attention to which websites or visuals to use as examples and to plan accordingly.

Text/instant messaging

Is it OK to send a text message to a customer during a Screen to Screen mobile meeting? Absolutely, as long as you have texted them before, you tell the customer what you are doing in the moment, why you are doing it, and how it will benefit them. For example, a customer might ask you to send them the PDF that outlines a product description to view after the call. If their preferred form of communication is text then you can send the file as a link or attachment to the message. Attaching the document to an email you send afterward is fine, but they may want immediate access on their device to save electronically in their preferred app.

Wearable technology

Would you find it odd that someone using a wearable technology with webcam like Google Glass started a meeting, recorded it, and broadcasted it without anyone else knowing? I know I would feel intruded upon. This could be the title of my next book, *How to Lose Friends and Piss Off People with the Latest Technology*, because of the number of social faux pas that would surface. People don't like to be recorded in general, and worse, you open up the possibility that their confidential conversations will be made available quickly. Check your wearables at the door please.

Checklist 10-5 DRONE IMPLEMENTATION

*This thing's kind of climbing like a pig. Climb, pig. ... Boy,
this is going to be tight. ... OK, interesting, we are
falling out of the sky.*

—ANONYMOUS DRONE PILOT

Areas inaccessible by foot require the use of drones in order to make decisions from mobile. This new form of mobile meeting can send a machine in the sky to capture video footage in the air, around buildings, and be the first one in case of an emergency response.

When you see that the next idea involves drones, you may be thinking, What does a remote-controlled aircraft have to do with sales? Is the drone a solution looking for a problem, or is it a solution that solves a problem?

Sales professionals who sell, lease, or supply access to spaces not easily accessible by foot, ladder or air, require a more cost efficient and safer alternative than hiring a helicopter to capture live footage to share with customers. Industries that can specifically benefit from using drones in sales include real estate, agriculture, emergency and energy. For instance, Richard Silver, a top producing REALTOR® with Sotheby's International Realty Canada hires a certified professional to capture videos and photos of his listings to be used in his marketing.

(Note: Salespeople, don't buy a drone unless it is a hobby. Flying a drone is serious business and requires several hours of practice in order to do it well. Your best use of time is to be spending time with customers, not playing with technology.)

Permission to fly

What would happen if everyone owned a drone and flew it on "drone day"? It wouldn't make much difference if you live on several acres, but if you are located in a booming metropolis, it could turn into chaos similar to a scene from the movie *The Birds*. That's maybe why the Federal Aviation Administration (FAA) in the United States has banned the use of drones for commercial purposes unless commissioned from a certified, licensed operator. But in other countries, there are no regulations yet to be approved. Keep checking the FAA's website to read the latest legislative updates concerning unmanned aircraft systems (UAS): https://www.faa.gov/uas.

Flight safety

Do you need to be drone certified in order to fly? Nope. Right now, you can buy a drone straight from Amazon, have it on your doorstep in two days, and have it up in the air. But before you do, imagine the risk involved if you flew your drone and it came crashing down on a house, a neighbor, or yourself. The FAA placed strict regulations on those using drones for commercial purposes in order to protect safety for everyone.

You can get drone certified through the Unmanned Vehicle University for $3,500, which covers aeronautical, electrical, and mechanical engineering topics, or you can hire a professional to fly your drone for you. Your role as a sales professional should be telling the story behind the footage captured, published, or live-streamed out to your customers. Your job is to make sure the operator flying your drone has the proper training, insurance, and credentials. Your job shouldn't be learning to fly drones.

Recording footage

If you were a customer and had wings, what would you want to see before making a major investment? That petroleum pipeline deal might look really good on paper, but you might want to send a drone to the site in order to verify it exists, inspect the construction, and share the footage with other key stakeholders before everyone signs.

An expert drone pilot will be able to capture footage as both still pictures and video to share among key stakeholders or publish to the web for marketing purposes. You, as the salesperson, are the director of the footage, and the drone operator is your camera operator. You need to highlight what are the most salable features of the site and request that the drone operator cover them in his or her recording.

An aerial view delivers a more comprehensive overview of the site inspection, whereas a close-up view demonstrates the details of features not accessible by foot. Make sure your drone operator uses a combination of both.

Publishing footage

Footage can be shared publicly or privately, depending upon the confidentiality of the transaction. Images and video can be shared publicly through LinkedIn, Twitter, Instagram, Pinterest, and Facebook.

Before you share the video recording, have a professional edit it to cut out any footage that doesn't add value to the customer. Once you are ready to upload the file, make sure you have researched the best keywords to include in the description and tags so it can be found more easily with search engines. Learn the tasks involved in publishing videos online, create a system that can be duplicated, and separate yourself from the process so you can focus on your biggest priority, more sales.

Live-streaming footage

The increase in accessibility of broadband wireless Internet has given us new options for delivering real-time video footage to the public. As long as the drone is Wi-Fi enabled, near the Internet connection source, and set up for broadcast, you can create your production studio from high in the sky. Also, new apps have been created so you can fly the drone right from your mobile phone.

But before you go all in and add a drone to your sales team, find out if the accessibility problem is big enough to justify using drones as a solution. Make sure you have permission from the federal, state/provincial, and local governments. Make sure you meet the safety requirements. And if you do, send your next video to me at doug@dougdevitre.com, and I will share it online for you.

Checklist 10-6 MOBILE NOTIFICATIONS

Everything beeps now.

—GEORGE CARLIN

During one full day, how many times does something beep or buzz? The alarm clock wakes you up. The electronic toothbrush tells you when the battery is low. And the coffee pot reminds you the coffee is ready. That's three beeps before you even get your day started. All of these notifications have been activated because you allowed them. In the case of Screen to Screen Selling, be aware of notifications you can send/receive in order to decrease meeting absenteeism, increase commitment from customers, and improve the customer experience.

Push notifications

Is it time to buy? Looks like the watch said so.

What is less intrusive than text messages and timelier than email? With texting, you have to consider that the customer might incur SMS charges. But if you have an important update to send, you don't want it to get lost in a customer's inbox. Another way to notify customers of an upcoming meeting is by sending a push notification through your company or meeting app as long as the customer has enabled push notifications on their device.

When your customer downloads an app, it usually asks them two questions: First, what is their current location? Second, will they allow push notifications from this app on their device? If they select yes, then anytime the app wants to send an announcement, their phone will buzz and ask them if they want to read the details of the message. Sales teams are sending push notifications straight to mobile devices whenever a new product is released, some other important announcement is made, or market conditions have changed enough to bring insights needed for customers to make decisions. When customers receive these messages to join Screen to Screen meetings it increases the likelihood more will participate.

Instant video chat

Do you find it weird that the phone is ringing less and that FaceTime, Skype, and Facebook video chat are blowing up (increasing in popularity)? Customers are becoming more used to using instant video chat to communicate rather than committing to a specific time for an appointment. Always be "Camera Ready" for when groups of customers who prefer video chat need your help—you have the technology and process to serve them according to their preferences. The expectation is evolving from hearing to seeing the person you are doing business with for the same reasons we still get on airplanes to make customer visits. Stay ahead of the curve by adapting to this increasingly popular trend as better technology is introduced into the market.

Bluetooth beacons

Have you experienced walking into a store and your phone buzzes to signal a message about the latest special that already matches your requirements? Retail stores with mobile apps, predictive analytics, and Bluetooth beacon technology now make this possible. When a customer enters in range of a store's Bluetooth Beacon notification system, the system sends out a notification to the store's app saved on the customer's mobile device about a new offer, sale, or announcement. The customer can choose to tap the notification to learn more or request the attention of a salesperson for help. The store's computer system identifies the customer profile from its database, analyzes past buying behaviors, and quickly recommends products or services the of interest to the customer.

Customers have demanded a better experience for years and those who have improved upon their sales practices to embrace new technology will be able to maintain their current sales productivity. And companies who are innovating with technology through practical differentiation will be those who experience growth. When you meet with a customer and they start telling you how to use the technology in order to serve them, then you have lost.

PART THREE

FOLLOW-UP

Is the fortune really in the follow-up? It all depends:

- It depends on how well you were able to build rapport with the customer during the conversation.
- It depends on how well you listened to the customer's needs.
- It depends on how well you were able to conceptualize the customer's problems, demonstrate your expertise, and determine the next steps that follow a sequential sales process.

With all processes being equal, it's not just how often you follow up but how you follow up differently than everyone else that positions you as the go-to person to solve customers' future problems.

The chapters in Part Three will discuss how visual summaries will add value to conversations to improve your conversion rate, how to keep electronic records confidential and secure with digital signatures, and how to improve the customer experience after Screen to Screen conversations.

CHAPTER 11

VISUAL SUMMARIES: HOW VISUAL SUMMARIES SUPPORT THE DECISION-MAKING PROCESS

I think in art, but especially in films, people are
trying to confirm their own experiences.

—JIM MORRISON, LEAD SINGER OF THE DOORS

Let's pretend you just ended a Screen to Screen conversation with a customer. How do you follow up?

- Do you send a handwritten thank-you note?
- Do you send an email with your proposal and next steps?
- Do you record a quick video to say thank you?
- Do you send the final agreements to be initialed?

And, there might be 10 other tasks you do in order to confirm the next appointment or make the sale. What matters most is how uniquely you have addressed the problems, uncovered the common pitfalls, and positioned your expertise in a way that makes you the only viable solution.

This chapter will show you how visual summaries create the point of differentiation over your competition, add value to the sales process, and decrease the amount of rework in explaining advanced concepts.

Checklist 11-1 VISUAL SUMMARIES

A visual summary is different from a written summary shared in an email or letter to the customer. A visual summary delivers these extra benefits:

- For the salesperson, less work is required for summarizing all of the details.
- For the customer, visuals provide greater clarity around ambiguous concepts.
- You can recap key points with stimulating images.
- You can annotate documents instead of compiling explanations of terms.
- Simple drawings can take the place of complex descriptions.

Consider the following examples of visual summaries to understand how they create more impact following your Screen to Screen conversation.

Offer a visual review of alternatives

Extremely busy customers sometimes forget about their decisions minutes after they make them, for many reasons. Perhaps they were multitasking at the time and didn't give you their full, undivided attention. Maybe several interruptions occurred during the conversation and distracted them. Or their short-term memory could have been hindered because something more important came up after the conversation.

Whatever reason they give, a visual review of the alternatives you discussed will reduce the likelihood of them forgetting critical moments in the dialogue because the screenshots and annotations support the verbal conversation.

Calculate profit and loss

Suppose an investor's sole focus is on the rate of return from an investment property and you demonstrated that return Screen to Screen. The investor may ask you to send them the summary of how you arrived at the satisfactory percentage. You could type out every step in the process you already demonstrated, but that would take just as long, if not longer than the conversation itself. Instead, take screenshots of the input fields and results from the calculations, and use these to create a visual summary. This gives them the same answer in a more visually stimulating format that takes you less time to produce.

Summarize next links

Have you ever had a customer ask you to show examples, processes, or tools using websites, and days later asked the same questions on how you performed the same functions? Save both you and your customer a repeated conversation by providing them annotated images of screenshots by highlight linked words, menus, or call to action buttons. This tip is especially useful for websites rich in content and navigation menus.

For example, suppose an insurance agent's client wants help navigating through the online customer portal to pay their bill, adjust their coverage, or file a claim. Accepting payment over the phone still doesn't solve their problem of paying online and enables this request to recur in the future. A better resolution would be to initiate a Screen to Screen meeting, open up the online portal page with the customer, and show them exactly where to click next to make payment. If the agent took screenshots of the process and made annotations to be shared by PDF, it would decrease the likelihood of having the same conversation again. The goal with Screen to Screen is to teach the customer how to fish, not do the fishing for them.

Reduce communication errors

Following a conversation, has a customer ever complained to you that they thought they were getting one thing but instead received another? Screen to Screen meetings clarify the gray areas of communication because both parties can see form fields being entered, data inputted into calculators, and contracts being completed in real time. You can further support this benefit by providing customers with visual summaries, which document the screenshots associated with how you engage with your customers Screen to Screen.

International real estate transactions involve many parties to complete tasks in a timely manner; otherwise the sale could be postponed or cease to occur if the details are miscommunicated. Visual summaries communicate input from the immigration attorney, real estate attorney, currency exchange partner, foreign buyers, and real estate agent and be used as evidence to rectify an issue caused by improper communication.

Checklist 11-2 TOOLS FOR VISUAL SUMMARIES

Men have become tools of their tools.

—HENRY DAVID THOREAU

You could take pictures of what shows on your screen with your mobile-phone camera, but it isn't always the best option. Why not? The camera might not capture the image in a high enough resolution for it to be readable. Also, if you send multiple images by email or another tool, the customer has to determine the right order for viewing them. Finally, this method requires more work, because you have to remember to pick up the camera every time you need to capture a screenshot. There are more efficient, more effective, and more user-friendly alternatives, which we will discuss here.

Screenshot images

Depending on your device, operating system, and software being used, you can create a screenshot of what appears on your computer screen by using one of the following keyboard shortcuts:

- With Mac OS X, press Shift-Command-F4.
- With Windows, press PrtScn (print screen) or Alt-PrtScn.
- With Apple iOS, press Home-power button.
- With Android, press Volume Down-power button.

A popular screenshot tool called Snagit will give you more options around annotating screenshots and repurposing images for marketing.

Collaborative documents

Consultants create visual summaries in real time with customers when they ask process-oriented questions and enter in the feedback during a screen share using a web-based collaborative technology like Google Docs. Benefits of using Google Docs include mobile access, minimal email correspondence, and collaboration on most recent file version. The most recent version is what the customer and consultant refer to as the working copy and previous versions are quickly accessible to view the evolution of the project.

Presentation slide annotations

Microsoft PowerPoint and Apple's Keynote presentation software already have a whiteboard feature; however, the problem I described before is that sales conversations are not linear. The order of the discussion takes place based on what the customer wants, not what you have prepared to delivered in the order you think the customer wants.

This is why sending over a slide deck as an email attachment doesn't work. A better way to send your slides is with customized annotations specific to customer needs. This way your slides become more about them rather than all the things your company can do for them.

The fastest way I've found to create screenshots of presentation slides that include annotations made during Screen to Screen conversations is to use the Doceri iPad app. One icon tap on the iPad takes the slide into annotation mode with a Microsoft Word-like toolbar you can use to start marking up the slide. One tap erases the annotations, another tap creates a second version of annotations on the same slide, and yet another tap exits annotation mode so you can continue with the next visual. Once all annotations are finalized, you can send a collection of annotations using one PDF summary, which is much faster than trying to piece images together individually using another tool.

Whiteboard drawings and sketches

As you saw already in Chapter 8, an interactive whiteboard provides many benefits in Screen to Screen meetings. With regard to follow-up, the chief benefit of drawing on the screen using a digital whiteboard is that the customer can't fall back on the excuse that they forgot details of the meeting because the dog ate their notes, coffee was spilled on the page, or they misplaced the napkin you were sketching on. Instead, you can save the images for future reference and to share with the client.

Check the whiteboard feature or application you are using to make sure it will save all of your annotations in a file or folder. This way, following the conversation, you have quick access to files you can share or use to remind yourself what was discussed.

Video recordings

As long as you have permission from your customer and you share how a recording will help them in case they want to review, you can record a video of the conversation as it happens on your screen. Most Screen to Screen meeting software has a premium feature that allows you to do this. Or you can use tools like Camtasia or ScreenFlow that are independent from the meeting software.

Save your recordings in a folder that is time- and date-stamped, which will save you time when you are accessing past conversations. In case there is ever a discrepancy between what was said and what was understood, you can play the video again.

Checklist 11-3 HANDWRITING ANALYSIS

> *Man is a strange animal. He generally cannot read the handwriting on the wall until his back is up against it.*
>
> —ADLAI STEVENSON

I admit my handwriting looks like it hasn't improved from the third grade. What about yours? If you have the same problem, here's some good news. Having used the digital whiteboard for the last couple of years during Screen to Screen conversations has taught me that you don't need to write every word that comes to mind in order to communicate an idea. Instead think of concise words, phrases, or inserting images that say the same thing.

Read on to discover ways to improve your handwriting skills on the digital whiteboard.

Replace words with sketches

In each of the following pairs, which activity can you do faster?

- Writing the word *time* or drawing a clockface
- Writing the word *money* or drawing a dollar symbol
- Writing the word *satisfaction* or drawing a smiley face

Drawing sketches is significantly faster, more accurate, and more memorable than writing words. For example, when I think "time,"

I know to draw a circle with a right angle inside, signifying the hour and minute hands of a clock face.

When you think of a word to write to explain a concept, the challenge can be determining which sketch will best represent the word. There are two exercises you can perform in order to increase your ability to draw the best sketch. First, play the game Telestrations with your friends, family, or coworkers. This fun game of handwritten charades will help you become more creative under the gun. The other exercise is to practice tracing icons. Icons used in computing, websites, and programs are essentially images that express the idea or brand as a sketch. Search Google images for "[name of your industry] + icons" for a list of commonly used images you might need to draw next.

Use big letters or all caps

If you have ever used a flipchart in a facilitation setting before, you know how hard it can be for someone to see the handwriting if they are seated at the far end of the room. Drawing big letters and using ALL CAPS in a group meeting will make your handwriting more legible for all to see, regardless of where they are sitting. It also is helpful when participants are using mobile devices to participate Screen to Screen, because these devices have small screens.

Use fewer words

Fewer words are better than long, written explanations when working with customers Screen to Screen. Less handwriting on the whiteboard is faster to draw and less copy on other visual aids (slides, websites, PDFs, etc.) is easier to read. Analyze the gestalt of what your customer understands their current position to be before summarizing anything in writing.

Here are some examples:

- "Preferences in using technology" becomes "technology preferences."

- "Keyboard shortcuts for mobile devices" becomes "software quick keys."
- "Integrating the calendar with software" becomes "calendar integrations."

Ultimately, your goal is to improve the speed and accuracy of your handwriting by using fewer words to describe the same meaning. Your customers will be able to focus better and make quicker decisions as a result.

Use multiple colors

During Screen to Screen conversations, you can easily differentiate thought patterns, categories, and lists by using multiple colors in your whiteboard remarks. For example, you could write cost savings, revenue-generating activities, and other intangible benefits in green. You could write overhead, time spent, and expenses in red. Can you use black for everything? Sure, but the problem with working in one color is that the customer will find it harder to mentally categorize information.

Also consider legibility. Choose darker-colored annotations on a lighter background and lighter annotations on a darker background. A color wheel will show the opposite colors that work well with one another on different-colored backgrounds compared to annotations. For example, black works great on white, yellow shows up fine on purple, and orange is best on blue.

Proofread before saving

If you sped up your handwriting in order to save time during the conversation, there's a good chance your English looks like Arabic or vice versa. This is why it's critically important to spend time reviewing your annotations before you save them and send the file to your customer.

When you proofread, don't just look for spelling errors. Your review should include but not be limited to meeting the following standards:

- Text is legible.
- Sketches are clear and concise.
- Lines are straight.
- Shapes are positioned properly.
- Calculations are correct.

Checklist 11-4 CONFIRMATION SLIDES

When we hear news we should always wait for the sacrament of confirmation.

—VOLTAIRE

Creating and sharing a visual summary involves a process that you can adapt across any size of sales organization, diverse portfolio of products or services, or any decision-making style for different types of customers. Ultimately, the customer decides what product or service they will buy based on how you presented options during and after the conversation. Here is the process you can use, customize, and then monetize from your visual summaries.

Options become bullet points

Make a list of all the products and services you sell, and write them on a piece of paper in an outline format listed as bullet points. The more complex your sales process is, the more you will need to identify categories that represent the subset of options. For example insurance agents have hundreds of options customers can choose from, and these can be categorized into auto, home, business, and life insurance. Each category is broken down into a subsequent subset.

Auto insurance can be segmented into liability, medical, and vehicle. Vehicle can be further segmented into comprehensive, gap, rental reimbursement, and so on.

Bullet points become visuals

With each bullet point, you now have a solution that is looking for a problem. Find all of the potential problems that exist that relate to one solution, and build a visual around how the problem leads to the solution. For example, if your car were wrecked, vandalized, or hit by a hailstorm and you were without transportation (the problem), you would have a car available at no extra cost, because it would be covered under rental-car reimbursement (the solution). Create multiple Infographic-like images that demonstrate the value of the money, time, and hassle customers would save by having multiple policies to protect them. If a customer asked about auto coverage, you would insert into the Screen to Screen conversation the image that breaks down the options of the policies, so the customer can see them, rather than trying to explain details that may or may not be important to this particular customer.

Visuals become check boxes

Now that you have visuals that break down the cost and benefits of each product, the images themselves act as visual forms that the customer fills in verbally while you fill in visually. For example, a visual for liability insurance might have check boxes for options including bodily injury, property damage, and umbrella coverage. If the customer says all three, you can mark the check box next to each one or explain the cost and benefits of other alternatives.

Check boxes become decisions

Before the end of the meeting, check boxes initialed on visuals summarize multiple decisions made during the Screen to Screen meeting and determine the next steps to follow. These decisions may require additional calculations if the customer investment is variable upon timing, units, etc.

These visuals—the filled-out check boxes—validate multiple decisions. If there is ever a disagreement or misunderstanding, these visuals can supply additional proof of each conversation. As the meeting reaches its end, review the final decisions with the customer, determine the next steps, and express your gratitude before saying good-bye.

Once all parties are in agreement with terms, the final step would be to confirm the sale in writing, or in the case of Screen to Screen Selling, obtain digital signatures. If the sale is made or not, still send the visual summary to reinforce the dialogue. Read on to find out how.

Checklist 11-5 SENDING THE VISUAL SUMMARY

A summary sent by email confirming the sale or to support the recent conversation should take minutes, not hours. The skill sets you develop around using the most effective tools will determine how efficient you are at producing this correspondence. You could send an email with attachments such as the annotations from visuals, checklists for accountability, audio/video summaries, a list of links mentioned during the call, and a summary of what needs to happen next.

Export annotations into PDF

All that matters after you have visualized the conversation with slides, annotations, websites, etc. is what the customer will do with the information you provide. Simple is better. It's best to send one PDF file that includes all of your annotations rather than several PDFs, images, and files. This way the customer doesn't have to worry about running Mac-to-PC file conversions or opening up several files in order to see how the conversation progressed.

The way you create the PDF depends on the software you used during the meeting. If you used Doceri, you can use the program's Export menu and select the Share as PDF command. Figure 11.1 shows what this menu looks like.

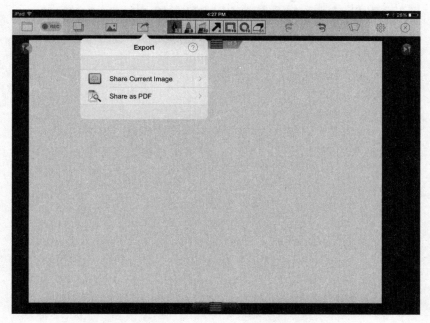

Figure 11.1 Creating a Visual Summary with Doceri

Collect links discussed

Every time a link to a blog post, video, or file download is discussed in your meeting, it's best to add it to a list for the customer, in order to save time for them. After the meeting, you can copy this list and paste it into the text section of your email to the customer. You can use a format that looks like this:

Links discussed

- http://doceri.com (iPad whiteboard app)
- http://zoom.us (videoconferencing app)

- http://wunderlist.com (checklist app)
- http://bit.ly/screen2screen (access to more Screen to Screen Selling resources)

Make available audio and video summaries

If the customer gave you permission to make a video recording of the Screen to Screen meeting, do not—and I say do not—send the video as an attachment to email. Chances are the email will take forever to upload to your email server, get caught up in the customer's email server, and not be delivered. Even if the email does get through, the customer might not have the right video player in order to play your video file format. Instead, find a tool or hosting solution that makes it easy to upload videos, creates a link to the video, and will play the video on desktop computers and mobile devices without error.

What if the customer would rather have the conversation in audio format because the only time they have to listen is while they are in transport? You can use online video-to-audio conversion tools like Online-Convert.com (http://www.online-convert.com). These can quickly separate the files so you can share them according to the customer's preference.

Write brief message

The email you send should be brief, highlight the key points discussed, and include any special instructions for using the multimedia provided. Here's an example:

Subject: 123 Main Street Listing

John and Sue,

Thanks for speaking with me today. I've summarized our conversation with a few key points:

- Need to sell in order to buy (no contingencies).
- Estimated home value = $375K–$450K.

- Desired closing date: December 20, 2016.
- Marketing and staging checklists will be sent once listing agreement is signed.
- Need relocation assistance to Warren, Pennsylvania.

I will follow up with you on the agreed date of September 5 (two days from now) to answer questions and collect signatures.

Links we discussed:

http://houselogic.com
http://mywebsite.com/sellers
Attachment: Visual Summary 123 Main Street Listing

CHAPTER 12

◆◆◆

MANAGING RISK: WHAT YOUR DEVICES ALONE WON'T TEACH YOU ABOUT SECURITY

It takes 20 years to build a reputation and five minutes to ruin it. If you think about that, you'll do things differently.

—WARREN BUFFETT

A security break isn't a matter of if. It's a matter of when. If someone really wanted to get your social security number, birth date, ATM number, and credit card information they can always find a way. Your goal with information technology security is to add as many levels of protection as possible against risks that originate from collecting customer data to exchanging files online. This chapter will give you security-related questions to ask your company's information technology (IT) department or your external IT support system to minimize risk while using technology.

Checklist 12-1 QUESTIONS TO ASK YOUR IT DEPARTMENT

You were taught to share your toys as a young child, but this doesn't apply to letting others use your Wi-Fi.

—ROBERT SICILIANO, AUTHOR OF *99 THINGS YOU WISH YOU KNEW BEFORE YOUR IDENTITY WAS STOLEN*

The safety of your data starts with the quality of the questions you would ask your IT department and/or the very questions criminals would ask themselves seeking to gain unauthorized entry into your systems. Since most of us don't think like criminals we need to rely upon trusted experts who specialize in data security and theft prevention. Conduct an internal security audit by a third party expert to identify potential security threats and adjust your organization's standard operating policies to reflect security protection best practices.

Liability factors

An employee might make the mistake but the leadership will take the fall. And with as many benefits stated from participating in meetings Screen to Screen with our customers, there are inherent liabilities to consider and work towards minimizing organization wide.

To protect yourself from potential risks, consider asking an IT expert the following questions:

- If hackers had access to our networks, what types of data could they collect from our customers that would put customers at risk of identity theft?
- Who else can access our Screen to Screen meeting and do they follow proper meeting safety protocol?
- How could someone else join our meeting without our permission, without an invitation, or without granted access?
- Which files transferred to or from customers across multiple media channels should be password protected, and which can have public access?
- How strong is the signal for the Wi-Fi network, and is access protected with a strong and memorable password?

Setup and maintenance costs

Your Screen to Screen technology might not function properly during a meeting if it isn't configured to the existing network security protocol. The network might block some software that may have been seen as a threat because it hasn't been tested yet for security or block users from opening certain websites.

Ask your IT department these questions regarding the configuration of your network:

- What is the cost for the initial setup of the network, including equipment, online services, and initial access to customer support for setup?
- Which Screen to Screen meeting tools have been tested and approved to protect the confidentiality of files, communications, and other apps?
- Which websites are known red flags to block undesirable behavior that might conflict with cobrowsing websites used in Screen to Screen conversations?
- How much will it cost to maintain the IT system with quick access to customer support on demand if and when an issue arises?
- How much would it cost our company per hour if we lost access to or had a security breach in our IT network, Internet connection, and intranet?

Confidentiality concerns

One key area of concern in network security is knowing how to protect confidential information from the eyes of unauthorized people. Strengthen your confidentiality shield by asking an IT expert these questions:

- What types of information do we collect on our customers and what would be the economic impact to our company if this data was stolen or lost?

- Are confidential files stored online, such as contracts, located in a secure, retrievable system for internal and customer use for quick and easy access?
- If a customer took a screen capture photo of the data appearing on a screen share, would it put our company at risk?
- Are the recordings of Screen to Screen conversations kept in a safe and secure digital file system?

Passwords and settings

Finally, you and the IT department must assess how passwords and security settings can help you protect confidential data related to your business and customers. All employees who operate technology representing your organization must discuss the following questions to avoid system breaches:

- Does each device have a password the employee must enter in order to begin use and an auto-lock feature to disable the device after prolonged non-use?
- Are employees' passwords unique, memorable combinations of upper- and lowercase letters plus numbers and symbols?
- What tools or methods must employees use to memorize account information, passwords, and personal details?

Checklist 12-2 QUESTIONS TO ASK YOUR ATTORNEY

Criminals do not die by the hands of the law. They die by the hands of other men.

—GEORGE BERNARD SHAW

What's the worst that could happen if you started meeting Screen to Screen? You wouldn't know unless you asked your attorney, so add that to your checklist. Furthermore, specific industries and law enforcement agencies have special rules and regulations regarding the use of technology as it pertains to privacy laws, disclosures, and communication of confidential records. Start by asking specific questions about recording meetings, handling confidentiality breaches, and protecting intellectual property and your online reputation.

Recording conversations

- Is it permissible for us to record conversations without prior consent from another party, according to national, state/provincial, or institutional law?
- What is the risk associated with recording a conversation without permission, and how can we be legally responsible for the distribution of its message?
- What do we need to document in order to demonstrate consent from another person to record a conversation?

Breaches in confidentiality

- What personal records are considered confidential and must be protected using secure passwords?
- What legal penalties exist when breaching confidentiality by (un)intentionally sharing electronic records?
- What protocol do you suggest following in case of an emergency when our network, database, and online communications are compromised?

Intellectual property

- How should our logo be trademarked and visuals be copyrighted?
- How can we seek resolution when there is a conflict concerning ownership of intellectual property?
- What is considered "fair use" by others who share images, annotations, and visual frameworks from Screen to Screen meetings?

Online reputation

- How do I request someone to remove incorrect or inappropriate descriptions that conflict with our company's image?
- How do I respond to an online review that includes libel, slander, or harsh statements about one of my employees?
- What risks are involved in the mishandling of online or in-person customer complaints?

Checklist 12-3 IDENTITY THEFT

Although security is never guaranteed, the right combination of tips and tools can decrease the likelihood of someone stealing your most protected data. You don't need an IT degree to understand the different options, and it sure helps to know how to protect yourself on your own. The following suggestions are a good start.

Password generators

To remember a password or not to remember a password, that is the question. Almost every one of your charts of accounts requires a screen name and a password to login. And, to create a more protected password, it must meet a set of requirements by capitalizing a letter, adding a number, and inserting a symbol. Remembering every single password is an onerous task and a lofty goal. A better option is to use a password generator. Some password generators are built into web browsers; others are add-ons like LastPass or 1Password. Either tool will create a password and remember it for many more visits after you first create an account.

Secure wireless networks

If you are on the go and have limited options, it might be tempting to visit a neighborhood coffee shop or hotel lobby to access the Internet using a public network, which doesn't require a password.

There is no guarantee that these open networks are safe, and you must depend upon your knowledge of network security for each location. An option is to BYOI (bring your own Internet) with a MiFi mobile broadband hotspot. The benefit is you can rely on your own connection, not someone else's judgment on how they protect their network security.

Internet browsing on other devices

Are you constantly on the go, checking up on work devices you don't own from multiple locations? If so, you may be putting the files and data you exchange at risk because you are relying upon the owner's Internet safety protocol, not according to your standards. Perform these tasks before and after every session on devices you don't use regularly:

- Restart the system by logging off and logging back into the computer, or restart the device by powering off and then on again.
- Visit only trusted sites you are familiar with.
- When logging in to any site or service, if your browser asks your log-in preferences, select the option "never remember password."
- Erase the Internet browsing history and cookies after using a computer other than your own when at a hotel, business, or home.

ID theft insurance

Some online forms require a social security number, birth date, and income level as part of a registration process. And, if that data were obtained by a criminal, that criminal could file for your tax refund, apply for credit cards to make purchases in your name, or impersonate your profile by creating records in your identity. Identity theft protection services allow you to receive updates on credit account enrollment activity, potential fraudulent charges, or reimbursement on unauthorized claims as stated in the provider's policy (e.g., LifeLock.com).

CHAPTER 13

◆◆◆

THEY SAID YES! HOW TO SAVE TIME AND MONEY FILLING OUT FORMS

There, I guess King George will be able to read that.
—JOHN HANCOCK WHILE SIGNING THE DECLARATION OF INDEPENDENCE

Sales professionals choose to either coordinate the transaction with a handwritten copy, or increase the productivity of their team and customers by using digital alternatives. At the end of the movie *Door to Door* staring William Macy, character Peter Bolton finally realized sales teams on the phone could outperform the door-to-door division and his career was in jeopardy despite being the #1 door-to-door salesman in the past. He unnecessarily persevered through his historic sales process as a dinosaur because he held onto his traditional beliefs about order taking, processing, and service. When you get caught up in saying, "that's the way it is supposed to be" because that's how it's always been done, you know you have problems.

This chapter will show you how digital signatures can remove the line "Wait till I get back to the office to send that to you" from your language and keep your focus on productivity when serving your customer.

A digital signature is like putting pen to paper to confirm a written agreement, however a different process and technology is involved in eliminating the paper. This chapter covers the benefits of using digital signatures, how to obtain them, cost savings, and how to comply with regulations concerning the enforcement of digital transactions.

Checklist 13-1 BENEFITS OF DIGITAL SIGNATURES

A verbal contract isn't worth the paper it is written on.
—SAM GOLDWYN

The antithesis of the productive is rework. A document produced and to be signed by the customer involves work. Delivering a contract involves work to get it in front of the customer. And, to gain acceptance sometimes involves rework of the original work in order to get a transaction to work. After reading some of the benefits of digital signatures, you will see how much rework you can eliminate in order to maintain a high level of productivity.

Commuting time decreases

When you need a signature on paper, you have to get the paper to the customer and then get the signed document back again. Often, that means a sales professional is running around to see customers just for that purpose. If a customer is a 30-minute drive or 300-mile flight away, remember that trip to obtain a signature from your customer also requires a return trip, doubling the total time. The cost to commute adds up every time you need a signature at one of these stages:

- A contract is executed.
- An addendum signed.
- A counteroffer is made.

- Terms of the contract need to be changed.
- Renegotiation of terms is necessary.

Correspondence time decreases

You can send your customers their contracts in a variety of ways. With many of the methods, however, there can be a significant delay between when the customer receives the documentation and when the customer responds, affecting how quickly you receive the appropriate signatures. Think about the delay in using each of these traditional forms of correspondence:

- Face-to-face (delay based on commute time)
- Mail (next day for overnight, longer for priority mail or first class)
- Courier (same day)
- Fax (5 to 10 minutes)
- Email (1 minute)
- Text message (instantaneous)

When you obtain signatures during a Screen to Screen meeting, essentially the customer is signing with you at the same time, because you both are using the screen share feature that eliminates the delay, skips reworking documents, and initiates a contractual relationship immediately.

Corruption of files decreases

Did the customer sign in the right spot on the form, or did they miss an entire set of pages completely? Certified public accountants are notorious for including little sticky notes on pages, positioned so as to remind you exactly where to sign on paper. You can do the same with the digital signatures by placing arrows or stamps and by highlighting signature areas using online form tools, in order to ensure the parties involved sign in the right spot.

Also, how do you know who signed the right form? Someone else, if they have access to the email account where the form was sent, could sign forms sent by email. Screen to Screen conversations allow the customer to sign with you at the same time, ensuring that the person signing is the person held responsible for the terms.

Files are never lost

A simple transaction might include a one-page PDF. A complex transaction might involve a series of documents, file formats, and versions that could easily get lost if there isn't a reliable system in place for both the salesperson and the customer to see everything in one place. For example, a commercial real estate transaction could include the following documents:

- Letter of intent
- Tenant documentation
- Operating financials
- Building, environmental, and soil reports
- Contract (attorney approved)
- Closing documentation

This stack of documents, if printed, can pile up over your head and be difficult to shuffle through to find the right one when you need it. Digital files simplify organization and provide quicker access.

Transparency of transaction

Sales professionals can quickly store and retrieve essential documents in a chronological paper trail using a secured electronic transaction management system (TMS). With digital signatures and a TMS, there will never be a dispute again as to who was supposed to sign what form and when. A reliable TMS allows each party to verify all of the details in one place. This is especially important when there are several other parties to the transaction and each is held accountable to perform in a timely manner to execute the transaction.

Checklist 13-2 COST SAVINGS

If saving money is wrong, I don't want to be right.
—WILLIAM SHATNER

In addition to how much time digital signatures save all parties in the transaction, they can also reduce some operational costs that can add up quickly, especially if you are paying close attention to the bottom line.

Here are some cost savings you might realize.

Paper

Guess the favorite food of the mountain pine beetle. You guessed right if you said pine trees. These beetles are destroying forests all across North America because they are devouring trees to feed their appetite. The weakened trees struck by lightning are causing forest fires, damaging homes, and ruining lives. Don't be a mountain pine beetle.

To show businesspeople how much money they spend on creating and managing paper documents, Thomson Reuters created a paper cost calculator, available at https://cs.thomsonreuters.com/FileCabinetCS/worksheet.aspx. Visit the site to calculate your paper-related costs. Consider how much money you could save if you didn't use all that paper.

Ink

Did you know that ink costs more than gasoline, milk, and some perfumes? Collecting digital signatures online instead of on printed documents is just one way to reduce the amount you spend for ink and toner cartridges. You can further reduce your ink costs by using the following suggestions:

- Create a team policy for best practices on printing.
- Decrease the font size of the text before printing.

- Print websites from PrintWhatYouLike (http://www.printwhat youlike.com).
- Use digital annotation tools.
- Stop faxing.

Office equipment and supplies

Will printers ever go away? I doubt it. There is nothing more reassuring than holding a piece of paper when making an important decision. It's easy to mark up, fold, or rip up. And sometimes ripping up a document can make you feel really good. Still, printing and binding reports can involve a whole set of costs for equipment and supplies:

- Printers (costs to purchase and maintain)
- Staplers
- Binding machines
- Labels and stickers
- Three-ring binders
- Miscellaneous office expenses

If you find more affordable and efficient ways of creating necessary documents, you can dramatically reduce your office expenses.

Automobile travel

If you work with printed documents, you need to get them to your customers, and sometimes that means a trip in your car. You'll have to fill up the gas tank, and your automobile gets wear and tear for every mile that you drive. Currently, the Internal Revenue Service lets you deduct 56 cents per mile for business trips, but that doesn't nearly cover the operational costs if you are driving a better-than-average vehicle. Other auto-related costs can pile up quickly, too:

- Gas
- Oil-change service

- Tires and brakes
- Tickets for driving violations
- Accidents

Lower each of these costs at once by adding the exchange of digital signatures instead of driving them all over town.

Environmental impact

What's better than recycling waste? Reducing consumption. Ron Zima, also known as the "idle-free guy," claims that Canada alone could save $33 billion in natural resources if individuals would simply shut off their engines, instead of letting them idle (the average idling time in Canada is three minutes per day). Similarly, small changes such as switching to digital signatures can add up to a big impact by lessening your company's environmental impact. Here are some areas in which you can reduce resource consumption and pollution:

- Carbon dioxide emissions from auto exhaust
- Processing paper waste
- Disposal of ink or toner cartridges
- Disposal of obsolescent printers

Checklist 13-3 TRANSACTION MANAGEMENT

A man is only as faithful as his options.
—CHRIS ROCK, COMEDIAN

Once you see the benefits of digital signatures and the costs of not using them, the next question is what programs, transaction management software, or apps you should use. The answer depends upon a number of factors that involve situations ranging from the simplest agreement to the most complicated deal. The following five considerations will help you make an informed decision if you are taking the plunge or considering switching platforms.

Web and app access

I've seen sales professionals scan contracts and then email the files to themselves so they can print out the contracts later and fax them to their customer. It works, but it's probably not the most efficient way to get signed contracts. A better approach starts with finding a way to get all of your standard forms stored as documents online, using a cloud hosting solution. This way, anytime you need access or a customer needs access, you can quickly send the document from a mobile device.

Your app-enabled smartphone can send off a contract without you ever touching a desktop computer, printing a page, or looking for a fax machine. Ask some of your industry peers who are already using digital signatures to give you recommendations that work well with your existing form types and are compliant with federal regulations.

Customer input fields

Have you ever received a PDF form but couldn't fill out the fields on your computer? Or have you ever received a form created as a Microsoft Word document with underlines and tables where you are supposed to enter information? When you start typing, Word adjusts the formatting of the whole document.

To improve the customer experience, save customers time filling out forms, and let you receive the filled-out form in its original format, hire someone to improve your form creation and data collection process. Some web-based platforms will capture data from a simple questionnaire and populate the agreement in a PDF format to be saved or printed for later retrieval. The easier you make the process for the customer, the more they will tell their friends when their friends talk about their bad experiences working with someone else.

Limited access

All of your documents for a customer can be stored in one cloud-based folder. That folder must be password protected, have multiple levels of security depending upon who needs to have access to certain files, and be easily accessible from mobile devices. For example, a real estate professional might give the title company access to the contract and mortgage payoff memo but not to the building inspection. The building inspection is available only to the agent, buyers, and inspector.

Systems integration

A common problem sales professionals have is that they use multiple databases from several sources. These sources include their website lead generation form, customer relationship management (CRM) software, and their transaction management. So to move the customer from inquiry to transaction, you need to enter the same data multiple times.

The most productive scenario occurs when your CRM automatically imports leads as new contacts from your website and automatically populates forms to be used as needed using the same data. Check to see which software integration systems are available between CRM, website, transaction management and digital signatures. Fewer, more powerful tools will help you eliminate duplicate data entry and streamline the productivity for all those involved.

Confidentiality and security

Think about all of the confidential information you collect about a customer.

Confidential records may include the following kinds of data:

- Information about spouse and children
- Social security numbers
- Driver's license information

- Bank account routing information
- Copies of checks
- Credit card numbers
- Accounting figures

You don't want a security breach to violate the confidentiality of this kind of information. Use a secure password on your devices or web-based software. If you don't, it could put the entire company at risk of a lawsuit.

Checklist 13-4 CO-BROWSING FOR SIGNATURES

A man's kiss is his signature.

—MAE WEST, ACTRESS

Analytical customers who need to read the fine print before signing or initialing each page will require a little more patience, hand-holding, and explanation of what terms mean. Also, those who are not as tech savvy might be able click a link to join your Screen to Screen meeting but not to scroll through your resources as quickly as you can. Here are some tips that can save both of you time when you are obtaining signatures but not physically present.

Review the agreements and terms

Have you ever emailed a contract to a customer as a PDF attachment to an email, with the intention of reviewing the contract over the phone? The phone meeting can sound something like this:

SALESPERSON: Open up the PDF, and scroll down to page 5 and line item 235.
CUSTOMER: I can't find it, but I'm still scrolling.

SALESPERSON: At the bottom of each page is the page number, and to the right is the line item.

CUSTOMER: I'm still scrolling.

You and the customer get frustrated because each person cannot see the exact line, phrase, or words in question. "Trust me" doesn't always work, especially if we are talking about a significant investment.

You can avoid these problems by launching a simple screen share during your Screen to Screen dialogue. Your display of the right version will save everyone time getting on the same page.

Highlight and discuss terms

When you are working Screen to Screen and the customer sees the relevant page of the contract, you may want to focus on a particular line, input field, or range of words. Here are some tips that will help you direct the customer's focus to the key terms you have in mind:

- Zoom in or out of text inside the Internet browser or file.
- Use the software's annotation tool to highlight the text.
- Fill in the blank with words, using the annotation tool.
- Pass mouse control over to the customer when you want to clarify their question.

Educate the customer about the best available options

While you are co-browsing the agreement collectively, the customer might ask specific questions that might not have been discussed in earlier conversations. The benefit of Screen to Screen conversations is that you have more tools to educate customers—for example, other visuals, the whiteboard, and links to other websites, as we discussed in Chapter 7. Use each of those tools to educate the customer about the best options available.

Be ready to discuss each of the following terms as it relates to the transaction:

- **Parties:** Who is funding the transaction? These are the names of the key stakeholders involved.
- **Price:** Initial investment, recurring charges, and interest rates, if applicable.
- **Duration:** Product or service life cycle or expected time lines.
- **Contingencies:** What happens if? These are clauses found in an agreement that protect one party's interest in case of a special occurrence, date, or event.
- **Trials, warranties, and guarantees:** These are offers made by the seller in order to add buyer confidence and value.

Troubleshoot digital signing

What happens if a customer has a problem signing the agreement after you have sent it electronically? Unfortunately, you can't sign for them, even though they agreed to the terms Screen to Screen. Therefore, understanding the problems in advance will prepare you to help the customer if they get stuck or make a personal visit to get the deal done.

Here are some problems you might encounter:

- Customer doesn't have an Internet connection or access to a device to open the agreement.
- Customer did not update their web browser to the most current version.
- Customer needs to download the latest version of Adobe Acrobat for reading PDFs.
- Customer fields are accidentally locked by document file.
- Customer can't remember password to update his or her own software.
- Customer can't find the document access code or link to see the file.

Have a plan in place for handling each of these problems.

Checklist 13-5 REGULATION OF DIGITAL SIGNATURES

No law or ordinance is mightier than understanding.
—PLATO

I am not you giving you legal advice to tell you if digital signatures are contractually binding in every federal, state, or provincial jurisdiction. For legal advice, ask an attorney who is familiar with digital signatures and your specific industry, and who resides in the region of the customers with whom you do business. The goal of this section is to inform you of existing regulations, supply you with questions to ask, and increase your confidence in obtaining signatures without paper.

Each country has defined its own terms, rules, and processes for how digital signatures may be used in commerce. In the United States, the Electronic Signatures in Global and National Commerce Act (ESIGN), passed in 2000, gave customers the option to sign enforceable contracts in the United States conditioned upon the approval of each state regulatory body. The Uniform Electronic Transactions Act (UETA) deals with how digital records are handled and the validity of digital signatures.

Internationally, the United Nations Commission on International Trade Law (UNCITRAL) prepared the Model Law on Electronic Commerce. The model law was adopted by the United Nations General Assembly and laid the framework for digital signatures on an international level. Also, the UNCITRAL Model Law on Electronic Signatures (MLES) advises states on how to put together a fair legal framework to improve how digital signatures are used in commerce.

◆◆◆

CHAPTER 14

ANALYZING THE CUSTOMER EXPERIENCE: HOW TO MAKE CUSTOMERS HAPPIER BECAUSE YOU MADE IT SO EASY

User experience is the competitive advantage.
—JAKOB NIELSEN

If you can do one thing differently than any of your competitors I would suggest improving the customer experience using the latest technology. Customers do notice the details as they relate to their preferences, not assumptions based on what your product/service offers. And, technology can either create a positive experience worth sending referrals on, or unintentionally create a problem due to operator error.

In this chapter we will reverse engineer specific parts of the Screen to Screen Selling process so you can improve the experience one byte at a time.

Checklist 14-1 CUSTOMER EXPERIENCE SCREEN TO SCREEN

Every recommendation you have read in *Screen to Screen Selling* has been an attempt to improve the customer experience, save them time making important decisions, while seeking counsel from a trusted advisor. In addition, the book has supplied sales teams with best processes and technology in order to meet those expectations. Let's explore these expectations further that represent the customer's best interest.

Easy to buy

Companies that make it easier to buy are more likely to outsell their competitors. Why is my credit card statement loaded with credit card charges from Amazon? It's not because I like shopping or to accumulate abundant possessions. I shop at Amazon because they make buying super easy. I don't have to leave my house, and I can get trusted opinions on items and get a customer service representative on the phone quicker than waiting for a clerk at the store.

Customers can enter in a social cobrowsing environment with one another or initiate a video-to-video conversation with a sales representative from live chat. The screen share and video make it much easier to ask and answer questions quickly than solely over the phone.

Remove unnecessary hassles

One big reason why I use Uber over a traditional taxi company is because I can make payment with a credit card, don't have to worry about my fare being fair or getting lost because we share the GPS coordinates to the final destination. Take your sales and support team through the entire buying process and create a roadmap of steps from awareness to following up after sale for referrals. Pinpoint opportunities to remove any discomfort experienced by the customer by using recommended tools in this book. Your customer will appreciate a more fluid process that involves them from the beginning, saves them time, and avoids unnecessary hassles along the way.

Real time customization

A road map of your sales process will help you customize your recommendations and demonstrate your expertise in real time without relying upon a set of ordered presentation slides. This involves rehearsing specific behaviors with technology in a conversational environment while honing the accuracy of making the right recommendations in real time.

Share your roadmap with your customer to prevent unexpected surprises and focus in on specific steps as needed while meeting through shared screen, whiteboard, or video-to-video conversation.

In order to improve your Screen to Screen time with customers, record a video (with permission from customer) of your next conversation, watch it for signals for when the customer looks puzzled, and develop better techniques at explaining issues that might arise in the future.

Checklist 14-2 USER EXPERIENCE TESTING

All through my life, I have been tested. My will has been tested, my courage has been tested, and my strength has been tested. Now my patience and endurance are being tested.

—MUHAMMAD ALI

Test several steps of the Screen to Screen Selling process for accuracy, speed, and customer satisfaction. Breakdowns occur in setting the appointment at the right time/date, starting the meeting, troubleshooting technology, and connecting to a strong Internet signal to name a few. Make a list of what doesn't work, figure out how to make it work using what you already have, find better technology to make it work, and get better at making it work better. The best source of malfunctions come straight from the customer's mouth. It's your choice to listen and take action or perpetuate the problems for others to experience in the future.

Feedback from surveys/reviews

50% of solving any problem starts by asking the right question. Many times surveys fail because they ask questions focused on how the company, not the customer, will benefit. Don't ask, "How did we do today?"; that's focused on you. Instead, ask, "How can we make your experience better?" The focus transitions from company-centric to customer-centric.

Table 14.1 lists questions that focus on the customer and suggests a format that is appropriate for each question. You can adapt these questions and create quick Survey Monkey links or Google Responses forms.

Table 14.1 Survey Questions for Customer Feedback

Sample Question	Recommended Format
Why were you not able to make any decisions from our conversation today?	Open-ended
What was your overall experience compared to similar conversations in the past?	Multiple choice
Which Screen to Screen meeting options do you prefer to use?	Multiple choice
Which Screen to Screen meeting feature caused a delay in the conversation?	Checkboxes
What is the likelihood that your trusted peers and colleagues could benefit from a conversation like this?	Rating

Analytics from your website

Once you capture an email address tied to an IP address, you can track online behavior as long as the customer doesn't consistently clear their cookies. In other words, you can see how many pages a customer visits during a session, how much time a customer spends on one web page versus others, and how often they return. Knowledge of this data allows to you have more meaningful conversations because you don't have to guess which web pages interest customers more.

User testing

The most common way to assess the customer experience with technology is by conducting user testing. The variables measured from user testing include the task completion rate, task completion time, and task satisfaction rate. For user testing of Screen to Screen meetings, you should measure results for the following tasks involved with user experience:

- Schedule meeting with notifications.
- Join meeting from calendar notification.
- Retrieve visual, document, or website.
- Adjust (or mute) participant audio.
- Carry out file transfers or link sharing using participant chat.
- Draw on visuals using an interactive whiteboard.

To prepare for user testing, list tasks you want to analyze, including the user's interactions with you and your website before, during, and after the meeting. Then from time to time, ask customers about their Screen to Screen experience using an informal evaluation by asking these questions:

- Were you both able to access the Screen to Screen meeting on time without delays?
- Were there any technical issues that could have been avoided?
- Did the use of technology get in the way of explaining a concept?
- What would you have likely done differently from our last meeting?

Card sorting and tree jacking

We can determine trends as to how customers navigate our websites with analytics, follow click behaviors with mouse tracking, and survey process execution with card sorting or tree jacking.

Card sorting is an online exercise (paper works too) that gives customers website tasks (1 task per card) commonly found in a website navigation menu and asks the participant to organize the cards according to the most appropriate label, submenu, and menu. A tool called Optimal Sort will help you conduct your own card sorting feedback exercise.

Tree jacking is a similar exercise. However, with tree jacking you are given a task and choose the order of the clicks according to the name of the next likely menu label you would select. And, the order of the clicks represents the thought patterns needed to find what they want much faster.

Card sorting and tree jacking will help you:

- Organize the information architecture of your website and find best labels for website menus. This saves you and the customer time finding the right link fast through menu navigation.
- Frequently used websites can be loaded into a favorites or bookmarks for even faster retrieval from multiple devices.
- Most-requested action items prioritize the order of which visuals to be used during screen share conversations.
- Increase online conversions because customers can find links on their own without assistance to make an investment.

Ethnographic feedback

The easiest feedback collection form for everyone is the online customer survey. However it isn't always the most reliable because:

- The survey collects data online within a specific response period instead of collecting real-time data through multiple feedback channels.
- Surveys do not reproduce customer behaviors in their natural environment and so results will be skewed.
- If responses are ambiguous, you can't schedule follow-up conversations to get clarity from anonymous respondents.
- Customers may not see an incentive to respond.

The most comprehensive feedback collection process conducts ethnographic research online and schedules follow up conversations with those willing to give their honest input as they are exposed to your website. For example, using a tool like Ethn.io, you can deliver a survey as customers are experiencing your website, ask them for very specific feedback on which products to offer or which service areas to improve, and schedule a time to visit with this customer to conduct deeper research if needed. This method allows us to see how customers behave in their natural environment and adjust our sales process according to their honest feedback.

Checklist 14-3 CUSTOMER JOURNEY MAP

When you have completed 95% of your journey,
you are only halfway there.

—JAPANESE PROVERB

There might be a difference between what you want your customer to do and what your customer actually does. Consider these examples:

- You might want customers to buy from live meetings, but they prefer Screen to Screen.
- You might think social media is helping, but your print media is driving sales.
- You might think your online customer portal is slick, but few of your customers use it.

If a differential exists in expectations vs. actual behaviors, then you have to ask yourself what changes to make: How do you do more of what the customer wants or improve the way the customer is exposed to each step in the process?

A helpful exercise to improve the customer experience is to create a customer journey map. When you create this map, you outline the

Customer Journey Map	Internet	Conversation	Follow-Up
📞 Phone	🎯 Calls from ad	📞 Teleconference	📋 Teleconference
Screen to Screen	Watches video	Screen share	Obtain signatures
@ Email	Newsletter	W Link share	Visual summary
www Website	HTML Visits website	Live chat	Live chat
Text message	Text opt-in	Link share	Visual summary

Figure 14.1 Customer Journey Map

steps in the sales process, the different channels used to communicate with customers, and the ways decisions are made using those channels.

Figure 14.1 is a sample customer journey map which demonstrates the stages in the Screen to Screen Selling process, media channel preference, and activity as performed at each stage for each media channel. As you tailor the Screen to Screen Selling process to your existing sales process, some of the activities will change as they benefit the customer's experience. Your next assignment is to create your own customer journey map using the following steps.

List customer decision stages

First, list the most common decision stages involved in the sales process that make a sale. For example, the home-buying process can be broken down into eight steps: obtaining preapproval, selecting an agent, finding the house, making an offer, scheduling inspections, obtaining loan confirmation, procuring title work, and closing day. Each step in the process involves a series of decisions to be made, advice to be shared, and actions to be taken. Identify which meetings, tasks, and transactional milestones can be completed by meeting Screen to Screen as opposed to face-to-face. Then, educate your team to provide a consistent experience with technology across different stages of the transaction.

Salesperson Journey Map	Preparation	Conversation	Follow-Up
Phone	Prospecting	Teleconference	Teleconference
Screen to Screen	Select meeting tool	Screen share	Obtain signatures
Email	Meeting notification	Link share	Visual summary
Website	Marketing	Live chat	Live chat
Text message	Meeting notice	Link share	Visual summary

Figure 14.2 Salesperson Journey Map

Preferred media channel options

Each decision stage allows the buyer to communicate with the salesperson and possibly others using different media channel options. For example, a first-time home buyer might seek preapproval over the phone, find an agent using online reviews, search for homes with a mobile app, make the offer in person, and so on. Once we spot patterns around media channel preferences we can then get better at making those experiences even better.

Walk through the process as if you were the customer and ask yourself at each stage, "What one thing did we do really well on this stage?" and "What one thing can I do better next time?" Some customers prefer email over postal mail, text messages over social media, or Screen to Screen over face-to-face. It's critically important to consistently analyze customers' preferred media channel processes and abandon tools and processes customers could careless about during the buying process.

Map the expected customer journey

Use the information you have listed to create a map of the customer journey you expect most customers will prefer. Customers are used to phone calls, emails, and meeting face-to-face, while more and more are becoming familiar with having someone share their screen. The contact page of your company's website should list the names and links to the channels so customers can initiate instant meeting as well as meeting scheduling options using an online calendar.

Revise your map based on the realized customer journey

Use tested behaviors to teach you how to improve the experience during each stage in the customer's journey with technology. For example, in competitive markets where bidding is common, time is of the essence and offers require immediate responsiveness, I would prioritize practicing Screen to Screen Selling skill sets around demonstrating value with visuals, co-browsing while creating online forms, and calculating home acquisition costs during screen share. This helps save you time by learning how to use less technology because you are focusing more on what customers want.

Table 14.2 shares two different customer types and their communication preferences during each stage of the process. Use a similar customer journey map of your own to map out expected preferences vs. actual behaviors.

Table 14.2 Adapting the Journey Map

Step in Process	Communication Channel to Use	
	Customer A	Customer B
Obtaining preapproval	Face-to-face	Website
Finding an agent	Open house	Website
Searching for homes	Driving	Mobile app
Making an offer	Face-to-face	Screen to Screen
Scheduling inspections	Phone	Website
Obtaining loan confirmation	Face-to-face	Website
Preparing title work	Direct mail	Email
Closing	Face-to-face	Face-to-face

Checklist 14-4 CROSS-CHANNEL MESSAGE DESIGN

Once you have created the customer journey map, your next assignment will be to ensure the right message appears in the right channel in a way that captivates the customer, breeds familiarity across channels, and enables decisions to become easier through every step.

First consider the language existing customers use to endorse your products and services. If you can identify common benefits as stated by the customer that demonstrate a significant increase or decrease in time or money, add the customers' language into these message delivery options most relevant to your customers:

- Website copy, call to actions, and order forms
- Email messages, newsletters and auto-responders
- Social media posts and discussions
- Mobile app copy
- Phone calls and voicemail greetings
- Events, conferences, and tradeshows

Think also about how many devices your customers are likely to use and how the messaging will vary according to how many characters will display on each device. For example, the amount of available characters to display on an Apple Watch notification will be far less than what you can display on a website. This forces us to be more selective with word choice to say more with less to accommodate technologies that have smaller screens.

Tone of the message

It's not so much what you say but how you say it that will take on new meanings for customers. And, how you want customers to feel after reading your message will dictate how you draft communications orally or electronically. If you want customers to feel inspired, choose descriptive words throughout all company correspondence with word choices analogous to passion, motivation, and enthusiasm. If your customers want to feel safe, consistently select detailed-oriented words related to analysis, pragmatism, and guarded. The logo of the company is to the brand as the tone is to the writing of the message. That message must be consistent with the theme of your company, express the values and personality of employees, and be delivered as the same theme through every channel or contact point established. More examples of message tones include:

- Fact based, as in a news report
- Consultative but not condescending
- Playfully humorous but not silly
- Pessimistic, aggressive, and destructive (consider to be avoided)

As you begin writing company correspondence, ask your team or customers to identify the message tone for you. The feedback you receive tells you if the tone resonates with customers or needs to be adjusted accordingly.

Writing for user experience

Website visitors skim more than they read. They are likely to overlook content-heavy web pages and electronic documents unless their interest is captured immediately. Similarly, visuals used by the sales team become confusing or overwhelming if they are overloaded with details.

Whether the marketing team is writing messages for the web or the sales professional works with graphic designers to build their presentation aids, effective, concise writing applies in all situations. Some tips include:

- Develop a strong vocabulary to choose more effective word replacements in messaging.
- Remove as many unnecessary words as possible that don't add value.
- Replace long paragraphs with bullet points for the web.
- Replace visuals with bullet points with fill-in-the-blank visuals.
- Draw attention to important words and phrases with highlighting, underlining, and boldface and italic type.

Content portability

Varying file formats cause problems for some customers, because they might need to download a specific type of software in order to view the file. For example, a .wmv video file (created on PC) will not open (viewed on my Apple iPhone) or if I send a .mov (created on Apple) it will not open on a PC. Add convenience to your content through its portability, meaning your customers can open it from any device regardless of the file format.

Instead of sending an email attachment of a file, upload the file to a cloud based tool and share the link to the file. For instance, the Dropbox cloud based tool will store a video file, and to share it you share the link to the Dropbox file for the customer to click and open. Dropbox supports most video file formats so the customer doesn't need to rely upon file type to open. So Dropbox, one of many file sharing services, cures the portability problem.

Wireframing

How customers experience your organization with technology all starts with great design. The design of websites, mobile apps, and other user-interfaces either will construct a positive experience or leave the customer annoyed depending upon how quickly they can perform tasks without error.

A technique marketing agencies and web developers use to build website design from scratch is called *wireframing*. This involves sketching what you want the user interface to look like before you have a programmer do all of the coding. In this mockup of what will display on the user's screen, you can choose the placement of menus, the relative sizes of images and text, and the appearance of web features on multiple devices and have a customer test new iterations of the design before the coding takes place.

User experience professionals will use one or more of these tools to create and test wireframes:

- Balsamiq Mockups (http://balsamiq.com)
- Fluid UI (http://fluidui.com)
- Moqups (http://moqups.com)
- AppCooker (http://appcooker.com)

App development

Apps increase brand loyalty, cross-sell from initial purchases, and automate the sales support process. Efficient design starts with making a list of customer outcomes and wireframing the app according to the sequential alternatives for how decisions are made. For example, use a tool Fluidui.com to create the wireframe of an app build-out to represent the steps, menu locations, descriptions, and link locations of how you want your customer to experience your company. This initial blueprint lays the foundation for mobile app developers to begin coding the project according to exact guidelines in the beginning and avoid rewriting code because a step was out of order. This can save weeks and thousands in developer work by being more intentional about customer behaviors in the initial wireframing process.

Checklist 14-5 FREQUENTLY ASKED QUESTIONS

A final way to ensure a positive customer experience is to make it easy for customers to get answers quickly when they have questions. For any given transaction type, the questions are always the same; only the answers might be different, depending on the specific input from the customer. By knowing the questions in advance and preparing stimulating ways of answering the questions, you can enhance the customer experience in a manner that sets you apart from the competition.

The remainder of this chapter tells you how you can package your frequently asked questions (FAQs) online and equip your sales team with the answers that appeal to the customer's best interest.

Collect responses from your call center

Your receptionist or call center, whoever answers the phone or initially greets customers, represents some of the best feedback you will receive because they are the frontline face of your organization. They know which questions are commonly asked, which questions take longer than others to answer, and which questions they cannot answer for themselves. This valuable feedback helps directors make decisions as to how to save time answering with templates, how to handle conflict, and how to route the message to the most appropriate representative.

In order to improve the customer experience from your call center take these steps:

- List what you think are the top 10 most frequently asked questions asked by your customer and received by your call center.
- Compare your list with the list of the top 10 questions that the call center actually receives in order of most recurring to least occurring.
- Ask your call center representatives to make notes into call records about type of task completed, person responsible for follow up (if needed), and follow up instructions. If this detail takes an extra 30 seconds now, it will save 2 minutes on the next call from the same individual by understanding previous dialogue.

- Ask what external resources will assist the customer in making the decision in order to keep conversations focused on the organization's core products and services.

Once this data is collected it must be shared with marketing to create better visuals to attract more attention, shared with sales teams in order to better handle objections Screen to Screen, and shared with IT in order to integrate the technology to enable faster communications with your customers.

Review results of trends searches

You don't need to wait for the news on TV or pop by the newsstand in order to find the latest trend in your industry which customers otherwise might surprise you with. Trends are being discovered daily through popularity in search terms, frequency of hashtags, and amount of website traffic available at our fingertips.

Try some of these online tools to help you identify the latest trends:

- Google Trends (http://google.com/trends)
- The Zeitgeist Movement (http://www.thezeitgeistmovement.com)
- Twitter Trends (https://mobile.twitter.com/trends)
- Trend Hunter (http://www.trendhunter.com)

Instead of relying on traditional media or hearing news from a second-hand source when someone asks you, "What is new in your industry?", now you have some tools to answer that frequently asked question as the pro.

Sources of common responses

Do you keep giving the same answers over and over again but to different people? If you hear the same question from three different people, bet it will come up again in the future. And, rather than creating the same answer to the same message, try to repurpose previous responses that exist. This saves time thinking of what to say each time you need to say it.

Find sources of these frequently used answers from these locations:

- Email messages saved in your Sent folder
- Audio recordings of past conversations
- Video recordings of past presentations
- Digital sketches drawn when conceptualizing concepts
- Popular websites visited or bookmarked

The intent is not to use the exact same message word for word because customers have different names, special situations, and different personalities. Look for when the explanation of the process becomes repetitive in your online communications and use them as templates for future correspondence.

Create tutorials and task aids

Customers are sometimes better off finding the answer to a question themselves rather than schedule an appointment, wait, and get the answer they could have found on their own. One way to improve the experience of solving problems online is by creating FAQ videos, visual aids and making them available on-demand.

Make a list of steps and decisions involved withing a buying process and create one or more YouTube videos that answer frequently asked questions for each product or service. Prioritize instructional over promotional when describing features, benefits, and intended uses. Keep these videos short and to the point. And, organize multiple videos into a playlist in order to save you time answering questions and save the customer time receiving quick answers.

Visual aids like checklists, process maps, and infographics also answer frequently asked questions to save everyone time. The only cost is the upfront creativity and time to design the visual. Fiverr and Graphic River are great places to find examples and get a head start with templates.

One approach is to summarize these answers in blog posts, images, or videos. A benefit of answering with a blog post is that customers can see a list of related posts, which could uncover other questions the customer might ask in the future. Images can diagram elements of the sales process, showing customers where they are in the process and where they need the most help. For videos, you might use a tool such as Camtasia, popular software for screencast recording (recording video with audio of a screen demonstration). Camtasia can record videos of you explaining steps in the sales process. Once you have created these task aids, you can post them online and provide links to them in the FAQ section of your website or in a link repository you share with your sales team (the next topic).

Create a sitemap for commonly consulted links

Have you ever said to someone, "Search my website, and you can find the answer". This statement may be true, but content-heavy websites don't always make it easy for others to remember information, especially when the link to the answer is a long URL containing letters, numbers, and symbols. If you add YouTube videos, SlideShare presentations, and map directions, it becomes impossible to remember the exact location of an answer you're looking for unless you have created a sitemap.

A traditional sitemap of a website organizes all of the links found on a website. And, since not all answers live solely on your website we need a new version that embraces both internal links and external sources. External sources may include:

- A link to a YouTube playlist that will play a determined order of videos.
- A link to a Slideshare presentation that contains slides that support the sales process.
- A menu to display the RSS feed of recent posts in a blog, upcoming events, or past episodes of a podcast.

These new sitemaps include direct links or are dynamic in changing content as they appear chronologically over time. Find ways on your website and Intranet to enable both to save your customers and colleagues time.

◆◆◆

CHAPTER 15

SCREEN TO SCREEN CULTURE: THE TRANSFORMATION FROM A VERBAL TO A VISUAL ENVIRONMENT

Working in the cloud has given us better quality of life and very positive ROI.

—GLENN SANFORD, CEO OF EXP REALTY

I f you ask the employees and agents of eXp Realty about what they love about working with their company, they rave about their ability to meet inside a virtual office from anywhere and have immediate access to real time from specialized experts from around the country. Working smarter is more than a mission statement. It represents the consistent behaviors demonstrated across the organization that live in a more productive environment.

In this chapter we will look more closely at how companies are making the transition to adapting to new technologies and designing a collaborative culture in the cloud like eXp Realty.

Checklist 15-1 TEAM PERFORMANCE

The highest levels of performance come to people who are centered, intuitive, creative, and reflective—people who know how to see a problem as an opportunity.

—DEEPAK CHOPRA

A positive mental attitude towards technology isn't optional, it's essential. And, a person's attitude toward technology becomes immediately obvious when they experience a problem in a team environment. Watch for when a job applicant becomes impatient, complains or blames someone other than himself or herself when technology doesn't work during the interview process. Does anyone on your existing team experience similar behaviors when technology doesn't work? The adoption of new technology requires that you try new things and make mistakes in the process. Anyone who doesn't fully embrace making mistakes as a part of the process will burden your support team with endless requests for when technology doesn't work. Add members to your team curious and resourceful enough to fix their own issues without hand holding every step.

Read on to explore ways to increase the performance of your virtual team.

Best interests beat excuses

If one of your existing team members prefers meeting face-to-face for all meetings and you know it is in their best interests to meet remotely, you must communicate the value of Screen to Screen as it appeals to them.

Table 15.1 highlights common excuses you will hear to avoid meeting Screen to Screen and emphasizes the enlightened self-interests of team members.

Table 15.1 Best Interests Overpower Excuses: Sales Team

Sales Team's Excuses	Sales Team's Best Interests
The cost of new systems is too high.	The cost of losing new business opportunities is greater.
This won't work for our customers.	Customers want to save time making better decisions.
The Internet connection is too slow.	Round-trip transportation is slower.
Our team prefers face-to-face.	Screen to Screen Selling lowers the team's costs.
Our team doesn't have time to learn.	Customers demand a personalized experience.
We prefer the phone.	Screen to Screen Selling solves problems faster.

Customers' best interests

Customers will certainly have their own excuses, too. You can overcome those objections by putting their best interests forward, using similar language. Table 15.2 offers some examples.

Table 15.2 Best Interests Overpower Excuses: Customers

Customers' Excuses	Customers' Best Interests
I'm not at the office to use my computer.	We can meet anytime, anyplace with your smartphone.
We need to meet face-to-face.	We can meet face-to-face from your computer or phone to save you the trip.
I don't want to download any app or program to my device.	We have several no-download options to choose from.
I have the files on my computer and don't know how to share them.	I can walk you through how by passing you control of the screen share, so you can share any file from your computer.
I don't want to learn to use technology just for one transaction.	I can show you how Screen to Screen conversations will help you make other important decisions in your life.
I would rather use the phone.	Screen to Screen meetings are more productive, and we make fewer errors in discussing terms.

Developing a learning culture

An environment running on all cylinders continuously excels because of how quickly operational teams can learn new ideas, collaborate with one another, and implement tasks that collectively produce results as a team. Sales leaders must collaborate with marketing, sales leaders must collaborate with IT, and so on. But before you know it, meetings can be delayed, important stakeholders show up missing, and then business units operate as information silos that are reluctant to share ideas to help one another.

Peter Senge describes in his book *The Fifth Discipline* how to create a culture centered around collaboration and learning. He breaks down mental models to create a shared meaning for how individuals learn and make contributions to the whole organization. And to support this, we can use some of the technology listed in this book to increase the amount of ideas shared between teams and how to have quicker conversations during regularly scheduled meetings.

Team decision making

Lee Johnsen, principal of Partners in Development, a consultancy specializing in virtual teams and workplace performance suggests analyzing your virtual team according to the *complexity of interactions* and *reliance upon team members to perform*. Drafting a virtual operating agreement as a policy will help your virtual teams set realistic expectations for how to prepare, make contributions remotely, and how to follow up to report results. An example can be found at http://www.partnersindevelopment.net/.

Screen to Screen meetings have many more benefits to only using the phone. These include:

- Visual role call. You can see who is present through their webcam rather than making guesses through voice recognition.
- Visual synchronicity. The meeting facilitator can focus a dialogue around a specific visual everyone can see rather than paint the mental picture with words over the phone.
- Less multi-tasking. Each person is unlikely to multi-task since its easy to spot visually who is and not respectfully paying attention.

- Observational cues. You can't see an eye-roll showing disgust over a teleconference.
- Instant collaboration. Reviewing and sharing files can exist on the same platform at the same time. The phone will only exchange oral dialogue.

One challenge teams face initially is gaining consensus as to which technology to use because each of us has our own favorites. Reference Chapter 3 on technology selection and Chapter 12 on questions to ask IT to help support those decisions.

Behaviors aligned with culture

How do you know when beliefs about the impact of Screen to Screen Selling have been ingrained into the culture? Here is strong evidence:

- Meetings happen on time without technology issues.
- All parties are present five minutes before the start of the virtual meeting.
- Participants enthusiastically exchange and support ideas.
- Informed decisions are made, involving all parties.
- Excuses about using technology have been eliminated.
- Emotions are minimized for the greater benefit of the group.

The behaviors in this list become the norm.

Assessment 15-1 TALENT QUALIFICATIONS

Many people not only fail to become outstandingly good at what they do, no matter how many years they spend doing it, they frequently don't even get any better than they were when they started.

—GEOFF COLVIN, AUTHOR OF *TALENT IS OVERRATED*

Before you invest in sales or technology training, you have to make sure you have the right policies using the available resources inside the best systems with the right people. If you don't have the right people with the best attitude about technology, the rest is futile. Before you make your next decision to hire new salespeople or administrative support, make sure they can prove they are strong in terms of the knowledge, skills, and beliefs listed in Table 15.3.

Table 15.3 Talent Table

Knowledge	Skills	Beliefs
Social intelligence	Listening	We understand our customer.
Emotional intelligence	Questioning	We empathize with our customer.
Cultural intelligence	Sensitivity	Our customers are diverse.
Technical intelligence	Adaptability	Technology saves us time.
Competitive intelligence	Researching	We understand the market.
Ethical intelligence	Integrity	We always do the right thing.
Customer knowledge	Analyzing data	We know who we help.
Value creation	Creativity	We have the best ideas.
Customer profitability	Financial	We increase fiscal strength.
Business acumen	Selling	We have customers for life.

Measuring mind-set

How quickly can you assess someone's comfort with technology? First I look at their phone. If they aren't using a smartphone, then chances are, the time it takes to get them caught up with using mobile operating systems will cost more than paying someone who already is familiar with best practices. But if we look deeper, why is someone not familiar with technology? Is it because they can't afford it, or have they not found a need yet? Or perhaps they have been holding off because they are too afraid of making mistakes.

What you need to be concerned about isn't so much technical ability; it's emotional strength and how the technology makes the person feel. In other words, if a salesperson is reluctant to start a Screen to Screen meeting in fear they are going to mess it up and it will make them look bad—fear that is stronger than just knowing there is a possibility of making a mistake, which is just part of the process—the salesperson is never going to search for new and faster ways to share information with customers. Find team members who already express a natural ability to use the tools they already have, and especially those who are eager to share how technology has improved their daily decision-making.

External locus of learning

Do your team members say to one another, "That won't work," or do they ask, "How do we make it work?" Do they think they have all the answers, or do they search for the answers as a continuous journey through life? There must be a consistent desire to learn, almost like an addiction, that fuels new ideas and better ways to implement daily tasks. You can tell someone who has an external locus of learning by how they behave:

- Continuously investing in their own personal development
- Seeing mistakes as minor roadblocks in the process of discovery
- Searching for definitions of unfamiliar words

Strategic thinking

Does each team member think about their responsibilities as these pertain to only their job, or do they see how performance in their role affects the overall customer experience in the future? If a salesperson sees Screen to Screen Selling as being solely for administrative support, and not as a way to influence customer buying decisions, the customer might not be as informed to act when "time is of the essence" transactions need to be executed by administrative support. In this case, the salesperson's reliance on face-to-face meetings crippled the customer's ability to buy in a competitive transaction, because the salesperson couldn't get the necessary signatures in a timely manner for administrative support to process. Ask your next recruit how they see their role contributing to the entire sales process.

Tactical skill sets

In Chapter 7, we considered many different types of skill sets that all team members, not just sales professionals, can use. Keyboard shortcuts, visual framing, and digital whiteboarding represent a few.

You can measure skill sets using a standard assessment, but skills are better demonstrated through observation. For instance, someone can say they are a perfect 10 at keyboard shortcuts but then fail to execute them during a live Screen to Screen meeting, which disproves their original claim. In addition to the live interview or as a replacement for the phone interview, host a Screen to Screen meeting to have them demonstrate their expertise. During the conversation, include the following questions:

- Can you show me how you would calculate the value of x?
- Can you show me how you would describe line 56 of this contract and explain why it is important to the transaction?
- Can you show us who our competitors are and what makes us different?

This way, the creativity of the answers is expressed through the Screen to Screen meeting, not just in words over the phone.

Deliver before deadlines

Results are good. Faster results are better. The response time for getting work done depends upon how quickly your team members can process their tasks using the latest technology. If you asked your team to send you a list of neighborhood restaurants, how would they do it? One person might search for the results on Yelp and send a link to the search results by email. One person might send the same list, but as a screenshot image of the restaurant listings. And another might look up a list from the phone book, write them down on a piece of paper, and then list them in an email to send (by that time, dinner might be over). The ideal recruits can perform the same tasks in less time without making excuses for not getting the job done on time.

Checklist 15-2 RETENTION TACTICS

*Control leads to compliance; autonomy
leads to engagement.*

—DANIEL H. PINK, AUTHOR OF *DRIVE*

How do you reward top-performing team members who have demonstrated consistent results over time? Companies in competitive environments are looking at alternative ways of retaining talent by providing benefits and options that others cannot scale.

Flexible hours and locations

Why would anyone want to sit in traffic longer than they have to? A company policy to be in the office by 9 a.m. only stresses each team member to fight their way through traffic, create more work to prepare for the meeting, and take more time to execute because of the personal chitchat that goes on.

Top performers are concerned with more results, not more activities. They will want the freedom and flexibility to execute their tasks on their own schedule while complying with company rules and regulations. Anything extra is considered extra weight dragging them down. New recruits will have to earn the privilege of working remotely by demonstrating results in the office first. Then you can set them free to handle responsibilities at their own choice of hours and locations.

Reverse mentoring

You might have some team members who are wise in experience but lacking in technology, and others who are wise in technology and lack in experience. This creates a perfect opportunity to have team members teach one another Screen to Screen skill sets. The experienced pro can share how they have helped a customer in the past, while the newbie tries to create the experience visually on the screen as a form of taking notes. The notes verify the understanding of key concepts while the experienced pro asks the newbie how they worked that technology. Sales managers can regularly schedule these reverse-mentoring meetings so their teams can collectively share knowledge with one another and improve one another's skill sets each time.

Achievement systems

Recognition among peers is a very powerful motivator. Some companies will reward their top performers with bonuses, take them on extravagant retreats, and award them plaques. Others create a competitive environment by using a system that rewards points for specific behaviors and motivates through the gamification process. In some offices, reps ring a bell when a sale is made and everybody stands up regardless of what they are doing to honor their co-worker. Regardless of what tactic you use, having some way to reward high performing behaviors is critical to maintaining goals to get done and keep your team happy along the way.

Group benefits

Executives and sales managers must see Screen to Screen meetings as a company-wide initiative to increase team performance, not just one tactic to increase sales and reduce costs. Here are some of the broad benefits available to teams that meet Screen to Screen:

- More meetings start on time, which increases the productivity of team members.
- The attendance rate of team members at meetings improves.
- Key stakeholders and team members make faster decisions.
- Faster collaboration and implementation improves team morale.
- Collaboration reduces rework of documents and supporting paperwork.

Checklist 15-3 PERFORMANCE STANDARDS

How does an organization examine their performance across a variety of metrics when adopting Screen to Screen Selling? Here we will explore performance metrics that apply to the whole organization, as opposed to just sales. I'll identify which metrics are most important and how to receive the most significant return on investment for larger decision-making teams.

Decrease labor intensity

The biggest cost for most companies is payroll. Salaried positions are more affected by this bottom-line variable than commissioned sales professionals, but the end game is still the same: Screen to Screen methods get more done in less time. And, the time saved by having better processes and tools saves payroll expense, allows you to pay your people more to perform the same tasks, or frees up time to focus on fewer, more productive tasks. The only way you and your team will be able to save time is by making time to learn how to use the technology smarter. Reading this book is a great head start and the payoff will come when these new skills become daily in their routine.

Increase bottom-line growth

Reduction in office space, reduction of technology, and decreased labor are all examples of how Screen to Screen Selling reduces costs, adding to the bottom line. When companies can eliminate unnecessary overhead by systematizing the sales process and increase their efficiency at performing tasks, they open up more room on the P&L sheet to invest in other initiatives or record profit.

Increase top-line growth

Sales professionals who can prospect for more appointments and meet Screen to Screen with more customers will be able to generate more revenue than those who limit themselves to face-to-face meetings. It might be true that face-to-face methods will yield better conversion rates than Screen to Screen conversations. However, the number of appointments with customers will be limited by how fast sales professionals can travel, the availability of customer schedules, and location of appointments, not by technological constraints.

Personal performance

The best standard is the one set by the individual, not the organization. In other words, the company might have lofty goals, but if team members don't seek out better and faster ways of performing outside normal business hours, then progress will be limited. I mentioned earlier that the best way to adapt Screen to Screen Selling is to practice on your family first, because they are more forgiving than your customer will ever be. I also recommend hosting Screen to Screen meetings for your own personal matters. Here are some examples:

- Plan your next vacation Screen to Screen with your family in order to choose flights, hotels, and tourist activities together.
- Meet with your CPA or bookkeeper Screen to Screen to find better ways of interpreting expenses and online accounting records.
- Review your investment portfolio with your financial adviser Screen to Screen to discuss new trends, legal updates, and investment alternatives.
- Update your estate plan with your attorney Screen to Screen according to life events that have changed how your assets are to be protected.

The more times you use Screen to Screen methods outside of work, the more productive conversations you will learn to have at work.

CHAPTER 16

◆◆◆

SCREEN TO SCREEN PRESENTATIONS: HOW TO ENGAGE PARTICIPANTS FACE-TO-FACE

The next time you get up in front of a group in order to inform, persuade, or influence others to take action I want you to think differently about the technology you and your participants have at your fingertips. And, in order to focus on creating the best participant experience, we first must start with participant outcomes, choose best technology to facilitate outcomes, engage multiple learning styles across multiple mediums, and increase the likelihood others take action with more accountability. The traditional classroom for training and development has flipped to focus from listening to traditional lectures to collaborative, peer-to-peer learning. Chapter 16 will supply you with the new roadmap to implement Screen to Screen Selling tactics into live presentations.

Checklist 16-1 AUDIOVISUAL NEEDS FOR SCREEN TO SCREEN PRESENTATIONS

Presentations without visuals can be extremely effective if the speaker can think extemporaneously and share their expertise with eloquence. However, this is the exception to the rule; most sales professionals are not also professional speakers. Flip charts work great to engage participants and they don't require any technology. However, when writing on flip charts you cannot erase if you make a mistake, flipping back and forth between pages causes unnecessary delays, and I guarantee there will be a lineup to snap photos from their mobile in order save to their notes. When you determine participant outcomes such as higher engagement, higher retention, and higher accountability result from the use of technology in the classroom, you will need a combination of the right audio/visual equipment to get started.

Figure 16.1 illustrates possibilities for your audiovisual setup.

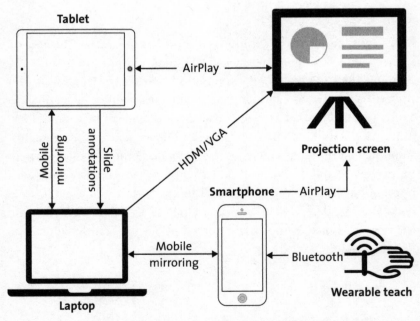

Figure 16.1 Audiovisual Options for a Screen to Screen Presentation

Speaker checklist

Any time you change from venue to venue it's important to work from a checklist to do the right tasks in the right order. Leave out one detail regarding the technology and it could mean the difference between rave reviews from inspired participants and anger because their time was wasted watching you troubleshoot your devices. Technology should never be an excuse for delivering a quality presentation. And, when used correctly, can really stimulate a group to collectively share and collaborate with one another.

This section will specifically benefit those who deliver training and development presentations, professional speaking, and meeting facilitators.

When I am working with meeting planners who are looking at several delivery alternatives created in the same environment, I give them this basic checklist of audiovisual requirements:

- Laptop, tablet, smartphone, and accessories
- Adapters, extension cords, and chargers
- Each device fully charged

Full speaker checklist: https://www.wunderlist.com/lists/134686133

Internet connection: Ethernet cable or Wi-Fi

The stronger the Internet connection, the more alternatives you have for using technology to deliver, facilitate, and capture recordings of live presentations. Presenting with PowerPoint and a clicker is the norm. But if you want to differentiate your session by walking around the room with your iPad to advance slides, mark them with your white-board, collect real-time data using SMS or web feedback, or broadcast your presentation to participants outside the facility, you are going to need a strong Internet connection on the same network.

The best setup for your Internet connection is an Ethernet cable plugged into a personal router or computer. You can use the Wi-Fi signal from the router to sync multiple devices with one another. This way, you can wirelessly connect your iPad to your computer to mirror displays or use different applications at the same time. This setup requires the following items:

- Personal router (Ex. Apple AirPort Extreme)
- Ethernet cable
- MiFi card (to use as a backup solution if no Ethernet cable or router exists)

Projector screen with screen sharing

A laptop computer usually has a VGA or HDMI port, so you can plug in a cable to connect a projector to be seen by all participants in the same room. But in large rooms with visual obstacles (i.e., large columns, big hair, and tall hats), it might be difficult to see what's on the projection screen from a distance. From the podium, activate your most user-friendly screen sharing tool and invite in-person participants to join the meeting from their mobile devices so they can view slides and whiteboard annotations in sync with your voice as you narrate along. Instead of participants taking pictures of what is displayed on a distant projection screen, they can now take screenshots to save slides as images in their photos stored on mobile. Remember to check with the facility before requesting participant access to Wi-Fi to ensure their network can support the bandwidth load requirements and simplify login as much as possible to avoid as many technical issues as possible. If you have invited remote participants using the same screen share link, they too can observe the same presentation and from anywhere.

Audio settings

How participants hear you from the stage will depend upon how well you integrate a wireless microphone, professional audio mixer, and speakers with sufficient amplification. In the case of the remote panelist or participant environment, you also have similar control.

On stage, multiple microphones might be needed to capture audio. One microphone for the speakers. One microphone for the recording device. A professional audio mixer will integrate the sound and consolidate to one microphone. Coordinate with A/V tech support to determine best options for live listeners and recording with audio/video.

Panelists that participate in the discussion remotely are responsible for their own equipment while the meeting facilitator is responsible for setting up the audio correctly. Test the remote panelist/participant microphone prior to any event as well as rehearse how to mute/unmute as if participating in a live event. These simple exercises will improve the quality of the audio and keep the presentation moving along without delay.

Recording options

Think of a live class as a resource that involves significant preparation in creating the curriculum, delivery, and follow up that only benefits those participating inside the walls. Would others benefit from watching the recording? Can you record to improve instructor development? Can the video recording be repurposed into an audio download, transcript, or other forms of content?

Anytime you deliver a presentation, speak at an event or run an office meeting, record yourself in action. And, if you dare to put yourself through what you have put others through, you will watch the video to find ways to improve your delivery.

Tripods come in handy; however, they will not follow you around the room to capture video. Invest in a Swivl base station to act as your personal camera. This tool is the size of a large hockey puck, has a placeholder for tablet or mobile phone to act as the camera, and has a built-in sensor that tracks a necklace around your neck as you roam throughout the room.

Invest in a quality microphone to capture sound from your mobile device if it's being used to record. Compare the SmartLav, a lapel microphone that connects to the audio jack input or Blue microphone model that plugs into the charging port of mobile devices.

Checklist 16-2 PRESENTATION ERRORS AND HOW TO AVOID THEM

I have personally made and observed just about every single mistake using technology during past presentations. In the worst instance, I was about ready to deliver a presentation, and right before the start, the Apple operating system experienced a kernel attack and forced shutdown of the computer. Because I had relied upon the slides as my outline, my delivery was weak. The evaluations from participants were poor, and I have not been invited back since. To this day I will never rely upon technology working exactly the way it should and I hope you don't either. What you can do is avoid making common mistakes when presenting with technology by advance preparation, repetition of common commands, and testing ahead of time. Allow me to explain more.

Difficulty navigating software commands

I find it appalling when professional salespeople or presenters fumble with technology. Even worse is when they ask their customers or participants, "How do I do that on my computer?" Any transition from switching the projection screen view from slides to web browser to video to slides requires deliberate and intentional practice so that customers don't notice a single delay. In Chapter 7 we discussed time saving shortcuts to navigate operating systems and software applications. The difference here in speaking to larger groups is any mistake is noticeable by more participants than having a private Screen to Screen conversation.

Predetermined slide order

A PowerPoint presentation with 60 slides to be delivered in 60 minutes assumes that those 60 slides:

- Appear in the logical thought sequence of the participants
- Each lists the problems to be solved
- Covers each solution's benefits and features
- Gives specific advice on personal examples

In Chapter 8 we discussed how to integrate a digital whiteboard to draw visuals extemporaneously, add visuals quickly as needed, and annotate slides. Choose the best whiteboard app and increase your confidence on delivering your message with fewer, more impactful sketches.

Excessive animation

Animation of bullet points, pictures, and slides rarely helps a presentation. Also, trying to perfect the timing of animation for a word to enter in a circle at the right time for multiple slides is a huge waste of time in itself. I have found that animations are more for the presenter (they think the animations are cool) than for the participants. Animation distracts participants from focusing on the message and can cause cognitive overload for participants if done in excess. The solution is simple: skip the animation.

Presenting with one screen

Adding an extra device (with screen) while presenting will increase your flexibility and adaptability to handle multiple learning experiences rather than relying on one device. For instance, when I'm presenting with my laptop only, I will typically use a PowerPoint presentation with slides. When I want to engage the audience with a digital whiteboard (iPad), conduct live polling (iPhone), or demonstrate a website (laptop), I could use as many as three different devices all at the same time. Presenting with one screen may not be a mistake—however, I see it as a crime to limit the impact you can create by settling on one screen.

Failure to test technology

An airplane pilot reviews a series of checklists before takeoff. The airline requires these checklists, and the Federal Aviation Administration enforces the requirement. Failure to perform a task correctly will put the pilot's safety and the safety of passengers at risk. In presentations, the stakes are lower, but not testing can cause your delivery to crash and burn.

To prevent your presentation from going into a tailspin, conduct the following tests before you go live:

- Ensure that the projector display takes up as much of the projection screen as possible.
- Test the laptop, lapel microphone, and remote-participant microphone.
- Test the strength of your Internet connection (I use Ookla Speedtest, at http://speedtest.net).
- Test the sync of mobile-phone apps with the laptop.

Checklist 16-3 TAKE CONTROL WITH VISUALS

Memory experts suggest that retention increases when a visual image is attached to a word, expression, or idea. Call it a mental hook to hang the word on. In the case of the professional speaker, the visual becomes the mental hook to hang the question on. Too often the conversation is one sided, about what the participant needs to know, rather than asking what the participant knows and giving them the opportunity to share it. In this section we will share how to take control of participant engagement using visuals and how to solicit the best ideas to create maximum value.

Ask a provocative question

Mark Hunter, also known as The Sales Hunter, says you can switch sales presentations into dialogue by asking a question that you and your customer cannot answer, so that you both can discover the answer together. This applies to both face-to-face meetings and Screen to Screen presentations in front of groups.

Use a visual to pose a provocative question to the group and, as responses are collected, they are annotated on your tablet and displayed on the projection screen. The simpler the question the easier it will be to collect answers. Brainstorm answers with participants by using process thinking to stimulate more ideas as others collaborate out loud or on mobile devices.

Frame a process with a digital image

A chart, diagram, or table will support a decision-making process faster than a verbal conversation without visuals. The more participants in the room, the less error margin you have in influencing the direction of the conversation as it benefits everyone involved. A presentation slide or saved image used as a template can solicit more accurate responses to questions by using fill in the blank, selection, and deselecting when narrowing down alternatives than a blank white canvas. Learn how to quickly insert images that frame specific conversations for specific groups or draw your own using a digital whiteboard.

Digital whiteboard delivery

Digital whiteboards also are superior to flip charts for taking control of conversations. Flip charts can effectively engage a small group. But when room sizes are large, say good-bye to your flip chart, because only the first couple of rows will be able to decipher them. A digital whiteboard provides you with a blank canvas to be seen on multiple projection screens and multiple devices depending on the type of presentation. This grants you creative expression to collaborate with the participants without the need for over-preparing and fear of not having all the answers. Working on the whiteboard requires less preparation than traditional slides because of your ability to focus on what the participants want, rather than what you might have prepared.

Request real-time responses

Some participants might not feel comfortable opening up to share their responses out loud. Maybe their answers are too confidential. Or, if someone does speak up, they might lose face in front of their colleagues. In either case, no one wins.

Screen to Screen methods offer faster, more effective ways of collecting feedback than asking participants to speak up or pass in handwritten notes. Enable your participants to make contributions by using any one of these tools to gather real-time responses:

- Poll Everywhere app (http://polleverywhere.com)
- KiwiLive (http://kiwilive.com)
- DirectPoll (http://directpoll.com)
- SMS Poll (http://www.smspoll.net)

Twitter, Facebook, and Instagram hashtags can also enable real-time feedback; however, they are public collection systems, not private, and are *free* for a reason.

Group exercises and participation

The more you can get participants involved with the data and discovery of the most practical solutions, the more effectively you will stimulate an environment to create change. To choose the best engagement exercises, discuss group participation preferences with the planner of the meeting. The meeting planner knows whether the participants are tech savvy. The meeting planner knows which methods have worked better in the past.

As an example, you can't expect a technically challenged group to be tweeting, taking pictures, and posting screenshot images to an online discussion board. If you try those activities with this group, you will spend more time providing tech support than making any points. To avoid that kind of mistake, answer the following questions about your group and the meeting location:

- Is there phone service in the facility location?
- How quickly can a participant join the Internet?

- How familiar is the group with sending text message responses?
- Is the facility's Wi-Fi signal strong enough to support the number of participants?
- What percentage of the group is used to participating actively on social media?

Checklist 16-4 LIVE POLLING

One way to collect responses is by asking a question and tallying responses on a flip chart. This works great in small groups because there are fewer participants. In larger groups, collecting responses becomes more chaotic because there are more votes to tally.

At our wedding reception, we asked our guests to pull out their phones to submit their favorite name for our first child. Random responses included Burton (name of our French bulldog), Dougie Junior, and Enrique. Guests needed to be reminded to keep the name clean and submit quickly because the answers projected on a screen for everyone to see. With live polling, seek to engage by asking a very specific question regarding their most pressing need and receive immediate answers to keep your presentation relevant to the group.

To make live polling effective in presentations to your customers, follow the steps described in this section.

Prepare your live poll

Questions to collect responses can be prepared ahead of time or created on the spot. Think ahead of how you wish to express the data before you map out the questions and potential answers. For example, if you want to report on media preferences as a pie chart and provide alternatives for participants to choose among, and 50% choose email, 25% choose text message, 20% choose social media, and 5% choose face-to-face, the pie chart fields are populated from the data collected in the live poll. In situations where a group is narrowing down a list of choices, you may have to ask the group to vote even though a live poll question wasn't prepared in advance. In this case, assign a letter or a number to each answer to save everyone time typing and to collect responses as fast as possible.

Participants locate device

My guess is that at any presentation you deliver, 95% of participants will have a smartphone with them. The other 5% don't have it charged, didn't bring it, or still don't know how to use it. Whether the phone is on top of the pile in a purse or buried in a briefcase, you will need to remind participants to access their phone, turn it on, and set the alerts to vibrate or silent. Ask individuals in a large group to show their phone to their seated neighbor to show that they are ready to participate with their devices.

Explain instructions in more than one way

Next, you need to explain how to respond to your poll question. Do your directions ramble on, or are they clear and concise? When a question appears on the projection screen, pay close attention to how you provide instructions for answering the question. If live polling is new for some participants, then you might need to explain the process multiple times in different ways. For example, you might use these two variations of the directions:

> "Send a quick text message to 44444, and share with us your opinion on the following question."
>
> "Open up your text message application, and just as you would send a text message to a friend, create a new message by entering 44444 as the cell phone number. Then in the body of the message, enter your answer to the question on the screen."

Interpret real-time feedback

The projection screen or live-polling website will start populating the answers in real time for everyone to see. Really juicy questions around hot topics create anticipation and excitement to see the answers as they are revealed. Some answers will be obvious. Others may not be. Your job as the presenter or facilitator is to interpret feedback as it relates to your customers in real time, and not wait for the end of the session to address top of mind concerns.

Checklist 16-5 VIRTUAL PANELISTS

We have access to more experts today than we have ever had in human history without requiring transportation, costs associated with transportation, or the potential delays of appearing in person. More groups are now inviting panelists to participate remotely in order to save on expenses and experts find the convenience in sharing their message without jumping on a plane.

Before you wire in another expert as a "virtual panelist" in your next conference or board room discussion, the following tips will simplify the process.

Connect to high-speed Internet

The facility for the presentation and the virtual panelist both must have a secure high-speed connection in order to make the arrangement work. Audio requires less bandwidth. Video chat or screen sharing requires more. An Ethernet cable used to establish an Internet connection is preferred over Wi-Fi because the cable connection is faster and risk of losing connection is less. Furthermore, urge the panelist to join using an Ethernet cable as their Internet connection to avoid interruptions in the conversation.

Panelist best practices

Not all subject-matter experts are effective at sharing their knowledge with participants they cannot see or hear. This environmental barrier can cause virtual panelists to ramble on, skip participant questions, or lose connection. Before you agree to have someone drop into a conversation from another environment, or you decide to participate yourself, practice these remote-delivery skill sets:

- Adjust audio settings, including ability to set the microphone volume, eliminate background noise, and mute and unmute themselves.
- Focus the camera position on center. Divide the screen into nine equal boxes, and ensure the head appears in the center box.
- Enable video chat during the requested participation time in the meeting, and disable it afterward.
- Enable and disable screen share to present slides, co-browse websites, and enable other desktop applications for demonstrations.
- Share important quick links using online chat and social media.

Share questions prepared in advance

Prepare your virtual panelist with the questions you are going to ask in advance, and request they share any questions they might ask the participants. This process suggests that you aren't going to blindside the panelist with a question they could answer better if they were prepared, and it discourages them from blindsiding you with a question that would disrupt the theme of the conversation you originally wanted to create.

Is the entire conversation supposed to be scripted? Heck no. You will always have surprises—some good, others not so much. Send your participant a list of questions you will ask, ask them if they would change any of them, and ask them to add a question that isn't listed that they think would add value to the conversation. This extra preparation helps them think more about what they are going to say rather than making something up.

Troubleshoot video and audio

In-person panel discussions usually equip each panelist with a microphone or supply one to pass around the room. It's pretty simple. But when you empower a virtual panelist to jump in, you are also relying upon the quality of their Internet connection, speed of operating system, and technical abilities over which your in-house audiovisual technician has no control.

You can at least exert some control over the quality of the audio and video signals. Before you add virtual panelists as regular contributors to your meetings, make sure you test the audio and video with your virtual panelist by asking these questions:

- Can participants in the back of the room see the visual elements of the panelist's screen share?
- Can the virtual panelist hear the participants, and can the participants hear the panelist?
- Is there a lagging delay in the conversation caused by a weak Internet connection?

If the answer to any of these questions signals a problem, try the suggestions listed in Table 16.1.

Table 16.1 Troubleshooting Video and Audio with a Virtual Panelist

Problem	Suggestions for Resolving Problem
Participants far from screen can't see panelist's screen share.	• Virtual panelist converts presentation slides to mobile. • Panelist zooms in and out of web browser. • Presenter expands Screen to Screen meeting application window to full screen.
Panelist can't hear participants, or they can't hear panelist.	• Presenter unmutes virtual panelist. • Panelist enables correct microphone for high-quality VoIP sound. • Panelist dials in conference call number provided by Screen to Screen meeting software. • Microphones are planted in strategic locations in room in order to capture sound.
Slow Internet connection is causing delays.	• Panelist and presenter use Speedtest to test Internet connection. • Presenter switches from video chat to audio from group location, because audio requires less bandwidth. • Panelist moves from video chat or screen share to audio only (last hope).

Teaching with technology is always a double-edged sword. When it works great no one ever knows, and when it doesn't they still will never know if they have never seen it used before based on what you now know is capable.

A benefit to using Screen to Screen for live presentations is that you use the same technology and skill sets as one would use to facilitate a meeting remotely, conduct an inside sales appointment, or coach another team member. The next few chapters will show you how to integrate these ideas to host better remote meetings, deliver webinars, and improve your marketing with technology.

CHAPTER 17

SCREEN TO SCREEN MEETINGS: HOW TO INFLUENCE DECISIONS DURING LIVE MEETINGS

Running our organizations lean, with slim or no travel budgets, and less and less time for real dialogue and engagement is challenging the quality of communications.

—DAVE SIBBETT, AUTHOR OF *VISUAL MEETINGS*

Most conference calls are lame, and here's why:

- You don't know who is on the call until they speak.
- The focus on meeting objectives is weakened when participants verbally wander off on tangents.
- Annoying teleconference prompts say, "The participant has now entered the meeting" every time someone enters and the opposite when someone leaves.
- Speaking up is more difficult on a conference call because it's hard to know who is more eager to contribute vs. those using silence to avoid confrontation.

- Voting over the phone requires repetition of responses, because you don't know who said what until they say their name with their response.

Need I say more?

You don't have to be in a sales organization in order to benefit from the concepts of *Screen to Screen Selling*. The principles are the same in other disciplines, though the examples are different. This chapter will share some of those examples and processes so you can use Screen to Screen methods throughout your organization in order to increase the effectiveness of your meetings.

Checklist 17-1 CHARACTERISTICS OF REMOTE MEETINGS

There are plenty of books on how to hold effective meetings, how productive meetings can help teams accomplish more, and how to deliver a remote presentation. Here I will uncover some best practices to help you and your decision-making team use remote meetings to eliminate unnecessary travel and meeting costs. You can think of these practices in terms of the characteristics that make remote decision-making more effective.

Smart uses of technology

Let's pretend ten individuals needed to get together in order to discuss an important project. Meeting face-to-face is an option; however, it isn't realistic because travel budgets are tight, and deadlines are approaching. Before this team decides to fire up a Zoom.us meeting to visit Screen to Screen, some advance preparation is required to integrate the technology in order to save everyone time.

Figure 17.1 lists some options.

Cameras. The Logitech Conference Cams can fit as many as 4–10 participants in a brick-and-mortar boardroom and individual webcams work great for single participants brought into

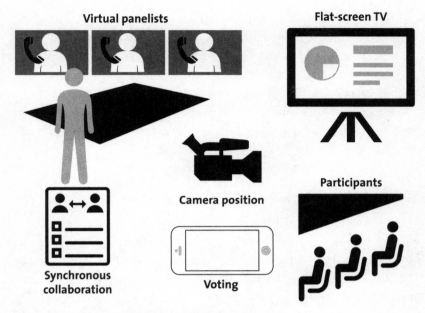

Figure 17.1 Options for Venue Optimization

a videoconference meeting. It is important in remote meetings that everyone is able to see one another at all times unless otherwise agreed upon. If someone is seated off to the side and hasn't been introduced into the meeting room or is not participating, other participants might perceive them as spying on the conversation.

Synchronous collaboration. Online or group chat are the simplest ways to send short, quick messages back and forth between team members. Adding tasks, assigning tasks, and completing tasks using project management software gets a little more tricky. Lee Johnsen, expert on virtual teams, recommends virtual teams spend as much as 50% of their work in preparation before the meeting begins. And with a virtual team operating agreement, teams can agree on setting realistic expectations on how quickly to respond and how best to collaborate.

Participants. Everyone has their own preferred ways of making contributions. Some people like to write on paper and some like to take notes on a device. Shouldn't matter. Team members must recognize the technical strengths and weaknesses in others and support them as much as possible. For instance, a tech savvy member might take a digital picture of a visual sketch from the tech challenged and share it on the social collaboration tool. Everyone learns and benefits from working together.

Voting. At some point during the meeting, participants will be urged to vote electronically or send feedback electronically through live polling.

Starting and ending on time

What does starting on time look like in the remote environment if you are the meeting host or the meeting participant? If you are on time, you are late. If the meeting starts at 9 a.m., that doesn't mean you click the join-meeting link at 9 a.m. You might need to adjust your audiovisual settings, open up important documents electronically to support decision making, or update your software. This is why the average online meeting takes 10 minutes in advance to start on time.

Ten minutes before the meeting starts, begin opening up any websites, documents, or programs you will need to use during your conversation. Joining the meeting early doesn't mean you have to start talking. Simply put the video on hide and audio on mute until others have joined and you are ready to engage with them.

Stop blaming technology

Rest assured, technology won't work when it is supposed to which is why it is completely unnecessary to react emotionally when it breaks down. There is no amount of yelling at your device or at a technical support representative that will solve your problem even though it might feel good temporarily. The best course of action is to think positively about how to overcome your challenge using existing resources. And, more times than not the answer to your problem is only a Google search away.

Less savvy members who blame themselves for a lack of technical knowledge, blame others for breaking their device, or blame the technology as if it had an ear of its own will need the most help. It's a self-imposed self-limiting belief that will require confrontation, maybe coaching or even cognitive therapy to self-correct.

Prepare visuals in multiple formats

Think of the elaborate PowerPoint presentations used for one meeting and never seen or used again. Someone had to sit down at their computer, gather all the reports from their colleagues, summarize the key points in slides, deliver the presentation and say, "Discuss!" There has to be a better way, right?

A diverse team with a wealth of experience doesn't need slides to be effective in team meetings. They need to be able to articulate their ideas in a way that makes a point using the support materials they already have. And, demonstrate them effectively enough that the entire group understands enough to obtain consensus or make an opposing argument.

For example, the vice president of marketing might share web promotions as websites or PDFs of brochures. The chief financial officer might share Microsoft Excel spreadsheet documents or use the Domo web-based app to provide the current status of all key performance indicators. Although the visuals are unique to the team members, the process of sharing them Screen to Screen is the same, using skill sets we identified in Chapter 7.

Team use of the same tools

There are hundreds of project management tools to choose from, but you only need one. Managers are consistently being challenged by their team members as to which is the best tool, because there are so many options that perform the same task, and each person has their own personal favorite. The options fall into several categories:

- Screen to Screen meeting tools
- Collaborative tools for editing business plans, mind maps, process thinking, and office documents in real time

- Secure and usable file-sharing tools
- Calendar integration with notifications
- Project management software
- Instant-messaging platforms

Create one decision-making process to analyze the best tools based on their features, use, security, and mobility as mentioned in technology review Chapter 3. Seek input from the team to narrow down the alternatives. Your team members' buy-in will be stronger if they had input on the decision than if you insist your way is always the best.

Optional video chat

There are some situations where team members agree not to enable video-to-video chat. Here are a few:

- Relationship with team and confidence with team members is already strong.
- There is too much distraction in the background.
- Video doesn't add any extra benefit to arriving at a decision.
- Your appearance lacks grooming or proper attire.
- Team members using mobile cannot keep their video camera still.
- The Internet connection is slow and/or bandwidth is limited.

Updated apps installed on all devices

Before you gift your entire team with an iPad for the holidays, supercharge their productivity by downloading the company-preferred apps, organizing them into the same locations across devices, and importing favorite website bookmarks onto the company-preferred Internet browser. This increases meeting productivity, response time, and training effectiveness because everyone is using the same set of tools and the same process.

Checklist 17-2 ABSENCE PREVENTION

Have you ever had to delay an important meeting because key stake-holders and team members weren't in the room to hold a quorum? Rescheduling is an option, but it's more efficient to avoid the absences in the first place. You can prevent absences by enabling team members to participate in remote decision-making. The following tips will help you increase your attendance, increase participation, and hold one another accountable for being on time to conduct effective meetings.

Offer options for sharing the meeting URL

Screen to Screen meeting software will give the meeting's host a link to share with the participants as a calendar notification, in an email, and as an email attachment. If team members forget to sync their calendars or don't have access to the meeting URL, the host or participant can share the URL in a variety of different ways, depending upon team members' preferred meeting channel. If someone is on the go and has no computer, you could send the link by text message. If someone else is in front of their computer, you can put the URL in a short email. Meeting software is making it easier and easier to let latecomers hop on, so you don't have to reschedule.

Monitor link tracking

Have you ever wondered why your team members weren't able to join the meeting? Did they try clicking on the meeting link you sent them by email, or did they just ignore it? Email software is now getting more sophisticated. You can use tools like LiveHive (http://livehive.com) or ContactMonkey (http://www.contactmonkey.com) that can track to see if others click on the links inside the email you send.

Also, if people aren't using the link, you can investigate why. It could be that the join-meeting link was too complicated to remember. Meeting tools such as Join.me allow you to customize the meeting URL so anyone can join as long as they have the link and are permitted access by the host. Or, as a last resort, shorten, customize, and track the join-meeting link using the free Bit.ly service.

Make participation mandatory

I feel as if the phrase "I'm going to be out of town" is the most over-used excuse in the business world today. Devices are portable enough that you can put them in your pocket to participate from anywhere. The Internet is available in most areas of developed countries and becoming more accessible with use of Wi-Fi drones and the installa-tion of fiber-optic cables. So if you are out of town, then what is the real reason for not participating in a meeting? Personal vacation and sick time are valid exceptions. Unless you are flying "Up in the Air", physically driving, or have blocked out the time for another commit-ment, excuses for not showing up are limited.

Hold peers accountable

When you participate in a Screen to Screen meeting to share your goals, demonstrate different working scenarios, and request input from your peers, you have opened yourself up to be held accountable for constructive criticism. Then, in the next meeting, your peers will ask you what you did differently in order to improve your current project, and they will expect you to answer questions Screen to Screen. Online collaboration tools (i.e., project management software, Google Docs, etc.) will show who has performed their work and who has not. If the latest policy revision is the same revision from two months ago, when the assignment was to have it done a week ago, this will become more obvious to all participants, not solely the managing director.

Checklist 17-3 VENUE OPTIMIZATION

Meeting facilitators will take a look at a room and decide how they want to arrange the tables and chairs, adjust the lighting for better vision, and arrange their own setup in order to help the group make a decision. Remote decision making requires more attention to what's being said, what's displayed on the screen, and how team members interact with one another to increase workplace performance.

Audio and screen control

At the start of a meeting, if everyone's audio is enabled, it might be difficult to understand who is in control. Once it's time to begin, the facilitator should mute all participants, greet everyone as if an in-person meeting were taking place, and start discussing items on the agenda.

When webcams are present, the Screen to Screen meeting tool will show who has video enabled and who is speaking through their microphone. Participants will mute themselves or the host will mute anyone who is shuffling papers or crunching on potato chips (participants should agree in the team operating agreement to use audio/video features appropriately). And, whoever is speaking Screen to Screen at the moment will be seen by everyone.

When the meeting facilitator or a participant requests to make a contribution using supporting visuals, either the meeting host will initiate the screen share inside of the meeting room or a participant can request to share their screen to deliver their own input using some Screen to Screen skills in Chapters 7 and 8.

Projection of screen share

In an in-person meeting room, the projection screen has competition for participants' eyeballs. The facilitator's body language, physical participation from others, and meeting room decorations can lure eyes away from the main points projected on the screen. And, those who learn visually or get distracted easily will have a hard time focusing on the message. In Screen to Screen meetings, the screen share feature acts as the projection screen.

Like a movie producer orchestrates a series of scenes, transitions, and sound, your role as the meeting host is to coordinate the visual environment in a productive and meaningful way. Now whatever appears on the screen is in control of the conversation navigated by oral commands and social collaboration through pre-selected technology tools.

Participant chat and voting

Laptop or smartphone participation opens up a value-added line of communication for sharing participant sentiment, links to useful resources, and comments unavailable in teleconferences reliant on the phone. Participants can share what they want, whenever they want, to whomever they want, all depending upon the participation controls assigned. For example, one Screen to Screen meeting might not allow participants to chat with one another, due to confidentiality concerns, while another might allow all participants to use a chat function as a way to enable collaboration and stimulate new ideas.

Multiple devices during meetings

In a conference room meeting, you might bring your mobile technology and pad of paper to take notes. If you were working from a home office, you might have a computer hooked up to two or more screens so you can view multiple applications open at the same time. For example, you have the Screen to Screen meeting application open on one screen, while the other screen shows your web browser open with multiple tabs ready for you to access and share information when needed. If someone asks for a link or file, you can move from screen to screen quickly without minimizing or closing an application.

Checklist 17-4 FACILITY UPGRADES

You have many choices to improve your office environment by making investments in technology. Some will take place in the facility where customers, colleagues, and managers congregate. Others involve upgrading the tools for those working remotely. Read on to see which investments in the conference boardroom, workstations, and facility make most sense for your environment.

High-speed Internet connection

As you already know, the speed of the Internet connection is of primary importance. Fiber-optic cable is the best, but it isn't always available. Satellite might get you access where broadband through the phone will not. Check with your Internet Service Provider to see what options are available in order to find the fastest speed.

Check your online meeting tool's diagnostics to see if the Internet connection is satisfactory or requires additional troubleshooting to ensure the best connection. Zoom.us support provides this list of metrics to test:

- Latency—the delay between when you speak and someone hears.
- Jitter—the variation in delay caused by network congestion or changes.
- Packet loss—the data that didn't transmit or was skipped because of poor connection.
- Resolution—the number of pixels shown on the screen.
- Frames per second—the rate the device can produce unique images or frames.

Ask your ISP, network administrator or meeting tool customer support if the above indicators are satisfactory and make adjustments as necessary.

Webcams with microphone

How would you feel if you were the only child who came to baseball practice and didn't have a glove? You might still try to catch the ball with your bare hands, or sit on the bench and wait until next time when you brought your glove. Besides, the other kids might think you were weird for playing without a glove.

In the Screen to Screen environment, if you are the only one who doesn't have a webcam then you might feel a little out of place too. Equip every team member's workstation with a webcam and a headset. If a team member doesn't have one, buy one and ship it to their location. Webcams are either built into the device or sold separately. Headsets connect wirelessly with Bluetooth or through the trusted USB cord. Even though the Bluetooth option allows you to be hands free, the USB cord model will not disconnect or run out of battery.

◆◆◆

CHAPTER 18

SCREEN TO SCREEN WEBINARS: HOW TO IMPROVE THE EXPERIENCE DURING WEBINARS IN ORDER TO GET RESULTS

I t's easy to get confused when you hear the word *webinar*, because it has so many definitions. In its most basic form, a webinar is an electronic means of presenting information over the Internet. And, in the most advanced form, a webinar reproduces a three dimensional learning environment which engages participants with the use of social collaboration tools. Each webinar environment is different based on what type of technology is used, how the presenter engages participants with respect to adult learning theory, and what the agreed outcomes or expected behavior changes are that will result. When someone says the word *webinar*, this next section will make you think differently about how others label them and how you can use them in your business.

Here are some common uses for webinars:

- List building. The sole purpose is to exchange valuable ideas for customer contact information.
- Special report announcement. Any timely resource that delivers customer value deserves a quick video introduction on how to apply the research. This is another form of list building.
- Virtual events. Organizations will host multiple educational sessions that involve multiple speakers in order to build a community of like-minded professionals.
- Customer onboarding. One way to increase adoption rate of the benefits received or features of products/services is to host a webinar with new users.
- Knowledge transfer. Updates on company policy, new legislation, or product features involving memorization and retention in the field, which when used, helps improve productivity.
- Skills training. Confucius wrote, "I hear I forget, I see I remember, I do I understand." In addition to teaching professional competencies, others can demonstrate their application of knowledge in real time.
- Coaching. Reminders to maintain a positive attitude, asking deeper questions to remove unproductive behaviors, and holding team members accountable can be delivered through webinar formats.

This chapter explores the process of using Screen to Screen Selling principles in whatever variation of webinar you choose in order to improve the participant experience while meeting your established objectives.

Checklist 18-1 WEBINAR SETUP

Think of your webinar setup as involving as many moving parts as we would typically see in a live classroom, and, depending on the magnitude of the impact, even more logistics. What a participant might see as a one hour show might have taken weeks of preparation by the organizer and the presenter.

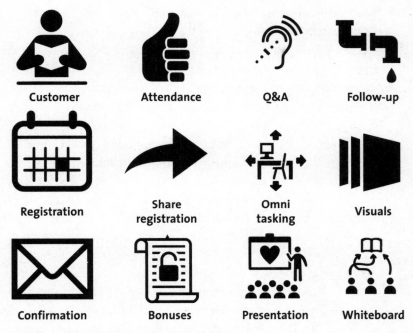

Customer **Attendance** **Q&A** **Follow-up**

Registration **Share registration** **Omni tasking** **Visuals**

Confirmation **Bonuses** **Presentation** **Whiteboard**

Figure 18.1 Webinar Funnel Process Map

Figure 18.1 provides a visual summary of the elements to add to webinar delivery in order to improve the experience for the participant. Here we explain each one in more detail:

- Customer. Know who your customer is and what problem you solve for them or what opportunity you create. Write webinar advertising copy to include the customer's interests as well as testimonials from current customers.
- Registration. Increase registrations by making the process easy and decrease absenteeism by sending reminders by email, text, or push notifications.
- Confirmation. This is the electronic ticket stub for webinars that contains the webinar join instructions. Automation features will allow you to customize the confirmation to include personal information, learning objectives, and bonus resources.

- Bonuses. Determine which informational assets or gifts are most relevant, and when shared, add more value to participants without extra work. Add a bonus as a market tactic to create urgency for signing up early.
- Share registration. If you want to increase registrations, ensure the social media share buttons exist on the page and ask others to share.
- Attending. Participants have their own audio controls but the host is on the hook for quality. Learn how to mute/unmute.
- Q&A. Control how questions are collected and answers delivered by limiting participation options.
- Omni-tasking. This presentation skill involves performing sequential tasks quickly as required by participant interaction. An example includes talking with slides and switching to a web browser to copy a link to share in the participant chat.
- Present. A Screen to Screen webinar is more than a presentation. It's a conversation consisting of dialogue involving using fill-in-the-blank visuals, webcam access, and interaction with engagement tactics.
- Whiteboard. Check your webinar platform to see if the whiteboard feature exists and use when appropriate.
- Visuals. These are retrieved quickly from a file folder to be used as needed, not in a predetermined order assumed to be best for the participant.
- Follow up. Send responses that remind participants to take action and ask what change took place as a result of the webinar.

The *Virtual Presenter's Playbook* by Roger Courville has over 250 ideas if you need more on how webinars play a role in your business strategy.

Set performance metrics

Your first step in hosting a webinar is to identify how you will measure its effectiveness. Certain objectives will apply if you are converting leads to sales, and others if the webinar's main purpose is to deliver training. In either case, you also should consider metrics for delivering the webinar. Here are examples for each category of metrics:

Conversion metrics

- Conversion rate from registration page to sign-up
- Number of registered participants
- Number of participants attended
- Average revenue per participant divided by number of participants per webinar

Training metrics

- Test scores from knowledge transfer
- Accuracy of skill execution
- Speed to execute tasks
- Change in key performance indicator following the training

Delivery metrics

- Percent of participants who joined the webinar on time
- Duration of participant participation
- Percent of participants who voted, used participant chat, or contributed to online discussion

Write registration copy

Don't make the mistake of marketing a webinar that encourages someone to do more work. None of us need more work to do. We need better answers to help us execute our predetermined goals. Instead, write the copy to reinforce expected outcomes. Trainers call these outcomes *learning objectives*. Performance change agents call these *performance objectives*.

Your measurement for success is translated into advertising copy and used to promote registrations for your upcoming webinar. Put another way, the copy must sell the presenter's performance objectives as quantifiable results, not supply a list to do more tasks. Reinforce outcomes that appeal to emotions of your target customer types, how to increase revenue/profitability, or save time.

Design the registration page

The best trainers are those who can train and market their training. Training and development legend Bob Pike said during one of his train-the-trainer sessions, "If there is one skill set I would improve every day, it is how to market your courses more effectively." I was surprised it wasn't learning a new training technique, design theory, or delivery system. If you want to consider yourself an educator, you must learn how to market your offerings better.

With that point in mind, make your webinar registration page part of your marketing effort, not solely the organizer's responsibility. Include elements on your registration page that help with conversion, such as testimonials, guarantees, and bonus offers for early registration.

Check your webinar registration systems for web page signup pages that have previously been tested for conversion on multiple browsers and mobile devices, and that execute a seamless experience from registration to receiving ROI. If templates do not exist, or more customization is desired, consider using LeadPages.net to design your own.

Each webinar registration page can contain the following elements:

- Headline
- Sub-headline
- Date, time, time zone options, and meeting tool
- Lead copy
- Extra bonus offers
- Testimonials from past customers or influencers
- Guarantee
- Number of seats available
- Add-to-cart button with email opt-in

Checklist 18-2 OPTIONS FOR INFORMATION DELIVERY

Many webinar platforms are loaded full of features that presenters will never use. And listing an unused feature sometimes creates a problem because presenters will try to make a delivery tactic work for its own sake rather than putting the participant first and selecting the most appropriate feature when needed. In summary, select the most appropriate delivery tactic based on what will help the customer best understand and take action.

In Table 18.1 we differentiate between webinar platform features and delivery tactics so you can choose the most appropriate that improves the overall participant experience.

Table 18.1 Options for Delivering Information in Webinars

In-Platform Webinar Features	Webinar delivery tactics
Teleconference, VoIP, or WebRTC for auditory participation	Introduce with live video
Webcam	Cobrowse a website, report, or financial statement
Screen sharing	Present and insert visuals as needed
Participant chat	Switch between applications during screen share
Online polling and voting	
Mobile mirroring	Mobile device mirrored to desktop screen share
Whiteboard	Comment on live polling responses
	Collaborate on language used on document while in screen share

Take some time to learn the delivery alternatives available through your webinar system or one belonging to your customer. The differences are discovered by clicking on menus of webinar features and applying the webinar delivery tactic you normally would since many webinar platforms offer the same features. In order to make the transition from one platform to the next more smoothly, know what task you want to accomplish first, and then ask for help on how to execute the same tasks step by step. And, if you get in trouble accessing a new platform, use another screen share tool to troubleshoot any problems.

WEBINAR DELIVERY TIPS

Webinars aren't presentations. They are conversations that translate performance objectives into actionable steps. The only thing that is being presented is one screen at a time, one chat at time, or votes as they are collected in real time. All it takes is a few adjustments in recreating the participant experience once the webinar starts.

Here are some tips to consider.

Pause in between points

A webinar is not a race to the finish line to see how many slides you can cover in *x* minutes. And "Does anyone have any questions?" is not a satisfactory means of ending the webinar. Each action with the keyboard, mouse, or stylus is intentional, aimed at helping the participants learn concepts at their own rate as they reach critical milestones during the webinar. Some participants will hold back from answering questions, not because they don't know the answer, but because they don't know how to share their answer and fear making a mistake. Be sure you give ample time for participants to answer questions in their head and participate inside the webinar platform before you move on to the next point.

Use a conversational tone

It's hard at first to sit down in front of a laptop and start talking to it as if another human being is listening. It takes confidence in knowing what you say during a webinar is the right message to communicate without the need to observe a gesture (like nodding) to tell you if the message is understood.

And, with more assurance, you will be ok with asking a question and hearing crickets if no answer is given.

Start a webinar as if you were sitting in front of a group of people live by asking, "Where are you from, what one thing do you want to take away from today, or what is bothering you right now that you wish would go away?" and ask them to answer these questions in participant chat. Read aloud responses where appropriate and acknowledge participants on a first name basis to build rapport in the beginning. A conversational tone shows you are with your group, not talking at them, which will improve your relationship with participants as the dialogue continues.

Tell everyone what you are doing

Anytime the screen moves without warning, a participant might think something is happening on the computer that is not supposed to happen, because many technical issues are possible during a webinar. For example, if the webinar host turns the screen black, a participant might think the system is down unless the host tells the participant what is happening. Every time you make a sudden leap from presentation slide to web-browsing application to participant chat, inform all of the participants what you are doing, so they can feel reassured that the movement on the screen wasn't on their end.

Support questions with visuals

Reinforce participants' questions with visuals to answer polls, share input, and provide critical feedback to the webinar host as to whether the performance objectives are being met during the webinar. This allows the presenter to dive deeper into specific topics or outline a quick overview of more generalized subjects.

You can ask questions by typing the questions and answers into the slide itself, adding them to the online polling feature, or posing them through the participant chat. As new answers come in, you can acknowledge responses aloud or in chat, or you can demonstrate answers as a new visual representation using other slides.

Contingency plans

What could go wrong on a webinar? Plan for everything, and execute as if nothing could go wrong. Here are some tips to prepare for the worst case scenarios:

- Before you start the webinar, dial in and put yourself on mute as a phone backup in case the Internet connection goes down.
- Use multiple screens to create more real estate to use multiple programs during the webinar. One screen might display the webinar platform and slides and another screen displays web browsers needed during the webinar and questions from participant chat.
- Locate multiple alternatives for Internet connection with the most secure connection in case one goes down.
- A stylus used on a digital whiteboard app installed on a tablet is more usable than a mouse-controlled whiteboard integrated into the webinar platform. However, if your tablet isn't working or connected then you will be forced to use the webinar's whiteboard feature as a useful backup.
- Record your webinars in a universal file format of appropriate file size (estimate 1 GB/hour), so you can easily edit it and upload it to a popular video-hosting service.

Checklist 18-3 WEBINAR FOLLOW-UP

Consider every webinar participant a customer. They submitted their name, email address, and other confidential information in exchange for the opportunity to learn more about what you do and how you might help them in the future. Check these tips to improve follow up in order get the most return on your time.

Add participant CRM

Webinar attendance grows webinar attendance. If you use webinars to build an email or customer list, you can grow your registration numbers by adding past participants into future webinars. Either integrate your webinar system to automatically exchange contact records with your CRM, or manually export contacts from the webinar system and import them into CRM for future follow up.

An overlooked benefit to using an integrated webinar platform with CRM is that the integrated platform saves time/cost on administering tasks that better systems can replace. Once the contacts are all in the same place with the most accurate information, then it becomes easier to follow up in multiple ways.

Follow up campaigns

A successful knowledge transfer occurs when a learned behavior is put into practice, it's not how good a participant felt after it was over. This is why collecting evaluations same day of the webinar training isn't effective because it takes time for a participant to take action on what was learned. Sometimes it can take as much as 60 to 90 days to see a performance increase from one webinar.

A better approach to reinforce measurable performance objectives and hold participants accountable for taking action is to use a series of email auto-responders that follow webinar training.

Review this sample auto-responder timeline to see what to include in your subsequent emails after the webinar takes place.

- **Day 0 (day of webinar):** Say thank you, summarize performance objectives, and provide access to learning aids that reinforce concepts discussed in webinar.
- **Day 3:** Remind participant of performance objective 1 and resources that supplement the execution of performance objective 1. For instance, the email contains links to process maps, checklists and videos that support the learning process.

- **Day 7:** Remind participant of performance objective 2 and list resources as in Day 3 of auto-responder campaign. Here, change the message to request feedback by email reply to uncover some challenges discovered while completing tasks. One response that shares problems might be experienced by all and, without asking, the perception is everything is ok when it is not.
- **Day 10:** Remind participant of performance objective 3, and request they share specifically what they have implemented that worked by replying to an email or submitting a quick online form.
- **Day 14:** Collect testimonials from participants who realized results from implementing the webinar training. Testimonials that support revenue generated, time saved, problems avoided, etc. are more effective in marketing webinars because the language comes from customers and not the trainer's perceptions.
- **Day 21:** Share testimonials from influencers who received results from implementing the webinar training. When participants see others have had recent success who experienced the same webinar, they will take the next webinar more seriously if there is an established pattern of results from the webinar host.

Share digital bonuses

Have you ever attended a training session, conference, or presentation and left empty-handed? A month later, you can't remember an action item—just that you had a good time. But don't give up hope. The next time you are considering one of these programs, you can make your decision based partly upon the takeaways offered by the provider and the facilitator.

Is there anything better than a well-recorded audio playback from training?

Yes, and then some. Try these on for size:

- Permission to upload PowerPoint presentation to SlideShare
- Copy of the whiteboard notes and drawings on presentation slides

- Live-polling survey results from participants
- Downloadable Evernote templates and files
- Downloadable Wunderlist checklists for project management
- Video recording of the slides synchronized with audio
- Video recording of presenter
- Video recording of the presenter synchronized with the slides
- SurveyMonkey follow-up 60 days later to measure percentage of those who implemented the training and perceived a return on attendance
- Photos of participants engaging with one another
- Videos of participants engaging with one another
- Summary blog posts that recap the pictures, testimonials, videos, slides, and written feedback
- Twitter and Instagram feed from the hashtag
- Follow up Screen to Screen conversations to coach participants on best practices

Call the participants

You would be surprised how many participants would buy if you picked up the phone and called them after the webinar. Use a power dialer to make the phone calls, or outsource your help with scripted questions from a company like Quality Contact Solutions. Have your inside sales team set up appointments, make recommendations to customers, or sell your product or service after answering all customer questions.

Set appointments

In an attempt to set an appointment over the phone with a customer to meet at a future date, the customer might request the appointment take place now. If that's the case refer to impromptu meetings as discussed in Chapter 7. If the customer wishes to set a time, refer to setting appointments in Chapter 4. Every contact point with a customer performed over the phone or another medium is a chance to improve your relationship, to help customers make wise decisions and ask for referrals from their peers. Follow up with participants as a form of prospecting, building relationships, and customer support. There's a good chance your competition isn't doing it.

Close transactions

Some transactions require formal proposals and others allow customers to buy from you online after conversations. Tools similar to Proposable, Quosal, and Qvidian will draft proposals online in order to streamline sales productivity. Shopping cart solutions including PayPal, 1shoppingCart, or Infusionsoft allow customers to pay online more easily than other systems. The type of product/service you sell and type of relationship you have with your customer will determine what tools you use to mark a conversation a closed sale.

CHAPTER 19

◆◆◆

SCREEN TO SCREEN MARKETING: HOW TO CREATE GROWTH OPPORTUNITIES FROM CONVERSATIONS

Some of the best marketing messages you will ever produce will come from the language that customers use to describe how they experience your business inside of its industry. Because our memories are not 100% perfect, it is impossible to remember every word of a dialogue. This dialogue could potentially benefit similar customers if we only had better ways of capturing it (with permission) and sharing it using marketing technology, also knows as MarTech.

This chapter simplifies ways to extract the best insights using the latest technology in order to gain more brand awareness, increase your marketing reach, and with the least effort.

Checklist 19-1 CONVERSATIONAL MARKETING

Leveraging previous and upcoming conversations with customers and industry experts is one of the easiest ways to create a consistent stream of new content. Customers will be able to relate to you as you relate to others while you either solve their problems or ask other industry experts to add their perspective to yours.

A common excuse that keeps entrepreneurs or corporate managers from posting videos to YouTube is, "We don't know what to say." Funny, because then I think to myself, "What do you say when you are with customers?" It's unrealistic to have all the answers and telling a customer you do might cause them to be suspicious.

Try some of these alternatives in conversational marketing.

Recorded interviews

A true expert knows how to craft a laser beam of a question that gets to the core of how to solve customer's problems and will sometime ask a specific question that customers haven't even yet thought to ask. Marketing expert Jay Baer recommends *becoming the chief questioner.* Your expertise is measured by the quality of the questions you ask, and by selecting the best guests to interview, your customers get their answers without you having to create each one.

In order to get the best answers regarding the Screen to Screen Selling process, we've recorded video interviews with highly sought-after experts such as Jeffrey Hayzlett to discuss C-Suite decisions, Alan Weiss, Ph.D. on the psychology of the environment, and Don Hutson on sales management.

Subscribe to the show on ITunes to see how we have packaged video interviews at http://devitre.co/s2spodcast.

Mobile broadcasting

In Chapter 10 we briefly discussed some popular tools to live broadcast video from mobile devices. In this section we will focus on how to be more intentional as it relates to having conversations with customers.

Anytime you are attending a special event, visiting an exotic location, or visiting with someone out of your office, you have the ability to start a live conversation with others who get to experience what you experience. That means we can invite others to join in on the party too from anywhere as long as you have a strong mobile Internet connection signal from your device. Here are a few tips to improve your mobile broadcast.

- **Set a time and date.** Most people aren't sitting at their computer waiting for you to get online to talk. If they do then they're probably not a customer, they're a stalker. Schedule the mobile as if it were an event in order get the most attendance.
- **Use a portable microphone.** The audio jack in your phone allows you to plug in a wireless mic to capture the best sound in a noisy environment. The Stony-Edge SIMPLE LAV-MOBILE Condenser Lavalier/Lapel Microphone for iPhone & Android Smartphones will work as your lavaliere mic to hang from your shirt. Or find an omnidirectional handheld microphone and add a mic flag to brand your logo into the experience found at (http://micflags.com).
- **Be camera ready.** The best journalists seem to always be there at the right place at the right time. They are always camera ready. You never know when you could be at the center of a historic moment in time, at the scene of the crime, or are an exclusive witness to a major announcement. With you at the center sharing from your phone, others will quickly spread the word depending upon how extreme the scenario plays out.

Video podcast syndication

According to the 2015 Screen Wars report by Nielsen, only 65% of viewers prefer to watch video programming at its regularly scheduled time. The other 35% will consume video when it's most convenient and there's a strong likelihood the video will be watched from a mobile device. As marketers, it's as important to pay attention to both the message inside the video as it is to which media channels the video will be watched on. Widen the exposure of your Screen to Screen conversations by publishing your recorded videos to one place, and it syndicates to many different channels. A video podcast publishing tool Libsyn (http://libsyn.com) will automatically publish to YouTube, iTunes, Android market, Windows devices, to a website/blog, and many of the popular social media channels.

Checklist 19-2 CAPTURING CONTENT

In order to capture the conversation to produce the best video file format for syndication, it's important to follow some important steps to ensure the best quality, and protect everyone's interests with respect to what gets shared. Read on to see how to obtain consent to record, choose which tools to record, and how to use those tools to everyone's satisfaction.

Customer consent

It is incredibly easy now with technology to record a video of a conversation that others don't know you are recording. A quick way to lose trust with someone is to record a private conversation and post it online for everyone to see without obtaining mutual consent. Beside being bad manners, it also may be illegal to record a conversation depending upon state law or the law of the state where you are conducting the meeting. Since each state establishes their own requirements for obtaining consent to record, research the Digital Media Law Project, which compares the laws for each state in the United States (http://www.dmlp.org/legal-guide/state-law-recording). Since I'm not an attorney I'm not giving legal advice and strongly urge you to seek appropriate counsel before you record any conversations for marketing purposes.

Software for recording videos

Most upgraded Screen to Screen conference tools allow you to press a button to record the conversation, and the same button to stop recording. Or, the recording will start when the meeting starts, and the video is saved as a file on the device or in the cloud to access when needed.

If your web-conferencing software doesn't have a recording feature, then consider using a screen capture video recording tool like Camtasia and ScreenFlow. These tools also have a built in video editor to add music and an introduction (intro), closing (outro) and captions to highlight important notes.

Video editing is a task for administrative support, not for executives, managers, or salespersons. If you manufacture your own labor (have kids) or have access to interns at a community college, or can hire a virtual assistant, the task can be left to someone who will most likely produce a production quality video better and faster than you.

File conversion tool

After a conversation has ended, have you ever wished you had captured the exact words the customer used to describe your product or service? A customer's praise, thanks, or compliments can be the most powerful marketing messages. You can repurpose a meeting video as a video testimonial, a testimonial as a recommendation, and a recommendation as a referral.

Either you or someone else can upload the video to an online service tool called Speechpad (http://speechpad.com) and convert the video into audio and text for $1 a minute. This way, you don't have to remember the exact words or attempt to type the words after replaying the video to use in your marketing copy. Since the words came from your participant and they gave you permission to use the video, it's always a nice gesture to ask them for use of the text even though it may or may not be required by law.

Look directly at the camera

If we were to talk right now and you saw my face looking down or off to the side it might seem as if I wasn't really paying attention even though I am looking directly at the computer screen or webcam. This happens because of the following reasons:

- The webcam placement is not centered in the middle of the computer screen.
- Your thumbnail video image (how you see yourself during the conversation) is located at the bottom corner of the screen. Drag the thumbnail video image directly underneath the webcam so you can be confident your appearance is appropriate while looking others directly in the eye.
- When using multiple desktop computer screens, the webcam might be placed on top of one screen while the meeting tool is using another. Make sure the webcam used is located on top of the same screen being used for the conversation.

Remember to smile

Has this ever happened to you? You ask someone why they are unhappy, they say they *are* happy, and then you tell them to notify their face. This kind of exchange happens when someone's face does not signal happiness.

If you don't smile, chances are the other person isn't going to smile either. A heated debate loaded with technical information can strip all enthusiasm right out of a facial expression. For your next conversation Screen to Screen, cue smiles by writing the word *Smile* on two stickers and affix them to your computer next to the webcam, so you won't forget.

Share video with participants

Video files can be cumbersome to send electronically because of the large file sizes, media player settings, and bandwidth of people's Internet connection. You could spend all day uploading a video, and customers could spend equal time downloading it to watch. You want to make the process easy for you and easy for them.

Here are a few ways:

- Upload the video to the Dropbox app and share the link to the file for someone else to download.
- Upload the video to YouTube and send as accessible through a private URL. This means those who have the URL can see it but the video cannot be found otherwise, unless they receive the link from someone who manages your YouTube channel.
- Upload the video to Hightail (http://hightail.com formerly YouSendit).

Screen capture image

Buried somewhere in the video recording will be a gem of a screen shot that highlights the answer to a question that other customers have asked before and you expect to answer again. You can use this kind of image to create teachable moments on social networks (assuming there is nothing confidential in the screenshot) so other customers will benefit and add more value, without having to think about where to get your next social media post.

Checklist 19-3 REPURPOSE WHITEBOARD SKETCHES

Visual summaries of conversations can be gold mines for the creation of intellectual property and be used in future conversations. Have you ever had a customer say, "I have never thought of it like that before?" Or you might have said to yourself, "I've never explained it that way before, and it worked better than my usual way." In both cases, you have found a visual worth sharing.

A digital whiteboard brainstorm with one customer can be shared as an image on social networks if you think your community will benefit. Check your visual summaries to see which whiteboard sketches you created from previous conversations and find ways to use them again and again.

Visuals for future conversations

After reviewing a visual summary, ask yourself, "What here is a frequently asked question or something that I haven't thought of before that other customers might want to know, too?" Wipe out any specific customer data, and you have created a template you can use again for the next conversation.

Then ask yourself, "How can I improve the way I explained x in order to help the customer understand better and faster?" This quick review with a coach or a manager will uncover some blind spots in your language, choice of visual for demonstration, and effectiveness at resolving recurring issues.

Exporting image files

When you export image files, what format is better: one PDF with all of the slides and annotations or individual image files of each slide with annotations? My recommendation is to use the feature in your whiteboard app that allows you to export your sketches as one PDF. This approach saves you time in producing the visual summary and saves the customer time required to open up images individually. Every little shortcut counts and improves the customer experience, because you are able to serve them in more visually stimulating ways.

Sharing watermarked annotations

Worry less about others stealing the intellectual property you share online by adding a watermark, logo, or at the very least your name to images you share online. Look for a watermark feature in your whiteboard presentation app to insert the logo (with contact info) of your choice into every whiteboard annotation you share. So if they get shared by others on social media, they know the source. Could someone copy the exact same sketch? Sure they could, but eventually those who regularly steal others' intellectual property and share as their own get found out.

Uses for images

Images are one of the easiest forms of media to create, because our cameras can capture them so quickly, and you can edit them from mobile devices. In addition, you can use these images across multiple media channels. Here are some options for where you might use your whiteboard sketches:

- Blog posts
- Slides for future presentations
- SlideShare presentations
- Online videos
- Social-media thumbnails

Social-media distribution

Real-time questions deserve real-time responses. When you have drawn whiteboard annotations, you can quickly send them through social media in order to deliver a specific point to one customer, rather than following up with a generic slide in hopes it connects. Deliver your annotations quickly by applying these tips:

- Engage specific customers by tagging, mentioning, and commenting in your replies.
- Add a hashtag to Instagram, Pinterest, Facebook, Twitter, and LinkedIn feeds.
- Syndicate picture posts using social-media tools for scheduling, publishing, and tracking.

◆◆◆

CHAPTER 20

MASSIVE EXECUTION: HOW TO MASTER SCREEN TO SCREEN SELLING ONE CLICK AT A TIME

What will set you apart from everyone else in how you communicate with the latest technology will come from how many new things you are willing to try, and that means taking risks.

There's the risk of missing an opportunity because you were busy learning something new. That might mean instead of making calls and fulfilling priorities you are experimenting with a new technology.

There's the risk of investing in a technology that gets outdated quickly and you have to eat the sunk cost. That might mean taking a loss before you receive a return on investment and switching to a newer technology in order to stay competitive.

And, there's the risk of losing a customer because the technology backfired because of some unpredictable problem. Or the risk of losing a coworker because they didn't want to change with the times. In order to get the competitive edge in the marketplace with technology, you are going to have to take some risks.

In this chapter, we will help you summarize the book by prioritizing your task list so you can minimize as many of those risks as possible and achieve your business and personal goals.

Checklist 20-1 PRIORITIZED CHECKLISTS

My goal was to start with the results first and then give you a process for using the technology you already have access to, showing you better and faster ways to use it. The following checklists identify the topics that have the highest priority as you practice new skills and implement changes in order to increase performance throughout your organization.

Performance metrics

- Sales metrics (Chapter 1)
- Productivity benefits (Chapter 1)
- Cost savings (Chapter 1)
- Global impact (Chapter 1)

Team member contributions

- Working arrangements (Chapter 3)
- Meeting alternatives (Chapter 7)
- Mobile-meeting etiquette (Chapter 10)
- Characteristics of remote meetings (Chapter 18)

Technology selection

- Barriers and irritants (Chapter 3)
- Technology review (Chapter 3)
- Mobile apps (Chapter 3)
- Managing your budget (Chapter 3)

Meeting policies and expectations

- Company transition (Chapter 1)
- Managing multiple buyers (Chapter 4)
- Balancing conversations (Chapter 7)
- Beliefs (Chapter 15)

Skills training and development

- Knowledge, skills, and attitudes about technology (Chapter 1)
- Consultative selling (Chapter 1)
- Participant applications (Chapter 7)
- Keyboard shortcuts (Chapter 7)
- Whiteboard analysis (Chapter 14)

Checklist 20-2 CUSTOMER CHECKLIST

The process of Screen to Screen Selling humanizes the customer experience because it customizes the entire process on what customers want, what technology they have, and how to decrease the amount of time making important decisions. In order to make the transition successfully, focus on the checklists in this section.

Value that exceeds price

- Questions customers need answered (Chapter 4)
- Visual creation and template types (Chapter 4)
- Extemporaneous visuals (Chapter 8)
- Setting the next visual agenda (Chapter 9)

Cross-channel experience

- Virtual trust (Chapter 2)
- Visualizing conversations (Chapter 2)

- Screen share conversations (Chapter 4)
- Cross-channel experience (Chapter 14)

Consistent flexibility

- Virtual trust (Chapter 4)
- Quick-access memory (Chapter 4)
- Keyboard shortcuts (Chapter 7)
- Impromptu meetings (Chapter 8)

Customer confidentiality

- Agreements when co-browsing (Chapter 8)
- Mobility connectivity (Chapter 10)
- Confidentiality concerns (Chapter 12)
- Benefits of digital signatures (Chapter 13)

Checklist 20-3 PERSONAL BENEFITS

When people ask me how I am able to use technology in so many different ways in business, I can share meaningful answers because of how I apply how I use technology in my personal life. I was able to be with my family when my second nephew was born because of Skype. I was able to have friends and family participate in my wedding through Google Hangouts On Air. And as a customer of other businesses, I'm able to make decisions quickly because we can get straight to the point Screen to Screen.

Retain information faster

Screen to Screen skill sets have helped me take better paper and digital notes. Pen-to-paper note taking might be slower, but it stimulates more brain activity than processing through keyboard strokes. You can easily employ creative note taking with visualizations by using pen and paper or the digital whiteboard. The skill set is the same, although the technology for processing the notes is different.

Nurture important relationships

You can visit with important contacts from all over the world in your living room. Valued clients and distant relatives living across the world can be accessible in seconds at literally no cost, so there are no more excuses for failing to stay connected Screen to Screen.

Your Screen to Screen meeting software can list a directory of favorites or let you categorize customers based on the media channel they prefer that you use to reach them. Also, in your customer relationship management (CRM) system, mark which platforms each customer prefers to use in communications. Then, the next time you call, you don't have to ask participant preferences all over again.

Build motivation into flexible work schedules

The ability to work from anywhere, sell to anywhere, and live anywhere you want comes at a cost, and that cost is self-discipline. When you are working from a remote location, you might miss the buzz of a thriving sales office where you and your colleagues talk continuously about sales quotas and how to handle customer complaints. You also miss out on getting relief from peers through challenging times. Find ways to create a similar support system through online communities. Create team interaction and motivation through gamification of sales numbers with your team. Finally, assuming your company's work schedules include mandatory times to be on duty, be sure you are easily accessible during those hours.

Power off

The one technology feature that you positively, unequivocally, and undisputedly have control over, regardless of operating system, belief system, and value system, is the power switch. In other words, you have the ability to switch your devices *off*.

Off will let the world know that you need to spend more time with your family.

Off will give you a stronger bond with your loved ones, because of the focused attention that you can give them.

Off will give your mind a break to regroup, refocus, and rework any strategies that didn't work in the past, so that you can improve upon them for the future.

I think that we all need to be able to turn off in order to make time for what's important. It's when you are ready to turn it back on that you will be able to impact other's people's lives when you next meet *Screen to Screen*.

INDEX

Place photo here

This book belongs to:

_____

My First Reading Log

Read to Me!

GROW A THOUSAND STORIES TALL

Written and Illustrated by
Martha Day Zschock

Commonwealth Editions
Carlisle, Massachusetts

A book is a gift you can
open again and again.

Garrison Keillor

To my baby birds—Bevin, Avery, and Jake

Copyright © 2015 Martha Day Zschock
All rights reserved.

978-1-938700-29-3

Book design by Heather Zschock

Published by Commonwealth Editions
an imprint of Applewood Books
P.O. Box 27, Carlisle, MA 01741

Visit us on the web at www.commonwealtheditions.com
Visit Martha Day Zschock at www.marthazschock.com and
www.growathousandstoriestall.com

10 9 8 7 6 5 4 3 2 1

Printed in China

Children are made readers on
the laps of their parents.

Emilie Buchwald

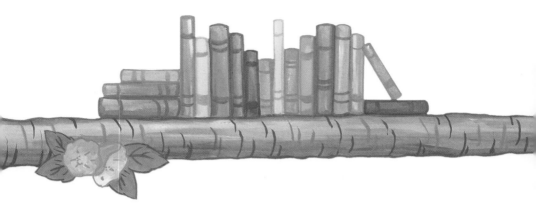

Read to Me!

Experts agree that the best way to prepare children to become readers themselves is to read to them. Learning to read is a process that begins long before your child enters kindergarten. From birth, your baby begins to learn important language and pre-reading skills. As a parent, you are your child's first (and favorite) teacher and you are the best person to help your little one learn and grow. When you make reading aloud a daily habit from birth, your child will enter kindergarten ready to read AND ready to succeed. As you record the books that you share, take time to celebrate your child's magical journey to becoming a reader!

Experts tell us that children
need to hear a thousand stories read
aloud before they begin to learn
to read for themselves.

Mem Fox, *Reading Magic*

Reading, Playing, Singing, Talking, and Writing

The years between birth and kindergarten show remarkable growth and transformation. During these early years, your little one is growing and learning constantly. As a parent, you are in a perfect position to provide opportunities for learning through everyday experiences that will foster pre-reading skills.

Each section of this log will explain how reading, playing, singing, talking, and writing can be used to help your child develop important pre-reading skills. You will also find fun and easy tips about how to incorporate these activities into your daily routine in meaningful ways that will help your child blossom into a reader!

The more that you read,
the more things you will know.
The more that you learn,
the more places you'll go.

Dr. Seuss, *Oh, the Places You'll Go!*

Watch Your Child Grow
A Thousand Stories Tall

Are you up for a challenge? Commit to reading 1,000 books before your child enters kindergarten! My First Reading Log is a fun way to encourage families to read frequently to their little ones before they enter school. When you make reading part of your daily routine, the numbers add up quickly and small daily investments pay off in big rewards in the years to come!

> 1 book a day for 3 years = 1,095 books
> 3 books a day for 1 year = 1,095 books

Reading aloud helps build vocabulary, develops language skills, introduces new ideas, increases listening ability, and fosters a loving bond between you and your child. The tips in this log will further enhance your child's reading and learning experiences. As you record the books you read, you create a tangible memory of your special time spent together. Grab a book, snuggle up, and start your reading adventure today!

1,000 Books?!?

A thousand books may seem like a lot, but don't let the number deter you. As you start to record the books you read, you will see that the list grows quickly. Like a child's attention span, most children's books are short, and it's easy to read a few in one sitting.

Choosing the right books for your child is the key to success. For infants, nursery rhymes and lullabies work well. For babies, books with bright colors, shapes, rhymes, and simple text are best. Board books are perfect for babies and toddlers who like to put things in their mouths. Toddlers are on the go, so short books are a must! Preschoolers can usually listen to slightly longer stories and may be ready for picture books. You are the judge and you know your child best. You will soon become an expert at picking out the perfect books for your child!

Your little one may have a favorite story and want you to read it over and over—that's OK. Children benefit from repetition. Each time you read the book, it counts! Books that your child listens to on a device (iPad, eReader, computer, CD player) also count. Remember to record books that family members and day-care providers read to your child as well. It all adds up! Although the goal is to read 1,000 books before your child enters kindergarten, the true reward is the time you and your child spend reading and bonding together. Enjoy every moment!

I think I can. I think I can. I think I can.

Watty Piper, *The Little Engine That Could*

Firsts and Favorites

Name: _____

Birthday: _____

Birthplace: _____

How we chose your name: _____

_____

_____

On the day you were born: _____

_____

_____

Family, Friends, and Special People: _____

_____

_____

_____

_____

_____

_____

Sometimes the smallest things take
up the most room in your heart.

A.A. Milne, *Winnie the Pooh*

Favorite Characters:

Favorite Songs:

Favorite Toys:

Favorite Food:

First Steps:

First Words:

Read to me!

Here is where people, one
frequently finds, lower their voices
and raise their minds.

Richard Armour

Read to Me!

Reading together is the best way to prepare your child to become a reader! When you read aloud, you are helping to develop important pre-reading skills in many ways that you might not even realize! You are—

- Building vocabulary
- Developing language skills
- Increasing memory
- Introducing new experiences, concepts, and ideas
- Growing knowledge
- Strengthening listening skills
- Teaching your child how books work
- Making connections between letters and sounds

And, most importantly, you are helping your child associate this time of comfort, discovery, and love with books. This makes reading a positive and happy experience!

Reading is important because, if you can read, you can learn anything about everything and everything about anything.

Tomie DePaola

Reading Log

1. _____

2. _____

3. _____

4. _____

5. _____

6. _____

7. _____

8. _____

9. _____

10. _____

11. _____

12. _____

13. _____

14. _____

15. _____

Make reading to your child a
daily routine. Bedtime? Snack time?
Upon waking up? Choose the
time that works best.

Ask questions as you read. For example,
"What does the cow say?" or, "Can you show me the
blue kite?" Your baby may not be able to answer
today, but soon you'll be in for a surprise!

16. _____

17. _____

18. _____

19. _____

20. _____

21. _____

22. _____

23. _____

24. _____

25. _____

26. _____

27. _____

28. _____

29. _____

30. _____

Once you learn to read,
you will be forever free.

Frederick Douglass

31. _____

32. _____

33. _____

34. _____

35. _____

36. _____

37. _____

38. _____

39. _____

40. _____

41. _____

42. _____

43. _____

44. _____

45. _____

46. _____

47. _____

48. _____

49. _____

50. _____

51. _____

52. _____

53. _____

54. _____

55. _____

56. _____

57. _____

58. _____

59. _____

60. _____

If your child is too squirmy to listen to a
whole book, that's OK. Several shorter sessions
are just as beneficial as one longer one!

Talk about the pictures as you look at a book.
For babies and toddlers, point out colors, shapes,
and names of objects. For preschoolers, ask
your child to tell you a story about the picture.

61. _____

62. _____

63. _____

64. _____

65. _____

66. _____

67. _____

68. _____

69. _____

70. _____

71. _____

72. _____

73. _____

74. _____

75. _____

76. _____

77. _____

78. _____

79. _____

80. _____

81. _____

82. _____

83. _____

84. _____

85. _____

86. _____

87. _____

Read stories that your child loves over and over.
Children learn from repetition. Someday soon,
your little one will "read" the book to you!

...you do not leave a library; if you do what it wants you to do, you are taking it with you.

Elie Wiesel

88. _____

89. _____

90. _____

91. _____

92. _____

93. _____

94. _____

95. _____

96. _____

97. _____

98. _____

99. _____

100. _____

101. _____

102. _____

103. _____

104. _____

105. _____

106. _____

107. _____

108. _____

109. _____

110. _____

Make trips to the library an adventure.
Bring a special bag for your child to carry books
in and create a place for library books at home.

Point out letters as you read and teach your child
the different sounds that each one makes. The letters
in your child's name are a great place to start.

A B C D

111. _____

112. _____

113. _____

114. _____

115. _____

116. _____

117. _____

118. _____

119. _____

120. _____

121. _____

122. _____

123. _____

124. _____

125. _____

126. _____

127. _____

128. _____

129. _____

130. _____

131. _____

132. _____

133. _____

134. _____

135. _____

136. _____

137. _____

138. _____

139. _____

140. _____

If you come across a new word, explain it as you read. For example, "Enormous means really big." "A hare is a kind of rabbit that has long ears."

Let your little one help turn the pages as you read.
This will teach your child how books work.

141. _____

142. _____

143. _____

144. _____

145. _____

146. _____

147. _____

148. _____

149. _____

150. _____

151. _____

152. _____

153. _____

154. _____

155. _____

156. _____

157. _____

158. _____

159. _____

160. _____

161. _____

162. _____

163. _____

164. _____

165. _____

166. _____

167. _____

168. _____

169. _____

170. _____

There is no frigate like a book, to take us lands away.

Emily Dickinson

Babies explore by putting things in their mouths. Board books will stand up to the rough treatment!

171. _____

172. _____

173. _____

174. _____

175. _____

176. _____

177. _____

178. _____

179. _____

180. _____

181. _____

182. _____

183. _____

184. _____

185. _____

186. _____

187. _____

188. _____

189. _____

190. _____

191. _____

192. _____

193. _____

194. _____

195. _____

196. _____

197. _____

198 _____

199. _____

200. _____

Be a role model!
Let your child see
you reading too!

Time to
celebrate!

Place 200 Books
Sticker Here

Play with Me!

Playing together is not only fun, it's an important time for your child to learn and grow. Play offers your child the opportunity to learn new skills, experiment with how things work, think creatively, problem solve, develop social skills, practice language, connect to stories, increase comprehension, and learn about the world all around! You are your child's favorite playmate, and you can help set the stage for meaningful play that supports your child's development. Playtime adventures are imaginative and magical. When learning is fun, your child learns best!

Creative play is like a spring that bubbles up from deep within a child.

Joan Almon, *Alliance for Childhood*

Act out stories with your child. Make a costume box and fill it with old clothes, shoes, and scarves. Use props from around the house.

201. _____

202. _____

203. _____

204. _____

205. _____

206. _____

207. _____

208. _____

209. _____

210. _____

211. _____

212. _____

213. _____

214. _____

215. _____

216. _____

217. _____

218. _____

219. _____

220. _____

221. _____

222. _____

223. _____

224. _____

225. _____

226. _____

227. _____

228. _____

229. _____

230. _____

Pretend a stuffed animal is speaking in a
silly voice and have it talk to your child.

Play gives children a
chance to practice what
they are learning.

Mr. Rogers

231. _____

232. _____

233. _____

234. _____

235. _____

236. _____

237. _____

238. _____

239. _____

240. _____

241. _____

242. _____

243. _____

244. _____

245. _____

246. _____

247. _____

248. _____

249. _____

250. _____

251. _____

252. _____

253. _____

254. _____

255. _____

256. _____

257. _____

258. _____

259. _____

260. _____

Play "rhyme time" during the day. Say a word and help your child think of others that rhyme with it. You can use prompts such as, "I saw a cat sit on a _____."

261. _____

262. _____

263. _____

264. _____

265. _____

266. _____

267. _____

268. _____

269. _____

270. _____

271. _____

272. _____

273. _____

274. _____

275. _____

276. _____

277. _____

278. _____

279. _____

280. _____

281. _____

282. _____

283. _____

284. _____

285. _____

286. _____

287. _____

288. _____

289. _____

290. _____

Make different faces, and let your child guess how you are feeling. For example: happy, sad, angry, or silly.

When you're curious, you find lots
of interesting things to do.

Walt Disney

291. _____

292. _____

293. _____

294. _____

295. _____

296. _____

297. _____

298. _____

299. _____

300. _____

301. _____

302. _____

303. _____

304. _____

305. _____

306. _____

307. _____

308. _____

309. _____

310. _____

Set the scene and then act it out with your child.
For example, pretend that you are at a restaurant
and your child is the waiter. Let your child be
the vet and take care of a hurt stuffed animal.
Bring toy trucks and cars to a sandbox
and build new roads.

311.

312.

313.

314.

315.

316.

317.

318.

319.

320.

321.

322.

323.

324.

325.

326. _____

327. _____

328. _____

329. _____

330. _____

331. _____

332. _____

333. _____

334. _____

335. _____

336. _____

337. _____

338. _____

339. _____

340. _____

Give your child safe plastic containers to play with in the bathtub. Describe what your child is doing... "Now the cup is full; when you pour it, it will be empty!" This introduces new vocabulary and concepts.

Make a fort using an old sheet and two chairs.
This can become a castle or a cave! Pretend
it's a library and read books inside!

341. _____

342. _____

343. _____

344. _____

345. _____

346. _____

347. _____

348. _____

349. _____

350. _____

351. _____

352. _____

353. _____

354. _____

355. _____

356. _____

357. _____

358. _____

359. _____

360. _____

361. _____

362. _____

363. _____

364. _____

365. _____

366. _____

367. _____

368 _____

369. _____

370. _____

I hear and I forget.
I see and I remember.
I do and I understand.

Confucius

Let your child be the leader and decide what to play. You can learn a lot about how your child thinks and feels just by listening.

371. _____

372. _____

373. _____

374. _____

375. _____

376. _____

377. _____

378. _____

379. _____

380. _____

381. _____

382. _____

383. _____

384. _____

385. _____

386. _____

387. _____

388. _____

389. _____

390. _____

391. _____

392. _____

393. _____

394. _____

395. _____

396. _____

397. _____

398. _____

399. _____

400. _____

Wrap up library books
in wrapping paper
and pretend it's your
child's birthday!

Wow!

Place 400 Books
Sticker Here

Sing to Me!

Singing and clapping to the beat are fun ways to add learning to your daily routine! Children naturally respond to music. Babies are soothed by the gentle sounds of a lullaby, and boisterous toddlers love to jump to the beat. Singing slows down language, making it easier to hear distinct sounds in words. Rhythms allow children to hear syllables in words. Jazzy tunes encourage dancing and clapping, which strengthens motor skills. Songs can also introduce new ideas and concepts. They often have repetitive words, rhymes, and verses which reinforce learning. Rhymes, letters, numbers, days of the week, animal sounds, and shapes—many things can be taught through songs.

If you're happy and you know it,
clap your hands!

Introduce your little one to all kinds of music—classical, rock, jazz, blues, and music from other countries. Talk about which ones your child likes best.

401. _____

402. _____

403. _____

404. _____

405. _____

406. _____

407. _____

408. _____

409. _____

410. _____

411. _____

412. _____

413. _____

414. _____

415. _____

416. _____

417. _____

418. _____

419. _____

420. _____

421. _____

422. _____

423. _____

424. _____

425. _____

426. _____

427. _____

428. _____

429. _____

430. _____

Singing the alphabet song will help to teach about letters. Soon your child will sing it back to you!

We are the music makers, and we are the dreamers of dreams.

Roald Dahl

431. _____

432. _____

433. _____

434. _____

435. _____

436. _____

437. _____

438. _____

439. _____

440. _____

441. _____

442. _____

443. _____

444. _____

445. _____

446. _____

447. _____

448. _____

449. _____

450. _____

451. _____

452. _____

453. _____

454. _____

455. _____

456. _____

457. _____

458. _____

459. _____

460. _____

Sing throughout the day—when your child wakes
up or as you go for a walk or ride in the car.
Make music part of your child's daily life.

461. _____

462. _____

463. _____

464. _____

465. _____

466. _____

467. _____

468. _____

469. _____

470. _____

471. _____

472. _____

473. _____

474. _____

475. _____

476. _____

477. _____

478. _____

479. _____

480. _____

481. _____

482. _____

483. _____

484. _____

485. _____

486. _____

487. _____

488. _____

489. _____

490. _____

Ask your librarian to help you find songbooks.
You and your child can sing along with the pictures!

If you cannot teach me to fly,
teach me to sing.

J.M. Barrie, *Peter Pan*

491. _____

492. _____

493. _____

494. _____

495. _____

496. _____

497. _____

498. _____

499. _____

500. _____

501. _____

502. _____

503. _____

504. _____

505. _____

506. _____

507. _____

508. _____

509. _____

510. _____

Some songs have words that can be easily changed to fit your current activity, such as "This is the way we...." Insert "take a bath," "go to the library," or "clean your room."

Make simple instruments for your child to play. Rice or beans in a plastic snack container makes a perfect shaker, and an oatmeal container is a great drum!

511. _____

512. _____

513. _____

514. _____

515. _____

516. _____

517. _____

518. _____

519. _____

520. _____

521. _____

522. _____

523. _____

524. _____

525. _____

526. _____

527. _____

528. _____

529. _____

530. _____

531. _____

532. _____

533. _____

534. _____

535. _____

536. _____

537. _____

538. _____

539. _____

540. _____

Get up and dance! Put on some jazzy music, and
spin, twirl, and jump to the beat on a rainy afternoon.

Many libraries have free children's shows and concerts that your child will love. Ask your librarian for a calendar of events.

541. _____

542. _____

543. _____

544. _____

545. _____

546. _____

547. _____

548. _____

549. _____

550. _____

551. _____

552. _____

553. _____

554. _____

555. _____

556. _____

557. _____

558. _____

559. _____

560. _____

561. _____

562. _____

563. _____

564. _____

565. _____

566. _____

567. _____

568. _____

569. _____

570. _____

Music gives a soul to the universe, wings to the mind, flight to the imagination, and life to everything.

Plato

Sometimes children will listen better to songs than to words. If you find your child isn't listening, turn your request into a song! Singing, "Clean up, clean up, everybody clean up now," works well.

571. _____

572. _____

573. _____

574. _____

575. _____

576. _____

577. _____

578. _____

579. _____

580. _____

581. _____

582. _____

583. _____

584. _____

585. _____

586. _____

587. _____

588. _____

589. _____

590. _____

591. _____

592. _____

593. _____

594. _____

595. _____

596. _____

597. _____

598. _____

599. _____

600. _____

Use familiar songs to teach new words. "The BIG ENORMOUS spider crawled up the water spout," or "Mary had a little lizard, little lizard," etc.!

Way to go!

Place 600 Books Sticker Here

Talk to Me!

It might feel strange to talk to a baby who can't yet speak, but don't let that stop you! Talking with your child throughout the day is very important. Babies learn to talk by hearing those around them speak. As children listen, they learn sounds, words, expressions, and gestures that make up language. Talking with children extends their vocabulary, and increases their understanding of the world. Reading and language development go hand in hand. When you have conversations with your child, ask questions, explain how things work, name things, tell stories, point out letters and numbers, and describe things; you are helping your child make connections between spoken and written language.

The sound of a word is at least as important as the meaning.

Jack Prelutsky

When your baby babbles or coos—continue the conversation! "That's right, Mommy loves you!" And "Yes, you are Daddy's little love," are appropriate responses.

601. _____

602. _____

603. _____

604. _____

605. _____

606. _____

607. _____

608. _____

609. _____

610. _____

611. _____

612. _____

613. _____

614. _____

615. _____

616. _____

617. _____

618. _____

619. _____

620. _____

621. _____

622. _____

623. _____

624. _____

625. _____

626. _____

627. _____

628. _____

629. _____

630. _____

Help to extend your child's vocabulary. "Yes, we
did see a dog at the park. It was a poodle!"

Keep a poem in your pocket
and a picture in your head
and you'll never feel lonely at
night when you're in bed.

Beatrice Schenk de Regniers

631.

632.

633.

634.

635.

636.

637.

638.

639.

640.

641.

642.

643.

644.

645. _____

646. _____

647. _____

648. _____

649. _____

650. _____

651. _____

652. _____

653. _____

654. _____

655. _____

656. _____

657. _____

658. _____

659. _____

660. _____

Speak to your child in your native
language. Children learn best when
language is spoken fluently.

Teach manners by using polite words. When your child gives you something say, "Thank you!" If you make a request say, "Please."

661. _____

662. _____

663. _____

664. _____

665. _____

666. _____

667. _____

668. _____

669. _____

670. _____

671. _____

672. _____

673. _____

674. _____

675. _____

HELLO

PLEASE

THANK YOU! GOOD-BYE

676. _____

677. _____

678. _____

679. _____

680. _____

681. _____

682. _____

683. _____

684. _____

685. _____

686. _____

687. _____

688. _____

689. _____

690. _____

Babies understand more than you think they do. Keep talking; they are listening!

Any book that helps a child to form a habit of reading, to make reading one of his deep and continuing needs, is good for him.

Maya Angelou

691. _____

692. _____

693. _____

694. _____

695. _____

696. _____

697. _____

698. _____

699. _____

700. _____

701. _____

702. _____

703. _____

704. _____

705. _____

706. _____

707. _____

708. _____

709. _____

710. _____

Help your child order things and events. For example, when you talk about your day say, "First we are going to the store, next we will go to the playground, and then we will go home for lunch."

Children love to touch things. You can use this as an opportunity to describe things. '"The bark on the tree feels rough. The puppy is soft, but his teeth look sharp!"

711. _____

RED

712. _____

713. _____

714. _____

715. _____

716. _____

717. _____

718. _____

719. _____

720. _____

721. _____

722. _____

723. _____

724. _____

725. _____

YELLOW

726. _____

727. _____

728. _____

729. _____

730. _____

731. _____

732. _____

733. _____

734. _____

735. _____

736. _____

737. _____

738. _____

739. _____

740. _____

Ask your child questions that encourage conversations,
rather than ones that can be answered with yes or no.

Point out the sounds at the beginning of words such as, "Bird and bug start with 'B,' and so does 'busy bee'!"

741. _____

742. _____

743. _____

744. _____

745. _____

746. _____

747. _____

748. _____

749. _____

750. _____

751. _____

752. _____

753. _____

754. _____

755. _____

756. _____

757. _____

758. _____

759. _____

760. _____

761. _____

762. _____

763. _____

764. _____

765. _____

766. _____

767. _____

768. _____

769. _____

770. _____

"And what is the use of a book," thought Alice, "without pictures or conversation?"

Lewis Carroll,
Alice's Adventures in Wonderland

Repeat nursery rhymes and teach finger games like "this little piggy went to market," and "the itsy-bitsy spider." These are oldies but goodies!

771. _____

772. _____

773. _____

774. _____

775. _____

776. _____

777. _____

778. _____

779. _____

780. _____

781. _____

782. _____

783. _____

784. _____

785. _____

786. _____

787. _____

788. _____

789. _____

790. _____

791. _____

792. _____

793. _____

794. _____

795. _____

796. _____

797. _____

798. _____

799. _____

800. _____

Add some numbers to your day! Count steps as you walk. Sing, "How many birds do you see? I see 1, 2, 3!"

Yea!

Place **800 Books** Sticker Here

Write with Me!

Writing, reading, speaking, and listening are all forms of communication. To be able to write, children need to understand that written words are symbols of spoken words, and that writing has a purpose. They also need to develop fine motor skills and hand-eye coordination necessary to form letters, words, and pictures. There are many small ways throughout the day that you can help your child become a writer! Help your child to notice words, letters, numbers, shapes, and colors in books and in the world all around. Let your little one see you write and explain what you are doing. Provide opportunities to play with small objects, such as blocks, puzzles, and beads to strengthen small muscles in your child's fingers and hands. From the very first scribbles your child is attempting to communicate, and you can help foster this magical progression from early lines to written words!

What wonderful paints and brushes they had! George could not resist.

H.A. Rey, *Curious George*

Children love to see their names in print.
Say each letter as you write your child's name.
Label your child's belongings and artwork!

801. _____

802. _____

803. _____

804. _____

805. _____

806. _____

807. _____

808. _____

809. _____

810. _____

811. _____

812. _____

813. _____

814. _____

815. _____

816. _____

817. _____

818. _____

819. _____

820. _____

821. _____

822. _____

823. _____

824. _____

825. _____

826. _____

827. _____

828. _____

829. _____

830. _____

831. _____

832. _____

Show your child how to use a pair of children's scissors. A stack of old paper or magazines is perfect to practice cutting skills!

Every child is an artist.
The problem is how to remain
an artist once he grows up.

Pablo Picasso

833. _____

834. _____

835. _____

836. _____

837. _____

838. _____

839. _____

840. _____

841. _____

842. _____

843. _____

844. _____

845. _____

846. _____

847. _____

848. _____

849. _____

850. _____

851. _____

852. _____

853. _____

854. _____

855. _____

856. _____

857. _____

858. _____

859. _____

860. _____

Help your child make birthday cards. Have your
little one decorate the outside, and then you can
write a message on the inside. Relatives and
friends will love your child's artwork!

Pour cereal on a tray and let your child pick it up and eat it. This helps strengthen the small muscles in hands and fingers, which improves fine motor skills.

861. _____

862. _____

863. _____

864. _____

865. _____

866. _____

867. _____

868. _____

869. _____

870. _____

871. _____

872. _____

873. _____

874. _____

875. _____

876. _____

877. _____

878. _____

879. _____

880. _____

881. _____

882. _____

883. _____

884. _____

885. _____

886. _____

887. _____

888. _____

889. _____

890. _____

Make a special box for writing supplies.
Fill it with crayons, markers, child-friendly scissors,
paper, stickers, paints, and glue sticks.

I found I could say things with color
and shapes that I couldn't say any other way—
things I had no words for.

Georgia O'Keeffe

891. _____

892. _____

893. _____

894. _____

895. _____

896. _____

897. _____

898. _____

899. _____

900. _____

901. _____

902. _____

903. _____

904. _____

905. _____

906. _____

907. _____

908. _____

909. _____

910. _____

911. _____

912. _____

Staple sheets of paper together to make a book!
Your child can write and illustrate their own story!

When you shop, notice signs in the store. Ask your child to look for words that begin with a certain letter, or to find something that's a particular color. For example, "Can you find something that is orange?"

913. _____

914. _____

915. _____

916. _____

917. _____

918. _____

919. _____

920. _____

921. _____

922. _____

923. _____

924. _____

925. _____

926. _____

927. _____

928. _____

929. _____

930. _____

931. _____

932. _____

933. _____

934. _____

935. _____

936. _____

937. _____

938. _____

939. _____

940. _____

941. _____

Puzzles, blocks, stickers, and beads are
toys that help to develop fine motor skills
and hand-eye coordination.

Serve alphabet soup for lunch and have fun looking for the letters in everyone's name!

942. _____

943. _____

944. _____

945. _____

946. _____

947. _____

948. _____

949. _____

950. _____

951. _____

952. _____

953. _____

954. _____

955. _____

956. _____

957. _____

958. _____

959. _____

960. _____

961. _____

962. _____

963. _____

964. _____

965. _____

966. _____

967. _____

968. _____

969. _____

970. _____

A, B, C, D, E, F, G, H, I, J, K, L, M, N, O, P, Q, R, S, T, U, V, W, X, Y, and Z. Now I know my ABCs; next time won't you sing with me?

Help your child make a pasta necklace—
and wear it proudly!

971. _____

972. _____

973. _____

974. _____

975. _____

976. _____

977. _____

978. _____

979. _____

980. _____

981. _____

982. _____

983. _____

984. _____

985. _____

986. _____

987. _____

988. _____

989. _____

990. _____

991. _____

992. _____

993. _____

994. _____

995. _____

996. _____

997. _____

998. _____

999. _____

1,000! _____

And I think to myself...
what a wonderful world.

Bob Thiele and George David Weiss

You did
it!

Place 1,000 Books
Sticker Here!

Kindergarten Skills

All children grow and learn at different rates—and no two are alike. This is important for parents and caregivers to remember when they are trying to evaluate whether or not their child is ready for school. The following list is a general guideline that will help you to identify your child's strengths and give you ideas about what skills to work on. It is best to check with your child's school to find out specific requirements and expectations. If you have concerns about your child's development, speak with a pediatrician, school, or day-care provider who can help you find the right support.

Learning Skills

- Shows an interest in learning new things
- Tries to solve problems independently
- Can follow simple directions

Self-Help Skills

- Knows full name, address, and phone number
- Knows age and birthday
- Is able to dress independently, putting on coat, mittens, hats, and boots
- Can manage zippers and snaps on clothing
- Is able to use the bathroom and wash hands independently
- Is able to ask for help
- Follows basic safety rules

Social Skills

- Demonstrates self-control
- Has had experiences sharing and taking turns
- Uses words to solve problems

Physical Skills

- Is able to hold crayons and pencils correctly
- Can do simple puzzles
- Builds with blocks
- Cuts with scissors
- Is able to bounce, throw, kick, and catch a ball
- Rides a tricycle
- Runs, jumps, climbs, and hops
- Can balance on a line

Language Skills

- Has a basic understanding of manners and uses "please" and "thank you"
- Talks in sentences
- Follows simple directions
- Remembers simple songs and nursery rhymes
- Is able to be understood by adults

Reading Skills

- Enjoys stories
- Can sit and listen to a story
- Knows how to hold a book and which way to turn the pages
- Can recite the alphabet
- Recognizes words that rhyme
- Notices print—text, signs, labels, etc.
- Makes predictions about a story—"What will happen next?"
- Can retell simple stories

Today a reader, tomorrow a leader.

Margaret Fuller

Top 10 Favorite Books

1. _____

_____

2. _____

_____

3. _____

_____

4. _____

_____

5. _____

_____

6. _____

_____

7. _____

_____

8. _____

_____

9. _____

_____

10. _____

_____

The journey of a thousand miles
begins with one step.

Lao Tzu

You may have tangible wealth untold.
Caskets of jewels and coffers of gold.
Richer than I you can never be—
I had a mother who read to me.

Strickland Gillilan

Congratulations!

Hooray for you! You did it!
You read 1,000 books!
Now you're a thousand stories tall!

Place photo here

Anything can happen, child.
Anything can be.

Shel Silverstein, *Where the Sidewalk Ends*

Special family and friends who read with me!

One of the greatest gifts adults can give—
to their offspring and to their society—
is to read to children.

Carl Sagan

For further resources, tips,
and ideas visit our website at

www.growathousandstoriestall.com